BMW GS
Adventure Motorcycle

A 30-Year Catalog

BMW GS
Adventure Motorcycle
A 30-Year Catalog

All two- and four-valve *Gelandsport* boxers from 1980 · All singles from 1993 · All F-series GS parallel twins from 2008

Hans-Jurgen Schneider (Rode a BMW R 80 G/S at its Press Launch in 1980) and
Dr. Axel Koenigsbeck (Freelance motorcycle journalist since 1974)

PARKER HOUSE

Contents

Opposite title: With its functional yet sober design, the modern four-valve HP2 completes the circle back to the legendary R 80 G/S of 1980 but with more than twice the power.

Preface:
Fascination with the BMW GS

When BMW introduced its first production enduro, the R 80 G/S, on September 1, 1980, success was far from certain. We now know it was the Bavarian's smartest move since the introduction of the Cardan shaft in 1923. With its frequently copied, but never equaled combination of sturdy technology, elemental power, endurance, and flair, BMW's enduro stole the hearts of the riding public.

Though the original G/S model had already sparked an unexpected surge in demand through 1987 (with more than 25,000 units sold including the R 65 GS), the Paralever models produced until 1996 went one better, selling more than 66,000 units, including Roadster versions, worldwide.

Then the fully redesigned, four-valve models with the Telelever frame came along to surpass all previous expectations. In just five years, BMW managed to sell almost 46,000 units of the R 1100 GS and from 1998 the nearly identical R 850 GS. As an individual model, the R 1100 GS, with 43,628 units sold, became the most popular boxer in history to that point and the second best-selling BMW motorcycle in BMW's history behind the R 25/3, sales of which reached 47,000 units in the 1950s.

And the trend showed no sign of abating. From its start, the R 1150 GS, introduced in 1999, was Germany's best-selling motorcycle bar none. Counting the Adventure, 71,138 units were produced and sold up to December 2003—a record. BMW's unbroken series of sales records since the beginning of the 1990s (101,352 motorcycles produced in Berlin in 2006, plus 2,407 in collaboration with Aprilia/Piaggio) can be traced to a continuing run on the enduro models. The R 1200 GS, introduced in January 2004, ensured that the amazing GS success story would continue, witness that to the end of 2006, the 1200 GS—including the "large" Adventure models—found 81,093 buyers around the world.

Success did not stop with the boxers. The chain-driven, single-cylinder models produced since 1993 never had trouble attracting buyers either, but with regard to image, the "Funduros" long stood in the shadow of the legendary GS boxer. Today this has all changed. With the F 650 GS, a sports model with an off-road look and feel that came onto the market in 2000, to be upgraded in 2004, BMW also aced its breakthrough into the single-cylinder segment. Within a few months, the new model had advanced to become the most popular single-cylinder enduro in all markets. It left all BMW production records behind it with 97,123 units built just for the period to December 2006.

The rise of the 650 from wallflower to true GS was encouraged by its competition success. After a false start in 1998, BMW won the famous/infamous Paris-Dakar rally twice in a row with the F 650 RR, a competition version. With this, the Bavarians not only succeeded in picking up the thread of four unforgotten boxer victories in the Dakar between 1981 and 1985, but also managed to make the single-cylinder bike acceptable to the hardcore "big" GS rider.

In 2000 and 2001 the boxer, now a four-valver, again took podium places in off-road competition. Yet, following defeat in the 2001 Paris-Dakar by KTM, BMW once more pulled out of desert racing, much to the fans' chagrin. On top of this, two-time Dakar winner Richard Sainct died in an accident in 2004 (on a KTM), making renewed BMW involvement in this discipline out of the question. Rather, the company moved in new directions. One such direction was to introduce a competition-worthy, production boxer in 2005 in the form of the HP2.

Since 2006, the three models of the G 650 X series have overturned much of which up to that point had seemed sacred to the Munich engineers. In off-road events, with its 450 Sport enduro, BMW is mimicking once again the glory days of the special GS boxers, which dominated off-road racing in the late 1970s.

It's because the GS models are so successful that this book, in its German version, is now in its fifth edition. This first English language edition follows the latest edition in full. It tells the fascinating story of the GS motorcycles, which are legendary not only in Germany but around the world, having topped vehicle registrations in all important export countries. Congratulations, Munich and Berlin!

Hans-Jurgen Schneider
Normandy, France

With the HP2, introduced in spring 2005, BMW once again commits itself unreservedly to racing. The elegant machine is barely heavier than the first G/S from 1980 but has more than twice the power.

BMW off-road boxers from 1923 to 1979

For BMW, the off-road testing of motorcycles and competitive runs belonged to the program from the very beginning. Even though in the days of the R 32, Bavarian Motor Works' first motorcycle (1923), most streets often resembled gravel tracks (for enduro riders?). Anyway, there was no reluctance to hold real cross-country off-road racing events. The famous "Ride through the Mountains of Bavaria" was a club tour with a varied program. It was here, on the May 5, 1923, that BMW's chief designer Max Friz rolled the prototype of his R 32 to the start line.

At the time, a certain degree of off-road capability in a motorcycle was simply taken for granted; there was no thought of any special equipment. To begin with, tires possessed a knobby, universal profile, and motorcycles were generally not so ponderous and top-

heavy. The engine output curve of the motorcycles of that era was rather flat and the good torque band allowed low-rev maneuvers even at walking pace.

At the time, the most extensive motor-racing activities took place in Britain. There, specialized off-road competitions were held; these often included difficult test stages. In 1926, two BMW riders from Germany, Rudolf Schleicher and Fritz Roth, first made the trip to the English town of Buxton for the International Six Days enduro. BMW's chief of development Schleicher and his friend Roth held their own on the fast R 37 street-racing machine, winding up with well-deserved gold and silver medals.

The motorcycles, with their cross-mounted boxer engine and advanced shaft drive, had elicited considerable interest in Britain, yet it would be years until their next international

BMW motorcycles were already successful in the off-road races of the 1920s and 1930s.

Far left: *Ernst Henne on a single-cylinder R 4 at the Three-Day Harz Race, 1933.*

Left: *Paul Greifzu (no. 65), 1925, the winner on an R 37.*

Below: *Josef Mauermayer and Ludwig Kraus on an R 16 sidecar machine at the 1930 Harz race.* **Bottom:** *The BMW team on a production ohv R 63 and R 11 SV before the start of the 1930 Piemont Race.*

appearance. In the interim, off-road racing in Germany survived rather feebly in the shadow of street racing. In the main, reliability runs were held.

▊ BMW triumphs at the 1933 Six Days

The larger events among these were increasingly organized with participating factory teams from local motorcycle manufacturers. In front of the public and the competition, the teams demonstrated the quality of their machines. Appearing for BMW at such events, besides the well-tried sidecar team of Sepp Mauermayer and Ludwig Wiggerl Kraus—both employed in the factory's testing department—were the street racers Ernst Henne and Sepp Stelzer.

These men went on to form the German national team at the 1933 International Six Days. A sidecar machine along with two solo R 16 motorcycles featuring a 750cc engine developing 33 horsepower and a heavy pressed-steel frame went up against the British single-cylinder machines, practically on their hosts' home course. To general astonishment, the BMW

At the sight of these complex designs, hardly anyone thought they would survive one day, let alone all six days, with stages of 400 to 500 kilometers. But they had underestimated the reliability and endurance of the men and their machines. Once again, the Germans won the trophy, their third victory in a row. It was only in 1936 that they finally had to bow to the competition.

With sponsorship from the National Socialists and the Wehrmacht, 1930s Germany witnessed a major increase in the number of off-road competitions. Intensive motorcyclist training in and outside of the military naturally also included a hard-driving cross-country component. At its conclusion, the young riders were expected to demonstrate what they had learned by racing. Thus, the larger off-road events such as the Winter Races, the Three-Day Harz Race, or the East-Prussia Tour soon came to be dominated primarily by soldiers.

Especially talented riders were entrusted with "factory material," usually in the expectation of eventual government contracts in the event of satisfactory performance. In this, BMW was favorably positioned, as it already provided the most popular training machine, the single-cylinder R 4.

Above: *Sepp Muller on an R 66 sidecar machine with an ohv boxer at the 1933 Six Days.*

Right: *Ake Laurin in 1939 on a modified R 51.*

riders prevailed in the overall standings, thus bringing the coveted Six Days trophy for the first time to Germany. The same team riding the same boxer motorcycles managed a repeat performance in 1934 as hosts to the following year's race held at Garmisch-Partenkirchen.

In 1935, the Six Days were once again held in Germany. This time, BMW had some special motorcycles on tap. The British, anticipating a cliffhanger for the overall victory lasting to the final race, had increased their reliance on more powerful machines. Ernst Henne, Sepp Stelzer, and Wiggerl Kraus, with Sepp Muller in the sidecar, were equipped with brand-new factory machines featuring light tubular frames, modern telescopic forks, and supercharged engines.

Production-oriented models for off-road racing

In the sales catalog, the R 4 was even touted as an off-road machine, though the awkward-looking motorcycle with pressed-steel frame and laminated-spring front fork lacked any sort of specialized optional equipment that might have distinguished it from an ordinary street bike. Rather, the "off-road" moniker could be traced to the numerous victories that three Bavarian motorcycle policemen—Fritz Linhardt, Josef Forster, and Georg Meier—had wrested with this machine. This trio prevailed wherever they appeared. Team victories, even under the most appalling weather conditions, earned the BMW veterans the admiring title of the three "Cast-Iron Men." From 1938, sleepwalker-like assurance allied to daring and tenacity also propelled the arch-Bavarian Georg "Schorsch" Meier to his impressive successes on BMW street machines.

Technical progress in off-road motorcycles was limited to ongoing development of production models; there were no specific innovations. Nevertheless, off-road tests remained an important part of standard testing procedure. It is thus hardly surprising that young design engineer Alex von Falkenhausen's suggestion to add a rear-wheel plunger-type suspension to the new tubular-frame models was first tried out at an off-road event. Von Falkenhausen also served as test pilot, being one of the best German off-road racers. He eventually raced a correspondingly modified BMW R 5 at the International Six Days of 1936. A few accessories, such as oversized handles on the knock-out wheel spindles, a compressed-air bottle for quick tire repairs, and a protective plate under the oil pan distinguished the factory off-road BMW Type 51 from the production street model.

Top left: *Josef Forster, Rudi Seltsam, and Schorsch Meier competed in the 1938 Six Days in Wales on an R 51.*

Top right: *Ernst Henne at the 1936 Six Days on a BMW 500 Kompressor.*

Middle: *Ludwig Wiggerl Kraus and Bernhard Huser at the 1952 Six Days.*

Bottom: *A Wehrmacht R 75 from 1941 with a 26-horsepower ohv boxer and powered sidecar.*

The Wehrmacht Motorcycle Department's intensive off-road racing program had led the army to consider the use of solo motorcycles and sidecar machines in the future not merely as liaison vehicles but also for combat purposes. Specialized machines would now be built for this purpose. Corresponding invitations to tender quickly went out to the manufacturers. BMW and Zundapp were especially interested in these contracts.

Before the onset of war, no thought had been given to a light, nimble motorcycle that could move its rider quickly in difficult terrain. Rather, priority was given to a sidecar machine for three fully equipped soldiers, including where possible a mounted machine-gun. As military equipment was then practically the only market remaining for BMW, the R 75 soon rolled off the line. It was produced in great numbers (more than 18,000 units) from 1941 to 1944. Today, it ranks among the most expensive collector's bikes.

This was a complex new design with a powered sidecar, differential lock, off-road gear reduction, reverse gear, and hydraulically actuated drum brakes (rear wheel and sidecar). The front wheel was steered by a massive, hydraulically damped telescopic fork. Drive was provided by a four-speed gearbox with reverse gear. Gear reduction doubled its number. The "square" ohv boxer engine with 78-millimeter bore and 78-millimeter stroke had a displacement of 745cc and developed 26 horsepower at 4,000 rpm. The sidecar machine weighed a formidable 420 kilograms; its top speed of 95 kilometers per hour was remarkable.

At war's end, street races once again captured the public interest. But the smaller motorcycle manufacturers wished to compete with each other in the familiar reliability runs and in long-distance events with off-road stages. BMW took part only in the larger races such as the ADAC Winter Tour or the 1950 1,000-kilometer German Tour.

Top, from left to right: *An R 67/2 for the 1953 Six Days; the 1956 Six Days silver trophy team in Garmisch-Partenkirchen: Hans Meier with an R 50; Alfred Hartner and Sebastian Nachtmann with an R 26; Konrad Welnhofer with an R 50; Ernst Henne on an R 47 racing version after his victory at the Karlsruhe Wildpark Race, 1926; and the team of Krauser and Peissl at a 1952 speedway race on a radically modified R 75 sidecar machine.*

Right: *Schorsch Meier on an R 68 at the International Austrian Alps Tour, 1952.*

Far right: *Sebastian Nachtmann on an R 69 S Special, 1960–61.*

Here, well-known factory racers Schorsch Meier, Wiggerl Kraus, and Max Klankermeier went to the start line on production machines. Klankermeier even tried his luck on a single-cylinder R 25. The Germans were only admitted back to the International Six Days race in 1951. That year, it was held in the Italian town of Varese. There, as

in 1952 at Bad Aussee, Austria, the BMW factory riders appeared on boxer models: There was Schorsch Meier and his brother Hans, Walter Zeller, Hans Roth along with the sidecar teams of Wiggerl Kraus/Bernhard Huser and Max Klankermeier/Hermann Wolz. Though the BMW racers could not revisit their earlier overall victories, they always managed to clinch medals in the individual placings.

Here, for the first time, the racing motorcycles quite clearly deviated in several respects from production models. There were front wheels enlarged from 19 to 21 inches and raised exhaust systems with a single silencer on the right side, rubber gaiters on telescopic forks, a seat cushion on the rear mudguard that served as a tool bag, a protective plate for the oil pan, along with crash bars placed here and there before the projecting cylinders. Initially, the R 51/3, with its 500cc displacement, was employed in the solo class along with the R 67, featuring a 600cc engine, in the sidecar category. In 1952, the 35-horsepower street-racing R 68 (600cc) replaced the 500cc boxer.

■ **Success also with full-swingarm models**

In off-road racing as elsewhere, the heavy machines with full swingarm suspension, which went into production in 1955, replaced previous models. Though 250cc single-cylinder motorcycles of the R 26 type were deployed here and there, BMW dominated the 500cc solo class with the R 50. In the sidecar class, the R 69 left few chances to the competition.

About the same time, in parallel to the machines, a generational changing of the guard was taking place among BMW factory riders: The new names at the apex of the German off-road championship were now Sebastian Nachtmann, Manfred Sensburg, and Karl Ibscher (sidecar).

With the decline of motorcycle sales in Germany from the mid-1950s, off-road racing increasingly developed as the province of independent riders on specially prepared machines. Against ever lighter two-stroke models, the heavy BMW factory motorcycles now seemed like dinosaurs from a distant era. Paradoxically, it was for this very reason that the public and the competition showed the BMW riders particular respect.

Maico, Hercules, and Zundapp all provided special racing models in small production runs to independent competitors. In the following years, these motorcycles quickly evolved, whereas the BMWs displayed no deviation from the 1955 models. Street models continued largely unaltered in the program; the available machines presumably seemed adequate to the off-road factory teams. Yet, this was hardly a time of stagnation at BMW's development department. On April 7, 1963, Sebastian Nachtmann first competed in the Biberach motocross on a modernized off-road machine. With its telescopic front fork derived from the R 25/3, lighter mudguards, and a small custom tank, the R 69 S cut a pretty startling figure. But this was only the beginning: In fall of the same year, a wholly a new frame and suspension were unveiled.

A compact double tubular frame with a light, bolt-on rear sub-frame for securing the shocks and a newly developed telescopic fork with long travel and forward axle clamps resulted in a shortened wheelbase and increased ground clearance.

Apart from the unaltered, precision-engineered R 69 S engine with its 44 horsepower, this BMW already rather more resembled modern off-road machines, such as those the British Triumph works were bringing to the start line in the larger displacement

In the 1960s and 1970s, BMW continued to be very successful off road. **Top:** *Karl Ibscher and Edgar Rettschlag on the R 69 sidecar machine.* **Above:** *1970 off-road racing prototype on an R 75/5 base.* **Right:** *Gunther Steenbock working the handlebars of his personal boxer sidecar machine at a 1972 cross-country event.*

classes at major international events. What's more, BMW engineers had succeeded in reducing the machine's curb weight by a whopping 21.5 kilograms. The factory prototype now weighed 193.5 kilograms.

Sebastian Nachtmann soon fulfilled the hopes placed in the new motorcycle: He won the German off-road championship in both 1964 and 1965 (over-500cc class). The BMW factory team was reinforced by Herbert Schek and Kurt Tweesmann for the 1966 season (in which Tweesmann won the championship straight off).

Once the idea that this off-road BMW offered clues to an upcoming generation of street machines had taken hold in the motorcycle community, the introduction of a new engine was keenly anticipated. But this expectation was initially disappointed, as BMW withdrew from off-road activities after the 1966 season.

Three years later, in 1969, BMW did eventually present a new model range, naturally with new engines. The R 50/5, R 60/5, and R 75/5 boxer powerplants were entirely new designs with plain bearings for crankshaft and connecting rods along with end-to-end tie-rod bolts for holding the light-alloy cylinders and cylinder heads as well as the camshaft located under the crankshaft. The frame and telescopic fork evidently derived from the factory off-road racer.

The circle closed in spring 1970 with renewed participation in the German off-road championship. Though the four machines for Herbert Schek, Kurt Tweesmann, Sebastian Nachtmann, and Kurt Distler (who had ridden the old 1963 prototype as an independent contestant the previous year) might have resembled the earlier factory machines at first sight, they now were based on the R 75/5.

▌ Off-road models on the R 75/5 chassis

The 750cc engine had undergone only minimal modifications (crankcase ventilation, a front cover of magnesium alloy). It retained its Bing carburetor as well as the electric starter. The production model's power output of 50 horsepower seemed more than adequate in view of extensive weight reduction. With its plastic gas tank (earlier aluminum) on empty, the new factory off-road machine tipped the scales at a modest 175 kilograms. In addition to the four motorcycles prepared by BMW's test department, authorized BMW dealers together with factory rider Nachtmann were to take on the assembly of additional units for independent racers. This project never materialized, however.

Schek, from Wangen in the Allgau, clinched the German off-road championship title in the over 500cc class in 1970 and 1971 on the BMW. He gave a repeat performance in 1972, though no longer on the factory bike. Meanwhile, BMW had (once again) lost interest. The result: Schek put together his own machine, with a Maico telescopic fork and reduced weight. But in 1973 it wasn't enough to propel him to a fourth title. He lost by a hair's breadth against a competitor on a two-stroke Maico 501.

The race was not nearly so close at the 1973 Six Days, held for the first time in the U.S. state of Florida. This time, for publicity reasons, BMW had opted for direct factory involvement. Preparations were taken over by BMW-Motorsport GmbH, a department whose involvement up to that point had been limited to auto racing. Again based on the R 75/5, the off-road bikes now only had kick starts. Though Schek ended up winning a gold medal, the factory's involvement in the Florida race was overshadowed by numerous problems at startup, split gas tanks, and even broken frames.

In the following years, the four-stroke boxer's low rumble vanished

Above: *Herbert Schek with the elaborately set up factory 600 (what an exhaust!) at the rider camp during the 1966 Six Days.*

Above left: *Kurt Tweesmann on the 600 off-road boxer, 1964–65.*

almost entirely from German off-road events. Only now and then would a Schek BMW appear in the hands of some independent competitor. Yet Maico's monopoly on the large-displacement class, thanks to its two-stroke one-cylinder 501cc, pleased neither the fans nor the organizers.

The remedy was the creation of an additional class for motorcycles with a displacement more than 750cc. In 1978, this was finally incorporated into the program of the German championship.

While Schek proceeded with his individual developments, Laszlo Peres, of BMW's test department, also began thinking about a new boxer off-road machine, with an eye on extending the racing rules. What eventually rolled to the start at the kickoff of the championship races in the spring of 1978 was convincing: Encased in a lightweight tubular frame of chrome-molybdenum steel with a central telescopic swingarm sat an 800cc motor assembled from various BMW parts. It possessed the R 45/65 series' shortened stroke (61.5 centimeters vs. 70.6 centimeters). The cylinder bore was 90.8

millimeters. This significantly reduced the boxer's overall width.

Also worthy of note: the new off-roader had 250 millimeters of suspension travel in the front, 200 millimeters in the rear, and a dry weight of only 142 kilograms. The prototype's terse designation was GS 800. These

machines were meant to usher in a new development at BMW. Still, in the final ranking of the German championship, Peres had to bow out to Rolf Witthoff on his individually modified 800 Kawasaki.

The trade press saw Peres's machine not merely as the forerunner of a

Top left: *A factory GS from 1979 with 55 horsepower for use in the 750cc class.*

Top right: *This Six Days factory machine from 1973 (745cc, 57 horsepower) already displays a vague resemblance to the later production GS, though it features a conventional swingarm.*

Middle: *Herbert Schek's legendary personally prepared 750 GS, 1978.*

Right: *The 1979 BMW off-road team. Left to right: Rolf Witthof, Laszlo Peres, team leader Dietmar Beinhauer, Kurt Fischer, Schek, and Richard Schalber. Note the prominent long-travel telescopic forks and the narrow tanks.*

future factory off-road racer but also as basis for the development of a new production enduro by BMW. A partnership with the Italian motorcycle manufacturer Laverda was adduced as more evidence of this. However, this collaboration only extended to construction of a series of chassis for the factory team and various tests outsourced for logistical reasons.

■ Victories on the GS 80 in the 1979 and 1980 German Championship

For the 1979 season, BMW lined up no fewer than six factory racers: Laszlo Peres, Herbert Schek, Rolf Witthoff, Kurt Tweesmann, Richard Schalber, Fritz Witzel, and Kurt Fischer. They were to compete in the German off-road championship, the European championship, and the International Six Days. BMW engineer Dietmar Beinhauer served as team leader.

The GS 80 factory bike had undergone further improvement,

now with a displacement of 798cc and a peak output of 55 horsepower. Maximum torque was 60 Newton meters (Nm); a couple of carburetors with 32 millimeters bore handled the air/fuel mixture. The two-in-two exhaust system was raised behind the engine. The rear central suspension shock already suggested the future R80 G/S. Tire equipment was 3.00x21 front, 4.50x18 or 5.00x17 rear. The narrow tank held 10 liters. Two drum brakes provided the stopping power for the 138-kilogram machine. The Six Days machine featured 270 millimeters of shock travel in the front, 230 millimeters in the rear. The motorcycle's appearance evolved markedly in the course of the season according to varying suspension linkages to the rear-wheel swingarm and differing exhaust systems.

As was to be expected, at each of their appearances the Munich boxers were the star attraction. The large and—relative to the competition—hulking BMW motorcycles hurtled impressively

The 1979 factory GS 80 weighed only 138 kilograms dry. This photo shows the version with conventionally mounted rear shocks. Other versions featured a long-travel central unit.

along the courses. Especially in the motocross special tests, high leaps on the growling four-stroke motorcycle held the public in thrall.

Richard Schalber won the German championship, placing third in the European championship. But the BMW team had even more in store for the Six Days, to be held that year in Neukirchen, Germany. With two factory teams of three riders each, BMW had decided to dethrone Zundapp from their leading position among the factory teams. Though it narrowly missed the overall victory because of a simple technical failure, BMW managed to dominate the individual results in the large-displacement class: Fritz Witzel won the medal for the over-750cc class.

Right: *Richard Schalber vaults his way to the 1979 German off-road championship.*

▌ Rolf Witthoff: 1980 European champion and Six Days winner

In 1980, BMW again sent two factory teams to the start line. They were particularly well prepared for the Six Days in Brioude, France. Team 1 was made up of freshly anointed European champion Rolf Witthoff, new German champion Werner Schutz, and vice-champion Fritz Witzel. The names in Team 2 were just as well known in the off-road world: Kurt Fischer, Theo Schreck, and Herbert Wegele. Domestically or internationally, BMW had no one to fear in the over-750cc class. Following a year in training, victories would now become practically routine.

The boxer engine had become both more powerful and more compact: The ignition system had vanished from its customary location on the front cover. The upper casing section along with the air-filter housing could also go; a low-profile air filter did the job. Both exhaust headers were directly connected via the engine housing. Displacement now reached 870cc (bore: 95 millimeters, stroke: 61.5 millimeters). Power output was rated at 57 horsepower. Torque had increased slightly to 64 Nm. For a 1495-millimeter wheelbase, the Six Days machine now tipped the scales at a dry weight of only 136 kilograms. The reconfigured silencer had been relocated to the left, at the frame's rear, as the "monoshock" shock

Left: *The 1979 G 80 with central rear shock and 55-horsepower boxer engine. Braking was evidently of no great concern—as apparent from the puny front-wheel drum.*

had migrated completely to the right, now resting only upon the right swingarm shaft. It's worth noting that at this final stage before the future Monolever single-sided swingarm, a thin swingarm shaft subsisted on the left side.

Werner Schutz won the German championship in his class, and the old hand Rolf Witthoff delighted himself, the factory, and BMW fans everywhere by clinching the European title. He was then drafted into the German team that competed for the Six Days cup in France. Running against light two-stroke machines, Witthöfft on his fat BMW accomplished his mission flawlessly and won the contest for Germany. BMW could not have wished a better backdrop for the presentation of its new R80 G/S production enduro.

The story of BMW factory involvement in off-road racing in Europe thus ended on a high note. In Africa, BMW would again gather a rich harvest of victories far away from paved roads. At the Paris-Dakar rally, BMW boxers soon won four times within a few years—a series revisited in 1999 and 2000 under completely altered circumstances on modern single-cylinder models. Following failure at the 2001 Paris-Dakar race, the factory officially pulled out of off-road racing until further notice, much to the fans' regret, now leaving the field for years to the KTM armada (see, Paris-Dakar page 128).

In 1992, riding a production R 100 GS, the Munich racer Jutta Kleinschmidt (overall 2001 rally victor on a Mitsubishi Pajero prototype) won the women's standings in the race, which at the time ended at Cape Town. BMW now opened a new chapter in off-road racing with the single-cylinder 450 Sport Enduro (see page 152).

Above: *The GS 80 of 1980, the victorious bike of the European and German championships.*

Left: *The 1979 team, from the left: race leader Ekkehard Rappelius, Laszlo Peres, Fritz Witzel Jr., business manager Karl Gerlinger, Herbert Schek, Richard Schalber, Rolf Wittoff, Kurt Fischer, and team leader Dietmar Beinhauer.*

The BMW enduro racing prototypes in action.
Top: *The team presentation for the 1980 BMW off-road racing season, Werner Schutz, left; Rolf Witthoff center; and Fritz Witzel, right.* **Above:** *Vice-champion Laszlo Peres on his special GS.*

Werner Schutz, German champion in 1980. The BMW off-road racer was an extremely lightweight construction. The Maico fork with the small drum-brake, the slender tubular swingarm with central rear shock, and the raised exhaust were all characteristic.

The marshal and the "Red Devil": Origins of the G/S concept

Large BMW enduros owe their existence to a crisis. During the 1977–78 model year, BMW's motorcycle sales in the United States, its largest export market, experienced a major downturn. Disagreements with its importer, Butler and Smith Trading Corporation of New York, only worsened the situation. Things finally came to a head with the wholesale resignation of BMW's motorcycle division top management, under Rudolf von der Schulenberg.

During the ensuing consolidation phase, successor Dr. Eberhardt C. Sarfert and sales manager Karl Gerlinger gave intensive thought to ways in which they might stimulate demand in the thriving market with a new, quickly developed motorcycle model. Putting this idea in practice was not so simple. The multicylinder K Series was already under development, but it was still a long way from the assembly line. On the boxer front, a four-valves-per-cylinder motor, albeit with pushrod valve actuation, had just been shelved because of negative thermal dynamics.

▌ GS prototypes on a street R 80 chassis

At the time it was only in the off-road area that things were moving forward for BMW. At the end of the 1970s prominent racers such as Herbert Schek, Rolf Witthoff, Richard Schalber, Fritz Witzel, Laszlo Peres, and Kurt Fischer were successfully competing in European championships and Six Days races under racing chief Dietmar Beinhauer. The motorcycles deployed there were ultra-light custom designs, under 138-kilogram curb weight, with 750, 800, and later even 1,000cc boxer

engines. But even a limited production run of these competition motorcycles would hardly have been marketable given high production costs and the resulting prohibitive price tag. Total production costs were in fact so high that there was no money left within the test department for training and replacement machines.

It's well known that necessity is the mother of invention. So the men under test department chief Ekkehart Rappelius set about building

a small number of "design-off road motorcycles" drawing widely upon components of the production R 80 street model. The telescopic fork was unmodified, though the front wheel went to a 21-inch rim. The rear of the motorcycle was lightened, and for the rear suspension there was something really special: a single-sided swingarm, later known as a Monolever, which in its essential features had been developed earlier. This prototype, built in 1978 without any specific development

Above right: The GS 80 factory prototype for the 1978 Six Days, with central rear shock and only 138-kilogram dry weight.

Right: The GS 800 prototype built in Italy by Laverda under contract to BMW in 1977–78; it featured a special lightweight frame and a front disc brake.

Project leader Rudiger Gutsche caused quite a stir at the 1979 Six Days with his self-built machine.

order and still equipped with the R 100's 1,000cc engine, formed the basis of a proposal to management and the board of directors for construction of a production-based, enduro motorcycle with an 800cc two-cylinder ohv boxer engine and shaft drive.

There had already been more than a few attempts to build an off-road machine. Thus, in the early 1970s then test department head Hans Gunther von der Marwitz had offered BMW sales manager Horst T. Spintler an American-style off-road version of the R 75, dubbed "Streetscrambler." This was von der Marwitz's answer to the enduro wave that, starting in the United States with the Honda XL 250 (and later Yamaha's XT 500), was then sweeping the world. But Spintler had no interest in an off-road bike, presumably because sales of street boxers were so good. BMW was already selling up to 7,500 units annually in the United States alone.

At the close of the 1970s, not even the Japanese believed that engine displacement for enduros could be increased beyond the half-liter mark. In this segment, lightweight construction was everything. Only a few Bavarian eccentrics tore through terrain on heavy two-cylinder juggernauts. And it surely didn't help that, wherever they went,

both cylinders jutted out ostentatiously left and right.

A decisive conceptual stimulus came in 1977 from the Italian builder (and Italy's Husqvarna importer) Moto Laverda in the form of two off-road prototypes constructed under contract to BMW. A special super-light frame, long travel Marzocchi fork, lengthened tubular steel swingarm, 800cc boxer engine, and five-speed gearbox were the salient traits of this Laverda design.

▌ Project blessing from the automaker

In January 1979, the BMW motorcycle developers presented their "design off-road motorcycle" (dubbed "Red Devil") to the marketing people as a product range gap filler. Incidentally, at that time the people calling the shots were not the motorcycle marketers (who had resigned along with the rest of the management) but, on a temporary basis, parent company BMW AG's auto marketing specialists. The interim team, headed by Karl Wimmer, immediately loved the idea and gave the project a green light. Now everything went quickly.

Rudiger Gutsche was named project leader. As a longtime competitor in the Dolomites Rally, he was the right man for the job, having also built an enduro on a BMW R 75/5 chassis in 1975. An improved version had followed in 1978, with Maico front fork, disc brake, R 100 S engine, special narrow cylinders, and 60 horsepower. The swingarm was supported by a monoshock located to the right. Dry weight of the machine: 168 kilograms. As a route marshal at the 1979 Six Days race in Siegerland, Germany, Gutsche had caused something of a sensation with this GS precursor. An American fan spontaneously offered him $6,000 for the bike, but the prototype was obviously not for sale.

From January 1979, development of the G/S went into high gear. The single-sided swingarm caused the greatest headaches. After all, such a solution had never before successfully gone into production. The IMME light motorcycle from the 1950s served as a cautionary tale for the engineers (and the board of directors). Admittedly, the drivetrain swingarms of many motor scooters were also single-arm suspensions, but the demands in terms of steering and stability made by a heavy, powerful motorcycle were of a completely different order.

The brothers Edgar and Reinhold Noss dominated the German championship for much of the 1970s. At the Odenheim Motocross in 1978 they took second place on an EML-BMW 1000.

Above and left: *R 80 G/S factory prototypes on test rides through Ecuador in the summer of 1980.*

The legendary off-road prototype of 1978–79, constructed with production parts, and referred to respectfully within the company as the "Red Devil."

■ Monolever: Swingarm innovation

The highlight was the fixing of the rear wheel: The crown wheel bearing in the rear-wheel drive was strengthened; the wheel was bolted directly to a flange on the crown wheel. The trouble was that this assembly had to withstand the most extreme stresses. And so it did, and continues doing so to this day, as with its elaborate descendent, the Paralever swingarm in the 1200 GS. That it has long been imitated (e.g., Honda RC 30/45 and the Ducati 916 and 1098 series) is further evidence that the BMW designers' thinking was right on the mark and quite forward looking.

The R 80 G/S went into production in September 1980. A mere 21 months had elapsed between project launch and production startup. A vehicle project implemented this quickly was unique at BMW. Today, the R 80 G/S, which was produced until 1987, enjoys cult status as the most problem-free, low-maintenance, and multi-use boxer enduro. If it is still in good original condition it will fetch high prices. The bike sold for 8,290 Deutschmarks (not euros!) in 1980. Those were the days. . . .

Trendsetter 1980: The R 80 G/S with single-sided swingarm

Avignon, September 1, 1980: a memorable day in motorcycle history. On this date, now almost 30 years past, BMW presented to the trade press assembled in the "City of Popes" a motorcycle with truly heavenly qualities, the legendary R 80 G/S. BMW press agents and technicians had not overstated their case when they described the eagerly awaited two-cylinder boxer thus: "The BMW R 80 G/S is designed as a leisure instrument with universal applications. The motorcycle's sporty features and high performance in daily use will open a new dimension in traveling by motorcycling. The R 80 G/S is comfortable while touring, fully passenger capable, and has the capacity to carry all necessary luggage."

Sure enough, this new BMW shattered the limits of everything imaginable in an enduro in terms of performance, riding characteristics, and style up to the day of its first public appearance in the south of France. Let's not forget that until the end of the 1970s, the off-road scene was dominated by clattering two-strokes, mainly with 250cc, at most 400cc displacement. Four-strokes, mostly

of Japanese provenance (e.g., the legendary Yamaha XT 500) only began appearing in numbers in 1974–1975 and had little more to offer than unruly one-cylinder engines without starters, bucking chassis with short suspension travel, and Spartan basic equipment with feeble electrical systems. As to displacement: 1/2-liter was the limit.

▍ "G" for "Gelande," "S" for street
Against this, BMW's brand new Super Enduro looked like something from another planet: a powerful and refined two-cylinder boxer engine with a generous 800 cubic centimeters of displacement and an impressive 50 horsepower, electric starter (initially as an option, then standard), plenty of space for two people with luggage, large gas tank with knee depressions for long nonstop stages, comfortable and directionally stable special frame and suspension. The entire machine had been specifically designed for a mixed application: off-road ("G") and street ("S").

From the original press release: "Largest in displacement, lightest in weight and fastest on the street in the

An unmistakable silhouette entirely devoid of baubles: The original R 80 G/S with distinctive rear end.

combined street/off-road class, the R 80 G/S is aimed at those motorcyclists who don't merely expect value in their machines but want riding pleasure on the road and off." The pleasure could be had starting at 8,350 marks.

As had been hoped, the epoch making "Monolever" rear-wheel swingarm got big headlines in the trade and general press. Unlike all previous BMW motorcycles and competing machines, the swingarm was supported by a lone gas pressure shock running along the wheel's right side. The swingarm itself did not display the usual dual tubes, but only one especially sturdy arm of cast light alloy. Protected from dust and humidity, the driveshaft ran rearward from the gearbox through this tube, imparting the rotary movement via universal joint and pinion to the large crown wheel in the differential.

The fixing of the rear wheel to the hub was another highlight: It was secured with only three bolts and could thus be removed as easily as the wheel of an automobile. On the R 80 G/S one searched in vain for the familiar knockout wheel spindle. As a bonus, the new design yielded a 4-pound weight reduction. Torsional resistance increased by 50 percent, and undesirable lateral forces at shock compression was reduced. "The BMW R 80 G/S is the first production motorcycle among the large field of street and off-road–capable machines to be equipped with such a swingarm design," as BMW's public relations department never tired of pointing out.

The R 80 G/S was at home on twisting roads and light terrain. The single-sided swingarm was perceived as revolutionary in 1980. Very wide: the classic ohv two-valve boxer.

New universal tires, good to 180 kilometers per hour

It is also noteworthy that the R 80 G/S was the first motorcycle of its type to be equipped with a racing-tested front wheel disc brake featuring asbestos-free semi-metal pads. The absence of asbestos helped the environment, and the semi-metal construction shortened the breaking distance on wet surfaces by 40 percent versus conventional pads. What's more, the pads were lighter, better at dissipating heat, and had no tendency to smudge .

Unlike the old R 75/5's conventional drum brake, the disc, with its ample 264-millimeter diameter, performed satisfactorily even when the bike was loaded with two riders and their luggage, tipping the scales at a hefty 398-kilogram total weight. In view of its performance and equipment and compared to today's four-valve enduros the bike's 167-kilogram dry weight was sensationally low. Gassed up, its curb weight rose to 191 kilograms.

The special Metzeler tires, approved to 180 kilometers per hour, also were a new development. Up to that point, off-road aficionados had to be content with tires that could only cope with speeds up to 130 kilometers per hour. But the R 80 G/S effortlessly reached speeds above 165 kilometers per hour in fifth gear, thus becoming the world's fastest enduro. BMW sang the new tire's

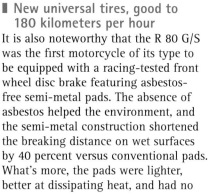

Top: *Author Hans J. Schneider with the first R 80 G/S at the model presentation in the south of France, September 1, 1980. At the time, with a top speed of 165 kilometers per hour, the R 80 G/S was the world's fastest enduro.*

Above: *The Monolever with the single rear shock.*

praises: "Working with tire designers, we've developed a tire which allows speeds of up to 180 kilometers per hour on the road, yet masters difficult terrain."

But in practice the tire's shortcomings were soon apparent: The Metzler tires' lateral stability proved inadequate on slippery surfaces such as wet grass. As a result, the machine tended to break out sideways. Traction also declined once the profile had filled up with mud. On gravel and asphalt, however, the tire design was convincing. Moreover, the Metzeler tires proved resistant to aqua-planing.

In the February 1981 issue of *Motorrad* magazine, the author, then a freelancer for that publication, summed up his experiences with the G/S tires on a 4,500-kilometer tour through the Alps and the Pyrenees: "On dry tracks, the universal tires' adherence was adequate. But on wet surfaces, the Cardan boxer would spin out." Decreasing front and rear tire pressure to 1.5 bar improved handling on rocky trails.

The 50-horsepower two-cylinder boxer engine was based on the R 80/7 street model's 797cc powerplant, though in many respects it had been adapted to its new role. Although the maximum torque of 56.7 (Nm) only became available at 5,000 rpm (later 4,000 rpm), the G/S still developed distinctly more steam in the "rpm cellar" than any other enduro of the time. "Especially in the new R 80 G/S, the famous powerplant for BMW motorcycles once again demonstrates its all-round capabilities and its superior design for extreme conditions." (From a BMW press release.)

The advantages of the proven boxer design really did reveal themselves above all on twisting mountain roads and far from paved roads. Anytime it proved necessary to elicit high performances at low speeds, the compact powerplant with the jutting, well cooled twin cylinders demonstrated Olympian poise. What's more, off-road the cylinders protected

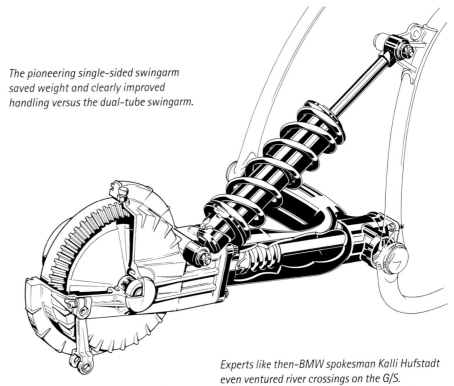

The pioneering single-sided swingarm saved weight and clearly improved handling versus the dual-tube swingarm.

Experts like then-BMW spokesman Kalli Hufstadt even ventured river crossings on the G/S.

the rider's lower legs from injuries caused by obstacles projecting into the bike's path. The mounting of safety or crash bars to protect cylinders and legs from the worse in case of a fall was recommended. During extreme mountain tours, the cylinders might still strike boulders. Gouged cooling fins were the result.

The boxer's quality and balance were outstanding. From the test log: "The two-cylinder boxer engine offers considerably improved operating characteristics versus the usual one-cylinder engines, both over long distances and off road." At the end of the 1970s, BMW had already demonstrated the design's competitive qualities with specially tuned forerunners to the R 80 G/S (see pages 6–18). Maintenance-free electronic ignition, Nikasil-coated light-alloy cylinders with correspondingly high heat resistance, oil pan protection, and a new two-into-one exhaust system all figured prominently among the G/S boxer's technical characteristics. The cylinder walls' high-quality Nikasil coating served primarily to keep oil consumption low and limit wear. As with all boxer engines of the then new generation, the dry air filter together with its dustproof housing sat at the back of the engine atop the transmission case and was easy to replace.

A specially developed, ultra-light clutch greatly reduced the required lever pressure.

The author tested the G/S on a 4,500-kilometer European tour in the fall of 1980. This photo was taken in the Pyrenees.

For added convenience, every G/S was equipped with both electric and kick starter from 1982. However, because of a weak battery, the electric starter often quit much too soon. This meant raising the machine on its stand, stepping up on the cylinder with the left foot, then kicking down forcefully with the right.

Two points impressed particularly: the bike's powerful halogen headlight

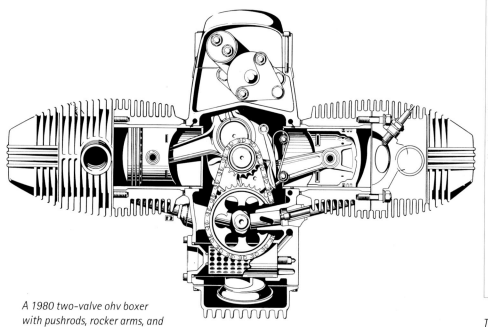

A 1980 two-valve ohv boxer with pushrods, rocker arms, and central camshaft.

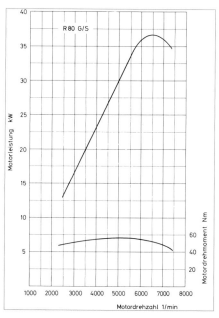

Typical: flat torque curve, continuously increasing power.

and its great range. While others had to more or less grope their way through the darkness with their weak 6-volt lamps, the G/S's 12-volt H4 headlight (almost) turned night into day. Despite its remarkable performances, the G/S proved quite frugal in fuel consumption (regular). In long-distance testing over many thousands of kilometers of freeway, highway, and open country, it had an average mileage of 5.9 liters per kilometer. This, together with an imposing tank capacity of 19.5 liters, yielded an impressive range of 330 kilometers.

The seat was entirely adequate for two riders, though the upholstery of the first G/S series left much to be desired. The looks of the rather crudely configured cockpit took some getting used to, yet the speedometer and indicator lamps were highly readable. Additional instruments (tachometer and voltmeter) were available as an option.

▌ 1984 Limited Edition "Paris-Dakar" G/S

Three months after its premiere, the BMW caused a sensation in racing. In January 1981, Hubert Auriol won the motorcycle-shredding Paris-Dakar rally on a specially modified competition version of the R 80 G/S. The Frenchman gave an encore performance in 1983. Belgian motocross star Gaston Rahier rode the BMW to victory in 1984 and 1985 (for details, see the "Almost too

Bringing dreams to life—with the most convincing two-in-one bike to date: How BMW marketed the G/S

In the '80s motorcycling will continue to gain new and interesting aspects. Today's desire to spend leisure time in the pursuit of stronger experiences, to realize oneself, one's desires and dreams will give rise to a very original style of travel: far from the beaten track of vacation RVs, with the aim of discovering the land and people, a country's authentic and intense character. Seek out and experience the back roads. Leave behind the main highways or the pavement altogether. For this, but also for everything else a motorcycle must offer in everyday riding pleasure, BMW has created a whole new class: the 80 G/S. G/S—as in off-road and street.
Sales brochure, fall 1980

The BMW R 80 G/S is the most convincing two-in-one motorcycle to date. It's both: an off-road and a street bike. Personality: bred for adventure, refined, fast, and confident on the road, built as the ultimate leisure time instrument for every situation. At a dry weight of 172 kilograms, it's the lightest production motorcycle in this displacement class. You'll experience it in the handling of this machine, which, with a payload of over 200 kilograms, can also serve as a touring

pack mule. Available for first time in an off-road capable production machine, the racing tested BMW Monolever guarantees precise tracking and accurate rear wheel guidance; what's more, it makes replacement of the rear wheel easy.
Press release, fall 1982

"Good times in open country"—that's the idea behind the new BMW R 80 G/S. Under "open country" the Munich motorcycle builders don't just mean gravel roads, meadow trails, and mud holes but first and foremost paved roads far from main travel and transport routes. The BMW R 80 G/S is designed as a leisure instrument with universal applications. This machine's sport features, its high performance in everyday use and while traveling open up a new dimension in motorcycling.
Text from press pack, September 1980

The R 80 G/S is the ideal motorcycle for adventure travel. Whether on asphalt or off, it's equally at home. Its off-road capable special tires are approved to 170 kilometers an hour. It's the right machine for individualists who blaze their own trails.
Press release, 1985

Cross-section of the 50-horsepower boxer and the compact five-speed gearbox.

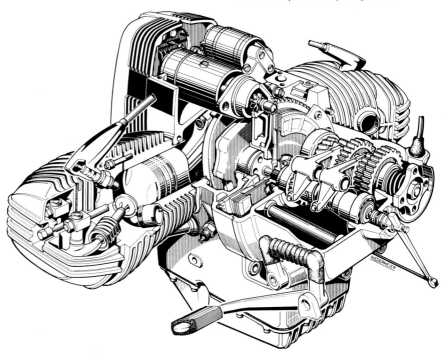

Down Spanish lanes with the G/S.

good for off road: the R 100 GS Paris-Dakar Classic" on page 50).

Quite logically, BMW crowned its rally victories with a special edition model. The Paris-Dakar R 80 G/S came out in 1984. It was equipped with an enormous 32-liter tank, a comfortable red solo seat, chromed exhaust, and large rear luggage rack. The mudguards and tank were painted Alpine White, and the kit included knee guards and "Paris-Dakar" emblems. Michelin T 61 tires, cylinder guards, and side stand completed the equipment. The special parts (tank, solo seat, luggage rack) were also available individually, or in a kit to upgrade the standard R 80 G/S.

It wasn't just in sport that the G/S quickly asserted itself. From year to year, it became more popular as a long-distance motorcycle. Riders from the four corners of the world crisscrossed the globe on the BMW enduro, leaving

tracks from China and Australia to Africa, Alaska, and Tierra del Fuego. To this day, BMW enduros are top drawer when it comes to exploring the world on adventurous trails. The readers of *Tourenfahrer* magazine again and again elected the BMW two-cylinder enduros "Touring Bike of the Year." Simply put, hardly any other motorcycle had (or has) so many good all-round qualities and is so perfectly adapted to sporting excursions on winding mountain roads or long-distance travel.

▍ Vigorous model upgrading year after year

Yet, as nothing in this world is 100 percent perfect, the R 80 G/S, like any mass production model, underwent constant improvement through the years. In September 1981, it received a wider rear-wheel rim (2.50x18) to improve handling. In addition, BMW reduced the diameter of the brake master cylinder piston to 12 millimeters, thus boosting the front brake's effectiveness. The seat's overly soft polyurethane foam was replaced by more resilient latex foam. Gearbox overshift prevention facilitated shifting. In April 1982, engineers upgraded the transmission gears.

From October 1982, there was an effort to improve the exhaust system's corrosion resistance with a new glossy, rather than matte, black coating. Two months later, BMW endowed the telescopic front fork dampers with a new valve housing, thus eliminating the occasional rattle. A major modification came in September 1983. Because oil would occasionally penetrate into the rear brake, the brake pedal was remounted. Clutch operability improved in January 1984 once the gearbox output shaft spline was nickel plated. In July 1984, the G/S received a new brake fluid reservoir with cap, new membrane, and modified ventilation. This effectively prevented the brake fluid from absorbing any water. Environmentally conscious G/S riders welcomed the fact that from December 1984 their machine could run on unleaded gas; specially hardened exhaust valve seats made it possible. However, upgrading the boxer engine was rather expensive.

In 1985, in order to reduce bearing play, BMW replaced the needle bearing in the differential with a tapered roller bearing. In March of the same year, the damper in the gearbox was modified

to absorb more extreme stresses. Then, near the end of the 1987 production, genuine love of detail found expression: the rear-wheel brake shoe return springs received a special coating to prevent swingarm breakages caused by cracks in the previously used zinc coating.

As a final modification to the original model, the return springs were also damped with rubber in February 1987. Counting the Paris-Dakar versions, exactly 24,309 units of the original series rolled off BMW's motorcycle assembly line at Berlin-Spandau.

▍ High standards of workmanship and long-term value

How well the R 80 G/S stood up to daily use was demonstrated among other ways by a long-distance test conducted by *Motorrad* magazine and published in issue 21/1981. Test results after 25,000 kilometers: "The frame paintwork was like new. The boxer engine's compression chart revealed

Munich, May 1982: Easy Rider *producer and star Peter Fonda becomes an honorary member of the European BMW Clubs. At left is then-club president (and ex-director of BMW motorcycle division) Helmut Werner Bönsch.*

Top and above: *The 1984 Paris-Dakar model offered at 10,120 DM.*

Above left: *Hubert Auriol in transit on the 67-horsepower 1,000cc special boxer at the 1983 Paris-Dakar Rally.*

Left: *Two-time Paris-Dakar winner Gaston Rahier with the 75-horsepower Rally 1000 from 1984 and the production Paris-Dakar R 80 G/S launched in the same year.*

Above: *An R 80 G/S at the end of 1984.*

Right: *The original G/S in its final 1986–87 version.*

no signs of fatigue. The Nikasil-coated cylinder barrels displayed barely measurable wear, just as the pistons and piston rings. The crankshaft drive looked as if it only had a couple of thousand kilometers on it. The R 80 G/S could have gone on like this for another 25,000 kilometers. Considering the extreme stresses to which we subjected it, on the road and off, the 80 G/S passed the long-distance test with

flying colors. With its low per kilometer cost, problem-free operation, and high reliability, the "all-purpose bike" earned a rating of "highly recommended."

▌ Low maintenance, to the present day

Nowadays, the R 80 G/S already rates as a classic. As always with BMW, spare parts aren't a problem. Maintenance is simple, but only machines in truly mint

condition justify the high asking prices for vehicles from the original series. Among the weaknesses of the older models are creeping oil leakage from the crankcase and gearbox area. Valve play requires regular checks; apart from the spark plug connectors, the electrical system is robust.

Quite pleasant to ride were machines equipped with the longer final gear reduction in the rear axle characteristic

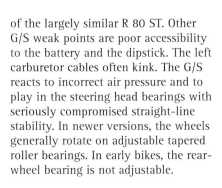

of the largely similar R 80 ST. Other G/S weak points are poor accessibility to the battery and the dipstick. The left carburetor cables often kink. The G/S reacts to incorrect air pressure and to play in the steering head bearings with seriously compromised straight-line stability. In newer versions, the wheels generally rotate on adjustable tapered roller bearings. In early bikes, the rear-wheel bearing is not adjustable.

Top and above: *In 1983, the author acquired this R 80 G/S in a fine Dark Blue Metallic. The bike was sold in 1987. Years later, he tried to buy it back, but the price was outrageous and the machine was in pathetic condition.*

Top left: *At the beginning of the 1980s, actor Gotz George did PR for the G/S. The machines were provided at no charge.*

Above left: *Kalli Hufstadt on the R 80 G/S in 1980.*

Leisure time motorcycle with universal applications—A reliable machine, suited above all to long distances

The G/S stands out through its amazing handling, supported by well balanced and comfortable suspension/damping adjustment; nothing seems to rattle this BMW, it goes exactly where you want it, with no vibration, no chassis instability. Wobble during fast straight line motion is not unknown in BMWs, but not with this new machine. It rides confidently and with good tracking stability over long straight-aways. Even at 170 kilometers per hour, ruts and medians were barely perceptible. The G/S is the best street motorcycle BMW has ever built.

Motorrad, August 1980

The unconventional rear-wheel suspension is technically remarkable: a single low-torsion swingarm secures the wheel while enclosing the driving mechanism, a Cardan shaft with all its components. Suspension and damping functions are accomplished by a single off-center suspension arm. Whoever settles on this new BMW should not misunderstand it as a Super Enduro, but see it rather as a maneuverable street bike with good riding characteristics on firm surfaces; 170 kilometers per hour are reached effortlessly. And the new tires hold up to this without a problem.

Lubecker Nachrichten, September 1980

The BMW enduro is no sport machine for hard off-roading. Nor is it a big touring bike like other BMWs. Rather, the new R 80 G/S is something in between. It's a good street machine with somewhat Spartan equipment, and it handles dirt roads and light terrain. Long tours are not a problem thanks to its 20-liter tank and adequate performances. It's a travel-enduro and as such a rather good compromise.

PS, September 1980

The torsion stiffness of the single powerful swingarm is considerably superior to that of a conventional dual swingarm. And wheel removal could not be simpler: there are only three bolts to unscrew, no more than with a car. What's more, 2 kilograms are shaved off the bike's weight by the use of a single suspension arm instead of the usual two.

mo, October 1980

I was surprised at how lightly this motorcycle can be swung left and right around bends and tight curves, even with a passenger. The new single-sided swingarm demonstrates its extra 30 percent of torsional stiffness when crossing pavement medians, ruts, and seams. On dirt roads and on moderate, dry terrain this bike is a lot of fun to ride. The BMW R 80 G/S should be viewed as a leisure time bike with universal applications.

Der Syburger, June 1981

Among all heavy enduros, the G/S features respectable suspension travel, even when fully loaded. And this also offers a security advantage on extreme trails. When the riding gets tough, the electric starter constitutes a real advantage. The Cardan drive, whose importance grows immeasurably on long trips, offers an additional comfort advantage. There's no more chain maintenance, no tightening, no extra chain, pinion, or riveting tool to lug around. Not to mention the ridiculously easy wheel removal. Incidentally, this becomes even easier with the center stand, something not offered on most other enduros.

Tourenfahrer, February 1983

After some initial doubts, word is out that this BMW is a tough, undemanding, reliable and above all globe-trotting machine. Whether traveling the Pan-American Highway from Tierra del Fuego to Alaska, crossing African deserts, the Australian Outback or winding up Himalayan passes, the R 80 G/S simply never quits.

VDI-Nachrichten, September 1990

On the first R 80 G/S, the rear spring was soft. The machine thus sank low even in normal riding.

Above: *Kalli Hufstadt, then a member of the BMW press department, gets the original 1980 G/S airborne for the camera.*

Right: *In 1984, this R 80 G/S equipped with protection bars reveals itself as a beautiful and timeless classic. Nowadays, it's rare to find machines from the initial series in original and well-maintained condition. Many of the 24,309 machines (including Paris-Dakar versions) built from 1980 to 1987 got worn out on long-distance travels. In its day, the G/S, equipped with cases, large tank, and every imaginable accessory, was the archetypical adventure motorcycle.*

Pioneering frame and suspension technology: Paralever models from 1987

In 1987, fans of the blue-and-white brand had their eyes riveted on Florence. For it was here, in picturesque Tuscany, that from August 24 to 29 the successor models to the now venerable R 80 G/S had their world premiere. The R 80 GS and R 100 GS, now written without forward slash, constituted a cautious and logical development of the proven concept. Design and fundamental principle remained unchanged, but in detail the BMW engineers had modified and optimized almost everything. The most far reaching changes concerned the twin-cylinder enduro's frame and suspension.

Thus the 1987–1988 models featured an essentially redesigned "Paralever" rear swingarm constructed of sturdy aluminum alloy. The double-joint swingarm principle, applied for the first time in a production machine, effectively reduced the typical driveshaft starting torque, sometimes perceived as unpleasant, along with front-wheel lift during strong acceleration. Other load alteration effects, such as lifting of the rear end while braking, now also belonged to the past. BMW's revolutionary Paralever design was equal in its effect to a swingarm length of 1,400 millimeters, thus providing a moment distribution of about 70 percent.

▌ Effective suppression of driveshaft-related spurious effects, longer suspension travel

The Paralever swingarm was made of a low-pressure die-cast light alloy. It retained the proven tapered roller bearing with superior adjustment possibilities. Two additional, equally adjustable tapered roller bearings were located in the joint between the swingarm and the transmission case. The weight of the new swingarm assembly was kept down by the use of light alloy. A truing of all details with a computer program applying finite element analysis had further improved the torsional strength of the rear-wheel swingarm. Despite its more elaborate technology, the new Paralever assembly was only 1.6 kilograms heavier than the old Monolever system. In order to keep the unsprung weight low on the new GS models, BMW retained the light drum brake with 200 millimeters diameter for the rear wheel. However, the brake was now no longer actuated by rods but by cable.

Rear-wheel suspension travel had grown from 170 to 180 millimeters. The more sharply inclined monoshock with Boge gas damper had slightly progressive characteristics, four adjustment positions, and was now directly anchored to the rear-axle housing. The front suspension was also new. Both models featured Marzocchi telescopic forks, each with a stabilizer between the fork sliders; travel was now 225 millimeters instead of 200 millimeters. The Italian off-road chassis specialist had clinched the BMW contract with forks provided for the Paris-Dakar rally and used to devastating effect.

The Marzocchi fork was a technical gem with especially durable plain bearing mounting between stanchions and sliders. The light-alloy sliders slid on bushings made of multi-layered Babbitt metal with a Teflon coating.

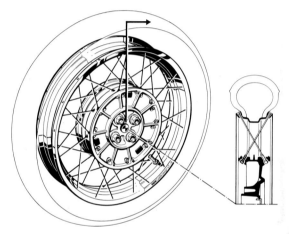

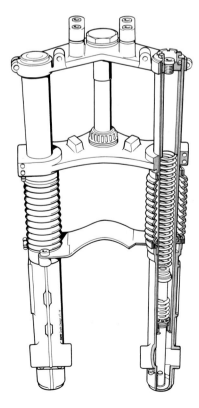

The drawings are of a GS model cross-spoke wheel and Marzocchi telescopic fork.

Above: *The Paralever swingarm of an R 80 GS from 1987, with brake actuation via a cable instead of rods, as previously.*

Opposite: *This press photo shows the first 1987 R 100 GS.*

The damping components operated with an especially high oil volume, high oil throughput, and ample bore cross sections. The result: adequate damping even under hard off-road conditions. The hollow front axle, with a diameter of 25 millimeters, was dimensioned like that of the K models of the time.

The markedly stronger fork assembly prevented warping of the fork while braking. The stanchion diameter had increased from 36 to 40 millimeters. The larger and more responsive solo brake disc on the front wheels of the new models (285 millimeters, as in the R 80 street model, versus 260 millimeters for

the old G/S) must also be considered a safety upgrade. The Brembo brake caliper was a notch larger and stronger. The brake's hydraulic system was modified to lessen required actuation pressure.

▌ Paralever GS with reinforced frame and new cross–spoke wheels

The BMW enduro's frame also underwent improvements. Thus, BMW reinforced the oval tubes running through the tank tunnel. Altogether, the new GS models impressed on the road and off with riding characteristics which, when compared to its competition, deserved to be called fantastic.

Just as innovative was the wheels' cross-spoke design. This new, patented solution offered multiple advantages. It allowed running the spokes through the rim flange; this in turn permitted the use of tubeless tires, with the added advantage that these could be changed without difficulty using normal tire irons. Moreover, the spokes, whose nipples were located on the hub side, could easily be changed, even with tire mounted and wheel in place.

A GS model of the 1987–88 vintage: an R 100 GS at top and an R 80 GS above. Paralever technology effectively suppressed the unpleasant Cardan reactions in the GS. The long spring travel of models from 1987 improved comfort, especially when riding with a passenger.

Paralever: Suppression of load alteration effects

When BMW engineers began designing the Paralever swingarm in the mid-1980s, they proceeded from the following set of considerations: All power transmitted to wheels produces specific reactions in cars, as it does in motorcycles. The effect known as "dynamic wheel load transfer" occurs even if all wheels are unsprung. Sprung-wheel suspensions are especially sensitive to drive torque. The extent of the reactions is dependent on the geometrical configuration of the suspension elements.

In motorcycles, the type of secondary drive also plays a part. Thus, in chain-driven machines there is a tendency to spring compression in a swingarm-guided rear wheel while accelerating. In shaft-driven machines, the reaction is exactly opposite: The wheel spring extends. On the other hand, the rear end settles when the throttle is suddenly released or while braking. Understandably, the engineers wished to remedy this.

In theory, lengthening the rear-wheel swingarm was the simplest, and most obvious, means to suppress these reactions. But in practice, this solution can only be partially successful. Calculations have demonstrated that

on a BMW, for complete compensation, the swingarm would have to be longer than the wheelbase, an incredible 1,700 millimeters. Obviously this is not easy to realize in series production.

Yet, with the Paralever the BMW designers came upon a solution of striking simplicity: The advanced double-joint swingarm produces the same effect as an extreme lengthening within a substantially smaller space. The technicians explain this in the following terms: "The parallelogram linkage increases the radius of the wheel path." Or expressed differently: the GS's double-joint swingarm (or that of the four-valve boxer or of the K models), designed according to the parallelogram principle, largely suppresses unpleasant load alteration effects.

In point of fact, BMW's revolutionary Paralever design corresponded in its effect to a swingarm length of 1,400

millimeters, thus providing a moment distribution of about 70 percent. On the road, this translates into a perceptible increase in riding safety and stability, especially in borderline situations: strong acceleration, braking in curves, or fast riding on sinuous courses with frequent load alterations.

Customized improvements are possible through individualized tuning of suspension to damping. Installation of a harder shock in the rear has proven itself for long-distance travel and riding with two persons. Corresponding parts for older models are available from parts shops and BMW.

The wheel's limited width at the spokes' intersection, a function of the design, offered useful clearance for the larger brake caliper at the front, for example, but also at the rear, for the Paralever's bulging bearing assembly, which in a conventional spoke wheel would have led to a considerable decrease in the spoke's strength, hence to an unstable rear wheel. The wheel's novel design also made it possible to mount a modern low profile tire (130/80x17) on the wider rear rim as opposed to the earlier standard 4.00x18 tire; this contributed decisively to increased tractive force. The advantage of easy rear wheel changes remained, now with four bolts to loosen instead of three, as in the old G/S.

For the first time, special enduro tires were mounted, rated at 190 kilometers per hour. These were new designs from Metzeler, with a herringbone profile. Comfort was not the new tire's forte (loud tire noise), but they offered solid grip and good tracking.

A view of the revolutionary 1987 Paralever swingarm: two universal joints, a cable-actuated drum brake, and an extremely inclined rear shock.

The R 100 GS in the 1987 original version.

▮ High-end model with 980cc and 60 horsepower

The powerplant made a large leap forward. The top of the line R 100 GS model had jumped to 980cc displacement and 60 horsepower (44 kilowatts) at a relatively low 6,500 rpm. The maximum torque also spoke volumes about the character of the new machine: an impressive 76 Nm at only 3,750. All round performance and top speed, well over 180 kilometers per hour, were equally outstanding. In the face of growing competition, BMW had once again managed to create a superlative: the strongest and fastest enduro in the world.

The confident Bavarians had this to say: "The 1-liter engine opens two entirely new prospects for enduros. It's a bonus for all those in a hurry on long trips and not adverse to occasionally riding at the top speed of 181 kilometers per hour (R 80 GS: 168 kilometers per hour); and, with its enormous tractive power from high torque at low rpm, it's also a boon to all those adventurers rambling in pairs with heavy loads through distant lands."

Left: *Riding twisting roads was a lot of fun on the maneuverable R 80 GS. Pictured is the 1987 model.*

Two Bing CV carburetors with 40 millimeters instead of 32 millimeters diameter provided the air/gas mixture. The valvetrain had become more "stable" through better bushing of the rocker arms. Modification of the valve seats allowed permanent use of unleaded gasoline, in keeping with the growing environmental consciousness of the 1980s. An oil cooler protected the 1-liter boxer engine from overheating when the bike was fully loaded. The redesigned electric starter, operating on the gear reduction principle and with lower amp consumption, was also 2 kilograms lighter. And the new GS had a distinctly more powerful 25-Ah battery.

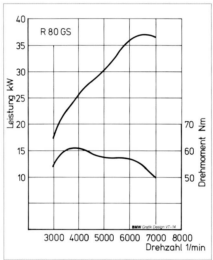

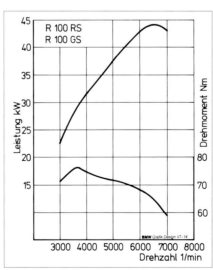

Top: *Torque and power chart for the R 80 GS,* **underneath** *for the R 100 GS.*

▮ Increased range through larger tanks

The exhaust system's pre-silencer, located under the gearbox, was considerably larger though only slightly heavier. Its volume had risen from 1.5 to 3.8 liters. The increase was good both for noise reduction and the torque band.

All these detail improvements naturally also benefited the R 80 GS, whose performances were otherwise identical to those of the original model: 50 horsepower (37 kilowatts). Large reconfigured 26-liter tanks with a 4.7-liter reserve and seats that rose in the front improved range and comfort of the new enduro models. When dry (without gas, oil, and tools), the GS twins each tipped the scales at 187 kilograms; curb weight was 210 kilograms. With 210 kilograms of payload, both machines offered the ideal basis for touring in pairs with luggage. A small cockpit windshield (standard on the R 100 GS) reduced airflow pressure.

The seats were now longer, wider, and more comfortable. Despite longer suspension travel, saddle height was not unpleasant; it was limited to 850 millimeters. For especially big riders, a seat with an 880-millimeter saddle height was optional. The upholstery had been distinctly upgraded with a layered construction of special polyurethane and elastic latex foam.

The motor and travel press reacted to the big new enduros with great interest. (See "Echoes from the press" box on page 48.) It was above all the Paralever suspension that elicited enthusiasm. Following an extensive GS tour through Tuscany, the author made the following report in *Abenteuer und Reisen* (June 1987): "Already after the first few feet, the redesigned R 80 GS astonishes with wonderful handling; in traffic, it handles like a bicycle. On the road, its handling of curves is unrivaled, even in sport bikes. And inexperienced riders will immediately do well on this new model. The old R 80 G/S required a lot more getting used to." There's more: "The entirely redesigned frame and suspension handle bumps and diagonal grooves with supreme confidence; the machine doesn't shake [and] displays absolutely no load alteration effects. There aren't many machines with which one feels so immediately at one as the new GS."

■ **An unsuccessful entry-level model: The Monolever R 65 GS**

In September 1987, a relatively inexpensive entry-level model, the R 65 GS (9, 200 DM), went into production. Frame, suspension, and equipment were identical to those of the old R 80 G/S: Monolever swingarm and smaller 19.5-liter tank. It was powered by the R 65's two-cylinder boxer engine curbed to 27 horsepower. With a maximum torque of 43 Nm at 3,500 rpm, the little GS delivered the same outstanding power from the bottom as BMW's other, larger displacement boxer models. Yet, at higher speeds the engine felt sluggish and overworked. The R 65 GS had a payload of 200 kilograms for a curb weight of 198 kilograms. To the end of 1990, 1,334 units of this classical, simply designed enduro-base model rolled out of BMW's Berlin plant. Production was then terminated, officially for "profitability reasons," more likely because the machine simply didn't sell.

A distinctive front view of the 1987 R 100 GS. The small wind deflector and the laterally mounted oil-cooler are characteristic of that model. The Metzeler tires specifically developed for BMW offered adequate grip on asphalt but had only limited off-road capability.

Top: *A 1987 R 80 GS on the road.*

Above: *An R 100 GS at the presentation near Florence in August 1987.*

Left: *The R 65 G/S with Monolever swingarm, produced in limited numbers from 1987 to 1990.*

39

1987 GS presentation in Florence: "New patented solutions"

As the saying goes: better is the enemy of good. Besides the many acknowledgments of the R 80 G/S design to date, we have also received criticism and suggestions. You will see a great many of these wishes for improvement embodied in the new R 80 GS and R 100 GS. Based on displacement and torque, the R 100 GS is now the largest and most powerful production enduro in the world. Our central development task was to ensure that frame and suspension could successfully handle the increased power.
Richard Heydenreich, chief of BMW Motorcycle Advanced Development and Testing Department, at the GS presentation, Florence, August 1987

The enduro segment is currently in a trend toward increased displacement and performance and larger fuel-tank volumes. This also implies a movement from pure enduro machines to street/ long-distance motorcycles possessing certain off-road capabilities, an evolution initiated by the BMW R 80 G/S. The new GS generation of the R 80 GS and R 100 GS demonstrates our continuing commitment to this development. With two new patented solutions, the double joint swingarm, known as Paralever, and cross-spoke wheels, the new GS models

stand out with technical progress, which we believe in because it enhances riding comfort and functionality.
Dietrich Maronde, sales and marketing director, BMW Motorrad GmbH, Florence, 1987

Exactly one year ago, here in Florence, we introduced you to our new enduro models R 80 GS and R 100 GS. Their market success so far has exceeded our expectations. In Germany, at 1,870 units sold up to July, the R 100 GS is not merely the best-selling motorcycle in the over 750cc class, it's the best-selling motorcycle, period. This has more than a little to do with why we recorded a registration increase of 7.2 percent over the previous year and have been able to comfort our market leadership in Germany in the over 750cc class.
Dr. Eberhardt C. Sarfert, chief representative of BMW AG and chairman of the board of BMW Motorrad GmbH, 1988, at the IFMA in Cologne

With its new GS models, BMW has pursued one goal above any other: first-class enduro riding.
BMW motorcycle program press packet, 1988

■ **Model upgrading from July 1988 in detail**

For all GS versions, July 15, 1988, marked the first model upgrade: an improved kick-start shaft design. Readers of *Tourenfahrer* magazine elected the R 100 GS "Touring Bike of the Year." In September, BMW began building a GORE-TEX membrane into the tachometer housing to suppress the tachometer glass panel's annoying tendency to fog over. In November 1988, in response to widespread customer requests, the R 80 GS and R 100 GS models were equipped with a lighter and more responsive shock at the rear. The stiffer version continued to be available.

■ **Long-distance boxer: The R 100 GS "Paris-Dakar"**

The main attraction at the 1988 International Bicycle and Motorcycle Exposition (IFMA) in Cologne was the new R 100 GS Paris-Dakar. Yet another success in the notorious desert rally had preceded the presentation: Well known Munich BMW specialist Eddy Hau had won the race's independent rider standings on an R 80 G/S modified for the occasion by the Bavarian firm HPN and replicas were made available in a small production run.

The media presentation of the Paralever models took place in 1987 in Tuscany.
Opposite: *The R 80 GS with the author.*

Above: *The R 100 GS's long shock travel was great for riding with a passenger.*

Right: *Reviewer Wilhelm Hahne with the R 100 GS.* **Below right:** *Thanks to the advanced Paralever swingarm, the R 100 GS displayed distinctly better handling than the old G/S.*

The Paris-Dakar Kit, specifically developed for the R 100 GS, was primarily designed to meet the higher standards expected from a long-distance motorcycle. These were wind, weather, and gravel protection, and excellent adaptable luggage stowage.

From September 1989, kit components were made available, initially in individual form, for subsequent upgrading. Beginning in 1989, the Paris-Dakar version could be purchased as an individual model ex-works. The 35-liter special tank, made of paintable plastic and equipped with a locking stowage compartment, was imposing. The new fairing, bolted to the steering head at four points and at two to the frame, offered good protection from the elements.

In contrast to ordinary systems, a red tubular frame, which served as a fastener, ran conspicuously outside the fairing. This had practical advantages: the tubes protected the fairing from damage in case of a fall. The central section had ample space for standard and additional instrumentation. A new rectangular halogen headlight derived from the K 75 S was integrated to the fairing. An aerodynamically optimized wind deflector and rubberized turn signals rounded out the equipment. The fairing connected to the tank.

A sturdy aluminum engine guard plate was bolted under the oil pan; it

A new era dawned in 1987 with the Paralever models. **Top and above:** There were 12,063 R 100 GS units produced in 1990. **Right:** The concurrently offered R 80 GS sold only 3,938 units for the same period. Apart from the absence of a windshield, it was indistinguishable from the 1000. The cut-away shows the 1987 R 100 GS's brilliant "propulsion" technology. While the 1000's engine developed 60 horsepower, the 800's motor put out 50 horsepower.

technical art

"SLS" Secondary Air System

Since September 1990, BMW offered the so-called SLS (German: Sekundar-Luft-System) Secondary Air System on all R models with dual-cylinder, two-valve boxer engines. This device reduced emissions of hydrocarbons (HC) by approximately 30 percent and of carbon monoxide (CO) by approximately 40 percent through exhaust post-combustion, with no reduction in power output, torque, and mileage. Retrofit on older machines with boxer engines was impractical, however, because of the complex associated technical demands. By the end of two-valve production in 1996, new boxer motorcycles were being almost exclusively delivered with this relatively environmentally friendly system.

The SLS system had already been successfully deployed in the United States and Switzerland to comply with emissions regulations there. It exploited the pressure fluctuations pulsing through the two-cylinder engine's exhaust system during the four-stroke combustion process. The pressure waves acted upon two membrane valves within the air filter housing, which, when open, sucked in fresh air. This air was then conveyed via steel tubes to both cylinder heads, where, directly behind the exhaust valves, it entered the exhaust system. The resulting excess air together with the elevated exhaust temperature resulted in direct combustion of HC and CO.

Backfiring was avoided by interruption of secondary air supply during overrun. To this end, the left SLS valve possessed an additional valve that was controlled by the inlet tract and affected the required air shutoff. The right valve drew its fresh air directly from the left valve via a hose. This interrupted air intake during the critical overrun phase.

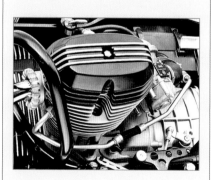

even protected the frame tubes and the exhaust manifold. As if this were not enough: a cylinder guard, hand protectors, a partial engine cover of impact-resistant plastic, and a widened and aluminum-reinforced front mudguard were also included in the Paris-Dakar equipment. The wide solo seat was ideal for trips alone. It allowed space for a distinctly longer luggage rack. The standard double seat with smaller luggage rack was also still available. Not surprisingly, the richly equipped 60-horsepower machine's weight climbed up to 236 kilograms (with a full tank); yet this didn't affect performance, with a top speed of 180 kilometers per hour.

BMW did not have to wait long for the success of its enduro strategy: at 5,865 units, the R 100 GS was Germany's best-selling motorcycle of 1988. Yet the Bavarians didn't see this as a reason to rest on their laurels. Additional improvements came in 1989. Both GS models were now made available with the choice of a softer suspension shock. On request, the machines could also be delivered with lower mounted front mudguards. In September 1989, all BMW boxer models, including enduros, received an improved rear-wheel drum brake with brake shoes, which had been widened from 25 to 27.5 millimeters.

From early 1990, BMW offered a sport frame and suspension jointly developed with the Dutch firm White Power for subsequent upgrading of GS models. It had somewhat longer, progressively wound telescopic fork springs with improved weight-bearing capacity and an adjustable sport suspension shock for the rear swingarm.

The company took a significant environmental step forward in 1990: All two-cylinder boxer models would henceforth be deliverable with the then fairly advanced secondary air system. SLS operated on the exhaust post-combustion principle, reducing emissions of hydrocarbons by approximately 30 percent and carbon monoxide by about 40 percent. Engine performance, torque, and mileage were not affected (see box, at left).

▌ Models with the new look from 1990

At the 1990 IFMA, on the 10-year anniversary of BMW's most successful motorcycle series, the R 80 GS and R 100 GS enduros displayed a new (though arguably not more beautiful) look. Like the Paris-Dakar version introduced in 1989, the new models featured a bolt-on cockpit fairing with exterior tubular frame and integrated K 75 rectangular headlight. The tilt adjustable wind deflector and both

The R 100 GS Paris-Dakar was particularly well-suited for long-distance travel (all pictures show the 1988 IFMA version). The fairing was protected by a tubular frame; the cockpit made a clean and sporty impression. The sturdy aluminum engine guard also came standard.

instruments (speedometer to the left, tachometer to the right) were entirely new designs. The indicator lights were located top center under a glass cover. The prices had risen to 12,800 DM and 14,950 DM, respectively.

The handlebar controls of the K Series now provided enhanced comfort.

The K Series' automatic blinker cancel mechanism could, however, not be adopted. Neither did the GS models possess an electronic speedometer. Steering head bearings with fine thread adjustment also from the K 75 now allowed a more precise setting of bearing clearance.

▌Floating brake disc

For effective attachment of the tank bag, the tank cover shut flush with the tank surface. The seat was rendered more comfortable and resistant through the use of still more advanced upholstery material. A rear shock developed in collaboration with the

Bilstein Company was installed from September 1990. Not only could the spring be preloaded in four positions, the rebound damping was adjustable to 10 positions.

The 1990–91 GS's muffler was constructed of polished stainless steel with practically indefinite durability. The front mudguard was mounted low as standard, but could also be delivered in the high off-road position upon request. Finally, the front-wheel single-disc brake had also been improved. The disc was now floating via buttons. This eliminated any squeaks, and it allowed nearly 100 percent utilization of the brake pad surface under any conceivable conditions.

A Paralever GS before and after the facelift.

Left: *The Spartan R 100 GS original model of 1987.*

Below: *The cockpit and views of the 1990–91 R 80 GS.*

All technical modifications of the 1991 model year also applied to the R 100 GS Paris-Dakar: adjustable windshield, new instruments, handlebar controls, and steering head bearings from the K series, new monoshock arm, and stainless steel muffler.

■ **Economical for sure:**
The R 80 GS with 27 horsepower
For beginners, there was the R 80 GS (and the street models R 80 and R 80 RT) also in a version down-tuned to 27 horsepower and correspondingly cheap to ensure. With little effort and for less than 200 marks, the engine could be brought back up to 50 horsepower.

All in all, it's clear that BMW's enduro concept precisely matched the public taste of the times. Of the classic GS two-valve models alone (R 80 GS Basic being the last), 69,050 units were produced and sold around the world from 1980 to 1996. The models shown on these pages were discontinued in 1994 (for special models, see the next chapter). There's little doubt that the sturdy and easily maintained two-valve boxers will continue to ply the roads and trails of the globe for many years to come.

Right and above: *The R 100 GS Paris-Dakar's 1991 version with low front mudguard.*

Below: *A 1980 G/S with simple Monolever swingarm and revamped Paralever R 100 GS of the final two-valve series from 1990.*

Echoes from the press: What reporters had to say about the R 80 GS and R 100 GS Paralever models

The 1000's 60-horsepower motor has gobs of torque. The 800, with 50 horsepower, was also improved. Its pre-silencer has grown from a volume of 1.5 liters to 3.8, increasing gas flow and thereby boosting performance.

mo, October 1987

The machine's powerplant delivers unadulterated pleasure. The powerful boxer pulls mightily and without vibrations from the lowest rpm. The responsive throttle did the rest to even enhance this invigorating sensation. It is this effortlessness that distinguishes this Super Enduro from the G/S.

Tourenfahrer, November 1987

A leisurely start-up already had this seasoned BMW rider waiting in vain for the shaft effect. And even when accelerating over bumpy sections, the rider may henceforth rejoice in a rear-wheel suspension that really does the job. Not a trace of the bouncing rear wheel because the driveshaft moment has taken up the entire negative suspension travel.

Motorrad, December 1987

Frame and suspension have no trouble handling the opulent power reserves. The newly designed Paralever rear-wheel swingarm contributes greatly to this. It reduces unwanted driveshaft reactions to a minimum. The front-wheel disc brake requires cautious application.

Abendzeitung Munchen, July 1988

We're glad to report that after 30,000 kilometers there were no weak points to criticize. All vital components such as pistons and engine bearings proved to be unaffected by the long-distance trials. Even the testers, originally skeptical of the GS, ended up carrying the bike in their hearts. For one thing cannot be denied: it possesses a character which has matured over the years, something that can't be said of many other motorcycles.

Motorrad, Reisen und Sport, April 1989

This enduro is wonderfully suited to long-distance travel, something for which it can be unhesitatingly employed as a pack mule (210 kilograms payload). What's more, this mule can run a good 180 kilometers per hour. Additional strengths are frugality (6 liters regular unleaded per 100 kilometers), the extended range allowed by a 26-liter tank and an extremely rugged chassis.

Neue Westfalische, August 1989

The 1-liter boxer has overwhelming torque. The magic carpet ride begins just beyond idle speed; the choice of gears is actually secondary. It's this exceptional torque that allows the BMW, despite its considerable weight of 230 kilograms, to look good off road: sand, mud, or dirt—it tore through everything with equanimity.

Suddeutsche Zeitung, October 1990

Among the GS's strengths is its maneuverability. The engine's low center of gravity, balanced axle load distribution, the well adapted steering geometry, and, last but not least, the ergonomically correct off-road handlebars all ensure that the rider always remains in control of this 215-kilogram (curb weight) machine.

Motorradfahrer, October 1991

Below left: *1991 R 80 GS.* Below right and opposite above: *R 100 GS Paris–Dakar, 1990–91 version.* Opposite below: *1990 R 100 GS.*

Almost too good for off-road: The R 100 GS Paris-Dakar Classic

Over the decades the BMW GS with its two-valve boxer has become the stuff of legends. It was above all the R 100 GS, for years BMW's best-selling motorcycle, that made history. Unforgotten were the four boxer victories in the equipment-shredding Paris-Dakar Rally during the 1980s; legions of bikers have heeded the call of faraway lands in its saddle. So it was a sad day for its fans when the announcement came that this mythical machine would be rolled out to pasture. The overriding cause for the end of production announced in 1994 was ever more stringent emissions and noise regulations. BMW could (or would) no longer comply with the new requirements using the outdated ohv engine technology. The future belonged to the four-valve boxers, hence to more environmentally friendly models such as the R 1100 GS.

■ **1994: End of production for the ohv base models**

The GS standard models, R 80 GS and R 100 GS, went out of production in 1994. The classic GS had remained unchanged since its 1990 facelift, when the rectangular headlight and the half-fairing with protective frame were introduced. Since the fall of 1993, there was also a 34-horsepower entry-level version of the 800 model (replacing the 27-horsepower version introduced in 1990—see previous chapter). Eventually, all types were equipped with the emission-reducing Secondary Air System (SLS) as standard. Other than this, BMW had been content with tweaking the colors and design from year to year.

Yet the old GS would not go out with a whimper but with a bang; the designers still had a few tricks up their sleeves. First, BMW introduced a racy Classic special model of the Paris-Dakar version, initially shown at the October 1994 IFMA and produced, like the other "Farewell Models," to January 1996. In 1996 came the R 80 GS Basic's turn (see pages 54 and 55).

High-point of the then 70-year BMW ohv tradition: The R 100 GS Paris-Dakar from 1994, in elegant black and noble chrome.

As expected, demand for the last two-valve GS with 1-liter engine was enormous. The black paintwork, silver tape, round valve covers, and the hardly enduro-typical chroming of numerous parts such as the fairing protection frame, handlebars, luggage rack, and passenger handles dressed up a motorcycle designed for hard riding into something more akin to an ornament for the front parlor.

Yet this luxury GS with Paris-Dakar trim was anything but a knick-knack. Whoever used it as intended discovered a bike that was tremendously fun to ride, even in winter. For the standard heated grips, hand protectors, windshield, and projecting cylinders offered effective protection from wind and cold.

With its rich sound unchanged, slight shaking while idling, and angry growl when going full throttle, the air/oil-cooled 60-horsepower 1-liter boxer was a worthy heir to BMW's then 73 years of boxer history. And whoever had last ridden a bike in the 1970s or 1980s and was now thinking again of buying a machine that could stir the emotions felt his or her heartbeat irresistibly quicken when twisting the throttle of this penultimate two-valve GS.

Although the large displacement twin-cylinder had lost nothing of its rough off-road heart, its manners had improved considerably. The GS Classic surprised with gratifying running

The final 1-liter GS with the proven Marzocchi telescopic fork and floating brake rotor. Typically BMW were the projecting boxer engine, the maintenance-free shaft drive, and the Paralever swingarm. Aerodynamics, however, were not the machine's strong suit, as apparent from this front view.

characteristics, above all in long-distance travel. The engine was quiet and smooth, with jolt-free pick-up from a low 2,000 rpm, nothing to take for granted in a large boxer and effortlessly achieved the nominal maximum engine speed of 6,500 rpm. It was remarkable to witness what the Bavarians have now realized by dint of model upgrades and detail work. Everyday convenience was further enhanced with details such as a locking stowage and tool compartment flush mounted with the tank.

Yet, whoever considered the numbers and measured values with a cold eye had to admit that this pushrod boxer derived from a 1969 design simply could no longer keep up with modern overhead camshaft (ohc) powerplants. Zero to 100 kilometers per hour in 5.8 seconds was nothing to write home about in the 1,000cc class, and 6.3 seconds to get through fourth gear was almost disappointing. What was missing from a twin-cylinder powerplant tuned to low noise emission was certainly not power but bite. On one of our test rides, we could not get beyond a top speed of 169 kilometers per hour, though this was admittedly acceptable for an enduro.

▌ Smooth-shifting five-speed gearbox

Among minor, typical GS shortcomings was the fact that the side stand could not be extended with the rider in the saddle, a definite handicap with a machine loaded up for long-distance travel. The choke lever, however, was located exactly where it belonged, on the handlebars. The obligatory couple of minutes required to delicately adjust the engine after a cold start had always gone with the boxer, like mustard with bratwurst.

The riding position was upright, befitting a classic, and especially an enduro. Even with a cold engine, the well chosen five-speed gearbox allowed easy and precise shifting, which was a giant step forward from earlier models. If the GS was not overtaxed, fuel consumption remained reasonable, i.e., under 7.0 liters/100 kilometers. Nevertheless, fuel efficiency (6.6 liters/100 kilometers average in tests) was not up to modern standards, let alone when considered in relation to performance. All the same, GS aficionados had to shell out 17,958 DM for a classic series R 100 GS.

With regard to handling and control, the 236-kilogram Paris-Dakar was clearly superior to the even heavier

four-valve GS. It could be effortlessly swung around corners. The bike's marked sensitivity to cross winds had to be taken in stride, along with the Metzeler tires' relative lack of comfort.

Although the Paralever rear-wheel suspension did a credible job of suppressing the typical boxer load alteration effects, it reached its limits on uneven surfaces. Though they worked no miracles, the brakes proved adequate within a normal, safety conscious riding style. All told, the Classic GS was a motorcycle with strong appeal to tradition-conscious riders who wanted to get some real dirt under their wheels, and banked on high resale value. The GS Classic held all the charms of nostalgia; in the end, what it offered was maturity.

Collector's item: The R 100 GS in retro-look with round valve covers. The 35-liter tank guaranteed extended range. Convenient: The integrated stowage compartment. Mature and dependable: The air/oil-cooled and SLS-optimized boxer powerplant with 980cc and 60 horsepower.

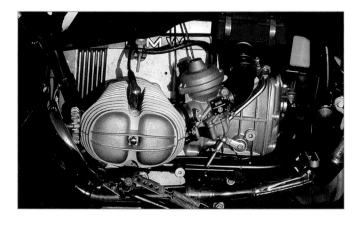

R 80 GS Basic: The parts bin two-valve boxer's last hurrah

By 1994, BMW had already written the two-valve boxer's obituary. There followed "farewell models" with "classic" design and moving funeral orations. But there was life in the old dog yet. This was demonstrated by the R 80 GS Basic: with it, BMW postponed the real goodbyes for another year. There ensued much speculation as to the reasons: perhaps there were valuable, readily marketable remainder stocks of engines, frames, tanks, and other parts from the long, successful boxer production. Whatever the reason, within a few short months, starting in June 1996, BMW's Berlin motorcycle factory cranked out exactly 3,003 of the nostalgia enduro. The final motorcycle of this type, hence irrevocably the last of the two-valve boxers, with vehicle identification number 0267503, rolled off the line on December 19, 1996, to take its place at the BMW Museum in Munich. The penultimate GS was raffled off on the BMW shop floor, the proceeds going to the organizer of a traffic safety campaign in Brandenburg. The GS only vanished from the BMW price lists in 1998: That's how long it took the limited production run to be sold out. Clients paid the 15,500 DM (plus 458.85 DM in fees) without grumbling.

▮ Blue-and-white livery— what else?

In design and technology, the Basic was a successful blend of parts from the original generation and modern components, like the Paralever rear-wheel swingarm introduced in 1987. The clunky cockpit with the large (and still not quite water tight) speedometer came from the R 80 G/S (1980 to 1985), and the tank came from the R 80 ST street derivative (1982 to 1985). The rest, BMW designers took out of their big toolbox: the two-valve boxer engine with 50 horsepower and 32-millimeter Bing carburetors, the long travel Marzocchi telescopic fork, the cross-spoke wheels, the Paralever, of course, and the double-loop tubular frame harking back to the /5 models. The latter, however, now painted Bavarian Blue contrasted well with the static parts, which were kept entirely white. The inclined rear shock came from the chassis specialist White Power. Like all two-valvers since 1995, the Basic was also equipped with the environmentally friendly SLS.

That the Basic was something more than a collection of inventory parts and

Above: *The Basic at the author's home chained to his K 1100 RS.*

Left: *The test bike, after the 700-kilometer ride from Germany to Normandy.*

toolbox components became obvious once riding down narrow country lanes. Here, it delivered thrills through exemplary handling and outstanding cornering. The wide handlebars and low center of gravity provided a feeling of security that the heavier and higher four-valve GS only granted after a longer period of acclimatization.

On rough trails, poorly patched-up roads and on light terrain, the Basic, like the second-generation GS models after 1990, was a sure footed and easily controlled mount. Fork and rear shock were responsive while providing adequate comfort even at a brisk pace. The farewell GS convincingly underscored that narrow tires actually constituted something of an advantage on difficult terrain. The beefy engine captivated with tons of torque and (unlike the original G/S) harmonized perfectly with the ideally stepped and easy-shifting five-speed gearbox.

■ Rather tiring for long-distance travel

With respect to aptitude for travel and long-distance riding, however, the Basic couldn't hold a candle to the more refined R 1100 GS. The hard seat and the relatively small 19.5-liter tank which, given an average mileage of 6.5 liters/100 kilometers, was on empty after a maximum of 300 kilometers, imposed frequent stops. What's more, the much too long center stand caused problems. The machine was a pain to raise, especially when fully loaded with tank bag and luggage.

The brakes were satisfactory, as long as the riding style remained reasonable. On the other hand, at high speeds or while negotiating sinuous mountain passes, one wished for a second disc, reduced lever pressure, and less brake fade. The cable actuated rear-wheel drum brake, however, was as reliable as ever.

All in all, based on his own experience, the author can only echo Gerhard Lindner's conclusions in issue 14, 1996 of *Motorrad* magazine: "You may wonder about the high price, moan about the lousy brakes, curse the difficult raising on the center stand. But when it comes to pure riding pleasure, there's nothing to criticize. Maneuverable, agile, and comfortable, on narrow country roads the old 50-horsepower airhead still gives the new boxer generation a run for its money."

Left: *On December 19, 1996, the last two-valve boxer came off the line; in the center, then-BMW motorcycle chief, Dr. Ganal.*

Center: *The author's son, Valentin, at 13, practicing his wheelies.*

Bottom: *The Basic in Normandy, after the author's move to France one year earlier.*

Compact Monolever models for the street: the R 80 ST to RT

Two years after presenting the R 80 G/S, BMW introduced its sister model in street trim, the R 80 ST. *Motorrad* **magazine had this to say: "Long awaited, better than expected: the new R 80 ST has brought the qualities of the G/S enduro to the street."**

With the richly chromed R 80 ST, BMW had responded to the calls of all those motorcycle lovers who had been so taken by the R 80 G/S's handling that they clamored for its street version. In basic structure, the ST was largely similar to the G/S: Monolever rear-wheel swingarm, compact lightweight construction, high torque 800cc boxer engine. Yet in appearance and in some important respects, it demonstrated an independent character.

Customers and the trade press were ecstatic: "This elegant 800 has unbelievable handling, the kind found, if at all, in a 250." (*auto, motor und sport*, Issue 16, 1982). "Despite its wide tires, the R 80 ST's handling is fantastic, there's no denying it." (Issue 9, 1982). "With the launch of the ST, the G/S is now only the second-best street machine BMW has ever built." (Issue 16, 1982).

These compliments rested on hard facts. The R 80 ST, with a dry weight of just 183 kilograms, was the lightest

motorcycle in its class. Even gassed up, it still weighed under 200 kilograms. In order to surpass the G/S on the street, the ST of course had to drop several specific off-road characteristics. One important modification was the shortening of spring travel: Monolever suspension travel had been reduced from 170 to 153 millimeters and front fork travel from 200 to 175 millimeters. The front end had been reconfigured: the 21-inch front wheel had given way to a 19-inch spoke wheel. The telescopic fork consisted of preexisting components: stanchions from the R 100 fork and fork sliders from the R 65. For BMW had only to reach into its richly endowed parts bin for the entire model range. Thus, development costs were close to nil.

▮ R 80 ST: G/S trimmed for the street

In any event, the ST stood lower than the multi-purpose G/S. One effect of shortening spring travel was a lowering of saddle height by 15 millimeters, down to 845 millimeters. The lowered oil pan came from the R 45 and R 100 RS models, the mudguard, which nestled closely to the front wheel, from the R 45/65 series. The wide low-profile tires

(100/90 H 19 front, 120/90 H 18 rear) were new. The BMW's massive dual-instrument cockpit with baffle and the round 160-millimeter H4 headlight also derived from the R 45/65.

A distinctive feature of the R 80 ST was the high handlebars. These had their origin in the R 65's U.S. version and allowed both relaxed or fast riding, according to the mood of the moment. The G/S's distinctive silhouette had largely been preserved. The line running from the tank, along the seat, to the high-mounted rear mudguard determined the bike's overall appearance. In contrast to the G/S, however, the tank was equipped with the other models' recessed, lockable cover tank. The high-mounted two-in-one exhaust had been retained. It featured a chrome rather than black matte finish and a reconfigured tailpipe cover.

A further distinguishing feature, besides the chromed cylinder guard, was a new livery: the buyer had a choice of Spherical Silver or Red Metallic with silver outlines. The entire G/S accessories range was compatible, down to bag holders and touring cases. A modified luggage mounting, in both models, now also made possible attachment of a bag on the left side.

The R 80 ST differed from the enduro R 80 G/S primarily through a completely altered front end with small front wheel and dual instruments.

With a payload in excess of 200 kilograms, the ST was a good choice for sporty touring in pairs and with baggage. In fundamental terms, the ST was absolutely identical to the G/S. The high-torsion strength Monolever swingarm provided precise tracking and accurate rear wheel guidance while markedly facilitating rear wheel removal and replacement.

The muscular 800cc boxer engine offered a pleasant torque band and an output of 50 horsepower (37 kilowatts). In tests, average mileage proved to be about 6 liters for 100 kilometers (the factory claimed 5.0 liters/100 kilometers); top speed was 174 kilometers per hour. "This BMW engine," the trade magazine *PS* reported in September 1982, "deserves much praise. It runs smoothly and quietly with that classic boxer feel. Lots of displacement and inertial mass in relation to performance lend this engine a forceful character. It's always confident and has power to spare."

▌ Progress in power transmission

In the Dutch periodical *Moto 73*, the author wrote: "Engine speeds between 3,000 and 5,000 rpm are sufficient to really start moving. Though there's already plenty of torque available below 3,000 rpm, the brawny dual-cylinder powerplant signals its displeasure at excessively low rpm with indignant shaking." The kick starter, up to then a perennial feature of BMW motorcycles, had been streamlined away; at least it was available as an extra.

Among the G/S and ST's typically boxer strengths were the "claw" shift five-speed gearbox, the single-plate dry clutch, and the Cardan drive power transmission. Thanks in no small measure to an entirely redesigned clutch mechanism, gear shifting was astoundingly smooth and effortless. After a few miles, one was no longer even conscious of the shifting process. The transmission had also become markedly more refined since the 1970s. Modern torsion dampers provided soft transitions at acceleration and deceleration.

In the G/S and ST, the "righting" moment so typical of the BMW Cardan drive was particularly pronounced. One reason was the limited inertia of the very light Monolever swingarm assembly. Because of this low weight, the light-alloy cast part had less inertia

As early as 1982, BMW recognized that a street version of the enduro would have good market prospects. The ST could be ridden quite briskly, not least because of its low-profile tires. Ready to tour: The wide handlebars. Nowadays, the ST is a rarity.

The slender R 80, launched in 1984, combined elements from the street boxer with others from the enduro.

twin-cylinder boxer with 800cc and 50 horsepower. Modifications of the rocker bearings, as in the other 1985 boxer engines, yielded a significant reduction in valve noise. Top speed for the 210 kilograms R 80 with full tank was 178 kilometers per hour.

The special part was that this model was also equipped with the now sufficiently proven Monolever rear swingarm. Contrary to the G/S and ST, however, the monoshock gas pressure shock with four adjustment positions and spring travel of 121 millimeters was not anchored to the swingarm but directly to the rear-axle housing. In place of the previously used needle bearing, a tapered roller bearing in the rear-axle drive, derived from the K series in production since 1983, increased both load-bearing capacity and reliability.

Also new on the R 80 was the responsive telescopic fork with 175 millimeters of travel, hydraulic damping, and progressive spring characteristics. The stanchion diameter was increased to 38.5 millimeters. Greater rigidity was achieved in the fork brace integrated to the reconfigured front-wheel mudguard. Eighteen-inch light metal cast alloy wheels, 285-millimeter disc brake at the front, a reinforced double-loop frame, and large 22-liter tank were some of the R 80's salient traits. Its elegant lines were highlighted by a two-in-two exhaust system. Highly readable: the round gauges for speed and rpm.

to oppose to the righting moment issuing from the encapsulated Cardan drive than a heavy steel dual-tube swingarm equipped with a couple of conventional shocks. What's more, the ST's swingarm had been slightly shortened in relation to the G/S. The ST's and G/S's pretty steel spoke wheels with Akront rims of highly polished aluminum alloy lent the bikes a certain nostalgic touch.

Apart from that righting moment, the ST's frame and suspension received nothing but applause: "With respect to road holding, handling, and riding safety, even at high speed on winding country roads with diagonal grooves, bumps, and hairpin curves, the ST is simply tops." In the front, the street racer was stopped by a perforated disc brake, fade free even under wet conditions. But this always required an iron right hand. Upgrading with a second disc was not possible. As in the G/S, the mechanically actuated rear-wheel full hub drum brake responded smoothly and evenly; brake effort could be well modulated.

Yet the R 80 ST wasn't cheap: Its price tag in 1982 was 8,490 DM. Balancing this were typical BMW low

maintenance costs, long life cycle, and above-average resale value. A well preserved ST has long been a collector's item. The early end of production for this distinctive and beautiful motorcycle came in 1985, to universal regret.

From 1984, Monolever swingarm for all boxers

But BMW had a replacement in mind. As early as 1984, they had presented the R 80 at the IFMA as a "logical development." It blended elements of the classic boxer street machines with essential traits of the G/S and ST series. Its core, once again, was the now thoroughly reworked air-cooled

From 1984, the full-fairing R 80 RT also featured the Monolever suspension. It was a roaring success, with 21,625 units solds.

The R 80 ST, from 1982, in the Eifel. The classically beautiful boxer model was as compact as a 500.

Technically, the enhanced R 80 RT was largely identical to the R 80 and from 1984 was also equipped with the Monolever frame—like all boxer models from that point on. An unusual feature of the 227-kilogram machine was the bulky touring fairing, taken from the preceding model with rear swingarm produced from 1980 to 1984. The windshield was adjustable; high handlebars and air inlets were standard equipment.

R 80 production to 1991 was 12,932 units. With 21,625 units produced from the end of 1984 to the fall of 1994, the R 80 RT/2 (Monolever) was one of BMW's most successful motorcycles of the time.

Just like the old days:
The neo-classic R 100 R and R 80 R

At the Paralever GS's 1987 introduction in Florence, the following question arose: In addition to the enduro, why doesn't BMW bring onto the market a correspondingly modified street version, as it had done earlier for the R 80 G/S and R 80 ST? It took four years, but on October 14, 1991, in Chiemsee, Germany, Hans Glas, then BMW Motorrad GmbH's chairman of the board, introduced the first production unit of the R 100 R to a handful of journalists. On October 23, the retro-look street machine, based largely on the R 100 GS, had its much heralded world premiere at the 29th Tokyo Motor Show.

The venue had been chosen carefully. The men from Munich had decided to hoist the Bavarian blue-and-white right in the lion's den, Japan. They were returning the call: a year earlier, at the IFMA in Cologne, the Japanese had set in motion a new classics wave with devastating success. Ironically, the trendsetter here was Kawasaki, which, until then had always been identified with uncompromising sport bikes. With its 1970s look, naked but technically very up-to-date "Zephyr" models, the builder had precisely matched the tastes of people who longed for motorcycles with relatively simple designs and straightforward, openly displayed technology. The other builders, from Honda to Yamaha, Suzuki to Moto Guzzi, soon followed suit, sending their neo-classics with retro design down memory lane, to the 1991 shows.

∎ The R 100 R: Cutting-edge classic design

BMW could feel comforted in its strategy. After all, the Bavarians, never fashion victims, had remained faithful to the classic boxer Cardan design since 1923! The R 100 R fit in perfectly. Like the R 80 and the R 80 ST, quite popular in the early 1980s, the R 100 R was logically marketed as "pure motorcycle," a classically sober machine without fairing or excess attachments. The second "R" in the model designation stood for "Roadster," clearly indicating

the intended purpose: untrammeled riding on winding country roads.

As a street machine directly derived from the R 100 GS, the R 100 R featured the largely identical dual-cylinder boxer engine with 1-liter displacement and 60 horsepower (44 kilowatts) at 6,500 rpm. Two Bing CV carburetors with 40-millimeter port provided the fuel/air mixture. The maximum torque of 76 Nm was already reached at 3,750 rpm. The oil cooler was not found on the cylinder guard, as on the GS, but was centrally mounted at the front of the frame. The exhaust system had also been reworked: the R 100 R inherited the modified, round stainless steel muffler from the 1991 K 100 models. What really struck the eye were the rounded valve covers, employed in the 1950s on the R 68 and the 1970s on the /5- and /6 series. It was above all these legendary old-time covers that imparted that touch of class to the Roadster.

On the other hand, with suspension/ damping systems, BMW applied modern production series technology. The R 100

The racy cockpit and 1994 R 80 R. Plus Wurm closed-loop catalytic converter.

R was the first BMW that came with a Japanese telescopic fork and rear shock. Renowned producer Showa was the subcontractor. The telescopic fork had a stanchion diameter of 41 millimeters; at 135 millimeters, suspension travel was markedly shorter than in the GS's off-road worthy Marzocchi fork (225 millimeters). Damping was hydraulic, spring characteristics progressive. The Showa gas pressure shock at the rear also had different characteristics; thus, its travel was only 140 millimeters, as opposed to 180 millimeters for the GS. Spring pre-load was adjustable in six positions, rebound damping continuously adjustable.

The rear single-sided swingarm, with the patented Paralever system detailed

The R 100 R Roadster was BMW's best-selling model of 1992 and 1993. **Above:** *As a farewell, BMW presented the R 100 R Classic at the end of 1994.*

on page 37, was taken over from the GS as was. The rear-wheel drum brake with a diameter of 200 millimeters conformed to the GS standard as well. Though the perforated single-disc brake at the front also had a 285-millimeter diameter, it featured the four-piston fixed-caliper of the four-cylinder K models. Like the GS, the slender roadster featured cross-spoke wheels allowing the use of tubeless tires. Naturally, the dimensions had been adapted to its new "road" purpose: mounted in the front was a tire with the low-profile dimension 110/80 V 18; the rear tire was a 140/80 V 17.

▌ Chrome extra, the R 80 R from 1992

Contributing appreciably to the R 100 R's classic looks, besides its sober silhouette and the round valve covers, were a fully chromed headlight from the K 75 along with the GS's round gauges (now set in chromed barrels). From March 1992, those who wanted the full-on American look could get the following parts chromed as a special option: fork brace, engine guard, valve cover, top carburetor cover, rear luggage rack, tank cover, rearview mirror, exhaust fasteners, instrument cluster, blinker assembly, and handlebar end weights.

The plastic handlebar cover, battery, and side panels, passenger hand-grips, and rear-wheel mudguard were not from the BMW parts bin but newly developed for the R 100 R. Yet the front-wheel mudguard came from the K 75. As on the GS, the K model's colored controls, with separate blinker switches, were located at the handlebar ends. But there was no automatic blinker cancel.

The rather clumsy-looking tank came from the GS, though with its new paint it was barely recognizable as an enduro part. It had a 24-liter capacity and allowed a range of more than 300 kilometers. The seat was not only reconfigured but better upholstered. The 800-millimeter saddle height was average. At 218 kilograms (full tank), the R 100 R was only 2 kilograms

lighter than the old R 100 GS. Payload was a good 200 kilograms, also in keeping with BMW standards.

No one doubted that the R 100 R Roadster would assert itself on the market. But the rush that ensued in the spring of 1992 surprised even the optimists at BMW. In Germany alone, more than 13,200 boxer fans had ordered the 1-liter base model by August 1994. Including all variants, 16,339 were sold by 1996. For a time, buyers had to accept longer delivery schedules.

However, the run on the retro-bike strongly subsided at the beginning of 1993 with the introduction of the R 1100 RS, first boxer of the new four-valve generation. The days of the classic two-valver were now clearly numbered. But it was a phased ending. BMW stopped production of the two-valve boxer in July 1994. For the little R 80 R roadster model introduced in the fall of 1992, this was the end of the line.

The R 80 R was powered by the famous twin-cylinder engine with 50 horsepower and 61 Nm of torque, available at a moderate 3,750 rpm. To the end of 1993, the R 80 R was

In 1991, BMW filled a gap in the market with the neo-classic R 100 R. There were 7,000 firm orders after only six months. Today, the Roadster is a collector's item. Seen here is the 1991 presentation model.

also obtainable cheaper to ensure 27 horsepower, then 34 horsepower versions. The oil cooler, indispensable for the 1-liter version, was missing on the 800. Other than this, there was no difference. The R 80 R was an economical but in no way puny alternative to the 1000 Roadster. For the 1993–94 model year, it came with a double front disc brake, standard. Exactly 3,444 units of the R 80 R were sold in Germany until production stop in 1994.

▌ R 80 R with regulated Wurm catalytic converter

A limited number of Roadsters were equipped with regulated catalytic converters from Stuttgart specialist Paul Wurm (see photo, page 60). Clever electronics overcame disadvantages of the carburetor technology and, employing servo-motors and membranes, provided exemplary emissions reductions with no loss of performance. *Motorrad News* found a top speed of 171 kilometers per hour

and average mileage of 5.9 liters/100 kilometers (Issue 8, 1994): "These good results are clearly attributable to careful tuning of the catalytic converter. The load alteration behavior, however, takes some getting used to."

▌ "Mystic" special model from 1993

The Munich BMW branch caused something of a stir in the summer of 1993 with the release of an R 100 R modified with Japanese special parts. Under the additional designation of "Mystic," the racy special model was initially only to be sold by the Bavarian branch. But then BMW decided to show off the elegant machine at the Frankfurt IAA and began offering it Germany-wide for 13,350 DM.

Selected options defined the Mystic's distinct look: red metallic paint, modified and chromed headlight mount, high-gloss metal cover plate for an instrument panel with new indicator lights, chromed blinker assembly, flat sport handlebars, sportier and narrower seat with slender tail section, new battery covers, shorter license plate frame, and a slightly inward-curving muffler.

Top: *The R 100 R Roadster undergoing tests in 1991; the two-cylinder BMW with the classic design had superb handling.*

Center: *At extra charge, the R 100 R was available with loads of chrome and special lettering.*

Bottom: *The R 100 R Mystic, 1993.*

Then, when demand for the two-valve machines persisted even after introduction of the four-valve boxer, BMW reversed itself and restarted production of the classic. This is how, at the 1994 IFMA, the Bavarians came to present four 1-liter classic models within the framework of a final edition: a redesigned R 100 R, the R 100 R Mystic, an upgraded R 100 RT, and the above-described R 100 GS Paris-Dakar in black and chrome. The clever marketing message ran something like this: "Fans, hurry and buy your Farewell-Boxer before it's too late!" Yet, in the end such preparation wasn't necessary. For though BMW had insisted that after 1995 the two-valve boxer would be history, in the end, as we've seen (pages 54–55), the company would hold out another year with the 1996 R 80 Basic.

■ **High-grade "classic" models**
While the Mystic Classic wholly conformed to the model presented in 1993, the R 100 R Classic featured some interesting details. It was delivered in retro-style Avus Black with classic white double pinstripes and special Classic decals on the tank. The seat (also entirely in black) had a new cover. In contrast, the headlamp holder, instrument cluster, passenger grips, brake, and clutch levers had a silvery gleam. The R 100 R Final Edition came standard with cylinder guards, side stand, dual-disc brake, SLS emissions control, hazard warning lights, and bag holder. The R 100 RT Classic came equipped in equally high style. The elegant touring machine also featured a bag, top case, and heated grips.

The R 100 R gained racing notoriety in the 1992 and 1993 Battle of the Legends held in Daytona, Florida. Ten famous American racing veterans, including Yvon Duhamel, Jay Springsteen, and Reg Pridmore, let the maneuverable classic boxers fly around the course as Schorsch Meier had on the Kompressor BMW of old. Then, in 1994, the R 1100 RS replaced the Roadsters at the classics race, a sign of the times.

An instant success: The four-valve boxer R 1100 GS

In January 1993 on Lanzarote in the Canary Islands, BMW presented the first model of the four-valve boxer generation, the sport touring R 1100 RS. Everything about this motorcycle was new: design, frame, suspension, engine, and equipment. Yet, the Bavarians had remained true to fundamental principles adhered to since 1923: twin-cylinder boxer design, a gearbox without power draining linkages, and a sturdy Cardan shaft drive.

A 1993 drawing of the R 1100 GS.

Below and opposite: *The R 1100 GS in the Motorrad News test, summer 1994.*

From the outset, it was clear that the future belonged to the modern, extremely quiet four-valve boxer, available with closed-loop catalytic converter, initially as an option, then standard. At the time, however, BMW was careful not to alienate friends of the two-valve design. This is why the enduro version of the R 1100 GS wasn't released on the market in tandem with the RS, though it was already well past the prototype stage and practically ready for production. The classic two-valve boxer continued to sell so well that a premature disappearance of the old GS from the product range would have caused a dealership revolt. This delayed the R 1100 GS's presentation for more than six months. It was only at the 59th IAA press conference on September 7, 1993, in Frankfurt, that the super enduro was finally introduced to the public.

The R 1100 GS came onto the market in the spring of 1994 and quickly caused a minor earthquake. Defying any number of skeptical predictions, customers waited in line for the imposing long-distance travel machine with the bold styling, and soon made the new BMW a sales hit. In Germany alone, 3,554 units of the new model were sold to the end of 1994. Even so, R 100 GS sales still reached 3,224 units for the same period. In any event, the R 1100 GS quickly became the best-selling enduro ever.

The bike, which sold for 17,910 DM (including fees), took fourth place in the overall German registration hit parade, well ahead of considerably cheaper Japanese single-cylinder machines like the Honda Dominator or the Yamaha

XT 600. In this connection, it's worth noting that with 3,783 units sold in the same year, BMW also held second place with its one-cylinder F 650 "Funduro." Three BMW's among the top five were quite a sensation. Altogether, the Bavarians gained 28.8 percent in 1994, while most of the Japanese experienced a steep decline. Never before had so many BMW motorcycles been sold worldwide: 46,500 units. Thereafter, the trend toward BMW (i.e., to expensive quality motorcycles "made in Germany") never abated. To the end of 2002, BMW managed to double its yearly production, to more than 92,000 units. Year after year, the later R 1150 GS, R 1200 GS, and F 650 GS enduro models asserted their leading sales positions.

What was it about this first four-valve enduro that was really much too heavy for off-road use? Without a doubt, many buyers were attracted to the prestige associated with the Jumbo BMW. The R 1100 GS was imposing, unconventional, massive, and simply impossible to ignore. And it was fast: In a highway test, we hit a top speed of 202 kilometers per hour. Apart from its reduced off-road capability, the four-valve GS surpassed the older model in every domain. Comfort and roadability were superior and handling was amazingly good thanks to the low center of gravity.

Technically, the GS was very much based on the R 1100 RS, evidencing clear differences only in chassis adjustment, performances, and, of course, in appearance and equipment. Its core was the air/oil-cooled 1,100cc twin-cylinder boxer engine with four valves per cylinder and a camshaft in each cylinder head (HC for high cam.). For use in the enduro model, however, BMW had reconfigured the powerplant for increased torque and acceleration. Thus, in the R 1100 GS the R 259 boxer's output was 80 horsepower (59 kilowatts) rather than 90 horsepower, and this as early as 6,750 rpm as against 7,250 rpm for the RS. Maximum torque had increased from 95 to 97 Nm, already at 5,250 rpm vs. 5,500 rpm for the R 1100 RS. The engineers had achieved this remarkable performance with modified camshafts, different pistons, altered valve timing, and a compression ratio reduced from 10.7 to 10.3. The central control electronics for ignition and fuel injection were adapted to the new setup, along with the exhaust manifold and muffler.

There was plenty of "steam" available even at the lowest rpm; the GS engine (also featured in the R 1100 R from late 1994) accommodated a riding style with little shifting. In Germany, for insurance reasons, the R 1100 GS was also available with 78 horsepower (57 kilowatts) at 6,500 rpm. In its time, it was not only the enduro with the largest displacement, but also with the greatest torque.

Like the R 1100 RS, the R 1100 GS featured a three-piece frame with a weight-bearing engine and transmission casing. Front suspension also featured the BMW Telelever, introduced in 1993, and employed to greatest effect, in our experience, in enduro models. And so the enduro's directional control was impeccable to 170 kilometers per hour; only beyond that point did the machine's poor aerodynamics cause slight instability. Ground adhesion on rough trails and damaged roads was exemplary; there was no shimmying, even under great stress.

In our testing, the wide handlebar's "tilting disengagement" mechanism was a welcome improvement over the RS.

The approximately 250-kilogram four-valve GS had an imposing presence. A good thing that the front seat was height-adjustable. Cockpit and controls had an exemplary configuration and functionality.

The upper fork crown did not rotate in a ball socket, but a large precision roller bearing; the inner ends of the inner bars were mounted on mobile Silentblocks to compensate. Thus, handlebars and triple clamps were insulated from the Telelever's swinging motion, with a very positive effect on steering stability. The GS was distinctly smoother than the R 1100 RS, especially on uneven surfaces.

Among the Telelever's advantages were excellent responsiveness and the anti-dive properties of the novel fork design, which, even while braking, provided an extra margin of suspension travel at all times. And, significantly, with its anti-dive properties and high lateral stiffness, the Telelever offered the ideal basis for ABS. The second-generation ABS II was also available as an extra on the R 1100 GS.

It had however been modified for the enduro. Some background: off-road or over loose surfaces, it can be useful, under certain circumstances, to block the rear wheel in a targeted manner. This is why ABS II could be switched

off on the R 1100 GS, though for safety reasons this was not possible on the move but only before starting, by actuating the ABS turnoff switch during ignition. Because enduros are ridden under a wide range of conditions, the front central shock, unlike with the R 1100 RS, was adjustable in five spring preload stages with a wrench from the on-board toolkit.

On the GS, rear suspension was also by Paralever swingarm with central shock. Unlike in the RS, however, the suspension preload was continuously adjustable hydraulically via an accessible hand wheel. Rebound damping could be continuously adjusted with a set screw. However, we ascertained that this was still not sufficient to achieve optimal adjustment, especially with respect to comfort.

▌ Specially configured Telelever chassis

At 190/200-millimeter front/rear, suspension travel was distinctly longer than on the RS (120/135 millimeters). With identical caster (111 millimeters), the wheelbase had increased from 1,473 millimeters to 1,499 millimeters. Like the GS models, the R 1100 GS featured the stable patented cross-spoke wheels, with diameters of 19 inches at the front and 17 inches in the rear. The special rims allowed the use of tubeless tires with dimensions of 110/80x19 and 150/70x17.

Adequate front-wheel braking was provided by the dual-disc brake with four-piston fixed calipers and 305-millimeter-diameter floating rotors derived from the RS. The rear wheel featured a reduced single-disc brake (diameter 276 millimeters vs. 285 millimeters) with dual-piston floating caliper. Like the RS, the R 1100 GS had a plastic tank, whose capacity had grown from 23 to 25 liters, thereby providing a range of about 380 kilometers (on the basis of an average 6.5 liters/100 kilometers). The front fender was attached to the frame as an extension of the cockpit fairing. With its integrated oil cooler, it contributed considerably to the machine's distinctive looks. The low splash guard at the front wheel was somewhat lengthened for the 1995 model.

In keeping with the R 1100 RS, the R 1100 featured an ergonomics package that included a windshield continuously adjustable by 13 degrees

and a driver's seat that could be set to 860 or 840 millimeters in height. For the rest, equipment and instrumentation were similar to those of the RS. In addition, the GS offered plastic cylinder protectors, an aluminum engine guard, and a luggage rack, standard. Removal of the divided seat's rear section increased the luggage rack's capacity.

The R 1100 GS's design set it apart from other enduros: It was original, expressive, and unmistakable. But the bike's weight was just as hard to ignore: 243 kilograms with a full tank (RS: 247 kilograms). Catalytic converter, ABS, and equipment such as travel cases quickly pushed its weight over the 250-kilogram mark. This left 200

The R 1100 GS's kingdom was the country road. Yet it was also amazingly agile on loose surfaces. The Telelever determined the bike's character, in looks and in technology. The photos show a machine from the initial series.

kilograms for payload and luggage; maximum total weight was 450 kilograms, as for the R 100 RS. All in all, the R 1100 GS, which was produced until 1999, indisputably set a new standard for the big long-distance enduro class, as its two-valve precursor had before it. With sales of 43,628 units (without R 850 GS, 1998–1999: 1,954 units), it ranks as one of the most successful BMW models in company history.

From 1994 to 1999, about 44,000 buyers chose the R 1100 GS over other enduros, even if these were lighter and cheaper. The extravagant technology captivated just as much as the unconventional design. Typically BMW: The passenger also rode in comfort.

As the archtypical touring and long-distance travel motorcycle, the R 1100 GS won numerous friends around the world. As heir to the two-valve models, it also fulfilled high expectations. All photos show machines from 1994—with and without travel case sets. At extra charge, BMW provided customized accessories.

Torquey and clean: The GS's four-valve engine

From 1986, BMW invested 150 million DM in the six-year development of a new generation of boxer motorcycles. The lion's share of the money went to design and testing of the R 259 four-valve engine. The motor was presented at the 1992 IFMA, had its street premiere in January 1993 with the 1100 RS, then to power the R 1100 GS enduro in slightly modified form and continuously improved has gone on to equip numerous subsequent models. Four-valve technology, digital engine electronics with fuel injection, and a closed-loop three-way catalytic converter were and remain the defining attributes of the modern boxer design. Whereas all two-valve boxers produced since 1923 were merely refinements of precursor engines, the R 259 represented a fundamentally new design, down to the details.

Yet it remained true to old principles. BMW's fidelity to the boxer went to the core, to the company's very identity. Hans Sauter, BMW Motorcycle spokesman until 2002, said this: "The boxer probably has more soul than any other BMW vehicle, on two wheels or four." Since the days of the R 32, the advantages of the boxer design are well known: excellent mass compensation, even without balancer shaft, good cooling of cylinders fully exposed to the airflow, direct power transmission from the longitudinally arranged crankshaft to gearbox and driveshaft, low center of gravity, outstanding access to engine components, low maintenance, reduced weight, long service life.

Yet, conventional parameters were no longer adequate for an engine intended to continue into the next century. From the 1980s on, legislators and an increasingly discerning public were constantly raising the bar in matters of environmental protection and economy; BMW now had no choice but to come up with a way to save the much loved boxer for the 1990s and beyond. Piecemeal alterations of the existing powerplant were insufficient. The old two-valve boxer could simply not be made any more quiet, economical, or environmentally friendly at justifiable cost. Hence, planning and design had to begin (almost) from scratch. The

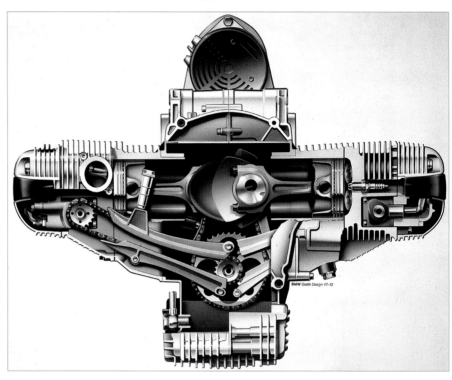

Four valves per cylinder—the 1993 boxer's prime innovation. The conrods manufactured through a "cracked" production process were a specialty. **Below:** Good acceleration: The R 1100 GS's torque band.

end result was a boxer engine that, even in appearance, was only remotely related to the traditional BMW twin cylinder. An explicit four-valve graced the cylinder covers, the cylinders tilted markedly forward on their longitudinal axis, induction pipes and injection nozzles had displaced old-fashioned Bing carburetors, and a central black cover tower for the alternator, itself derived from automobile production.

The revolution began with the engine housing. This no longer consisted of a single body tunnel assembly with bolted-on oil pan, but of two, highly rigid, light-alloy sections with integrated die-cast oil pan halves. The left half of the pan featured a large oil sight glass that indicated the level only when the motorcycle had been stopped for a while. Because oil was required for cooling, the new boxer's oil volume was an impressive 4.5 liters. The engine's front section consisted of a die-cast light-alloy housing and generator cover shielding the timing

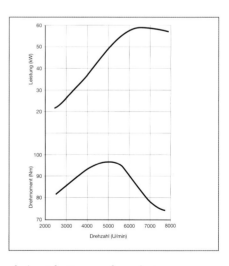

chain at bottom and serving as an alternator mount at the top. Among the R 259's special features were special three-electrode spark plugs, which drew current from a computer-controlled mapped ignition system. (More on the double-ignition system introduced in November 2002 in "GS Adventure, model upgrading" on page 82.)

A 1994 GS engine with cylinder and oil-pan guard.

In the four-valve R 259 boxer, first installed on the R 1100 RS in 1993, the crankshaft powered an intermediate shaft that drove both overhead camshafts via chains. The valves were actuated via short tappets and forked rockers with set screws (right).

The new engine's valvetrain was original in design. It was certainly a sign of the times that for efficient combustion each cylinder head was now provided with two intake and two exhaust valves. These, however, were actuated neither by overhead camshafts nor by vertical shafts, as in the BMW racing engines of old, but in the following, exotic manner: a chain led from the crankshaft to an intermediate shaft with 2:1 reduction; the latter was located where the camshaft had once rotated in the two-valve boxer, i.e., under the crankshaft. This intermediate shaft actuated one camshaft placed next to the intake valve for each cylinder head (Hc principle, well known in 1960s Opel engines); two long chains transmitted the power. A light-alloy holder to take up the entire valvetrain was bolted to each cylinder head.

The overhead cam actuated two tappets that in turn moved two forged forked rocker arms via short pushrods;

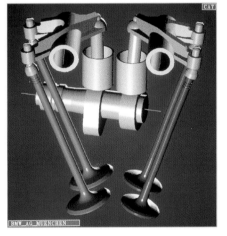

each rocker simultaneously actuated two valves. Practical and well-tried: set screws (four on each side) to adjust valve clearance. The result of all this detail work was the extension of adjustment intervals from 7,500 to 10,000 kilometers.

The explanation BMW offered for why it had done without an ohc or dohc valvetrain (such as in automobile or the K engines) sounded reasonably plausible: the R 259 would then have been 4.0 centimeters wider and thus not offered the required lean clearance of 49 degrees, unless mounted higher, which

in turn would have changed the whole design.

The distinctive cylinders were of cast light alloy. Rigid crosspieces prevented any unpleasant whirring from the closely spaced cooling fins. A friction-reducing nickel silicon coating (Gilnisil) was applied to render the cylinders fully gas tight and wear resistant. The cast light-alloy pistons had a diameter of 99 millimeters yet weighed a third less than the old 1000's pistons. This allowed high rpm with minimal vibrations.

The "cracked" conrods were a motorcycle world premiere: As with the V-8s in large BMW sedans, at production the conrod was no longer cut at the big end but "precision-broken." This made dowel pins to screw the halves together unnecessary. The R 259's crankshaft was one piece and revolved on two plain bearings. Among other things, the shaft drove two oil pumps, one for lubrication, the other for internal cooling, primarily of the exhaust valve area. Both pumps were located in a separate housing at the front of the intermediate shaft. The hot exhaust zone received additional cooling through the cylinders' pronounced forward tilt. A further refinement consisted in an external oil separator that removed the residual oil from the so-called "blow-by gas," oil vapor in the crankcase, through isolation and afterburning.

The aimed-for increase in output and torque with simultaneous reduction of fuel consumption and emissions would have been impossible without electronic engine management. So the new boxer was equipped with the Bosch-Motronic MA 2.2 unit, known from the K models. An overrun shutoff interrupted the fuel supply when rpm fell below 2,000 during overrun. At 8,000 rpm, the electronic governor kicked in to prevent over revving.

The 90-horsepower engine of the R 1100 RS was the standard powerplant of the new boxer generation introduced in 1993.

R 259 valvetrain with bearing structures for camshafts and rockers.

Telelever, Paralever, ABS: The four-valve GS frame and suspension

The heart of the Motronic system was the control unit, which was constantly fed all relevant data while adjusting fuel volume and injection duration. An electric fuel pump and electronically controlled injectors also formed part of the system. The elevated compression of 10.3:1 (R 1100 GS) mandated the use of premium-grade gasoline. Fortunately, the electronic control system provided the basis for installation of a closed-loop three-way catalytic converter. For all models of the post-1993 four-valve boxer generation, the drive unit is integrated into the frame as a load-bearing component. In relation to the RS, the R 1100 GS's engine characteristics were more decidedly oriented to torque. In return, it sacrificed 12 or 10 horsepower (there were 78 and 80 horsepower versions).

Front-wheel suspension by telescopic fork: This had been the norm at BMW since 1929 (R 16), and it remains so to this day for the majority of its production motorcycles, including the one-cylinder models of the F and G series. In 1993, however, the R 1100 RS sport touring boxer broke with this tradition, introducing downright revolutionary chassis technology: the BMW Telelever system. One year later, the R 1100 GS was the second model to receive the advanced front suspension. Nowadays, all BMW boxer models are equipped with the Telelever.

In a way, the Telelever represents a synthesis of telescopic fork and swingarm design. The long outer tubes and the triangular longitudinal control arm immediately strike the eye. The structure is amazingly simple: for the Telelever essentially consists only of a telescopic fork gutted of its usual entrails; and it is not connected to the frame via ball bearings and steering head but by two ball joints (GS: ball joint at bottom, roller bearing on top) and a longitudinal control arm, as in auto design.

Let's take a closer look at this unique system: First, we have two inner tubes a mere 35 millimeters in diameter. The lower outer fork crown is connected

From this perspective, the R 1100 GS looks quite compact. Among the Paralever's advantages is freedom from maintenance. The sidestand was improved in 1997 for improved stability; the pivot was better protected against dirt.

Components of the GS's disengageable ABS II.

absolutely no spring and damping components but only oil, for lubrication between inner and outer tubes. The result: extra-fine responsiveness. The inner tubes move along Teflon-coated sliding bushings.

With this advanced telescopic fork, steering no longer occurs via conventional ball or tapered roller bearings but (as in an automobile suspension) by way of a clearance and maintenance-free joint/bearing system at the outer tube and fork crown. The bulk of the forces generated by braking are transmitted to the stable load-bearing engine housing via the lower ball joint bolted to the longitudinal control arm. The control arm triangle, clearly visible as the most important design component, is pivot mounted to the engine housing at the ends of both its left and right branches.

This results in a complete decoupling of springing/damping from steering. In other words: in the BMW Telelever system, the telescopic fork's only remaining functions are wheel control and steering, while springing and damping occur independently of the central suspension shock. The GS handlebars' "tilting disengagement" is a significant feature: here, the upper ball joint is replaced by a heavy roller bearing; two elastic Silentblocks fix the inner tube ends to the upper fork crown.

Riding Telelever machines, it's immediately apparent that, because of the special geometry, the front end

The very long-stroke GS Telelever with 190 millimeters of spring travel.

dips only imperceptibly when braking compared to conventional systems. The overall effect is that of a mechanical anti-dive system. There's always sufficient marginal spring travel when braking. The large overlap between the inner tubes and the conspicuously long outer tubes also contributes to the Telelever's stability. The handlebars are only affected by extreme external conditions.

to the longitudinal control arm by way of a sturdy ball joint. The upper fork crown is pivot mounted to the frame's forward section; in the RS, this occurs via a second ball joint, in the GS, by way of a special roller bearing. A central shock, with 190 millimeters of spring travel in the GS, secures the longitudinal control arm to the frame's forward section. Unlike in the RS, the shock of the R 1100 GS, which was produced until 1999, had adjustable preloads (five stages, adjustable by wrench). The steering damper equipping the Roadster models to the end of 1994 is missing in the GS, however.

One Telelever innovation was that the telescopic fork's legs contained

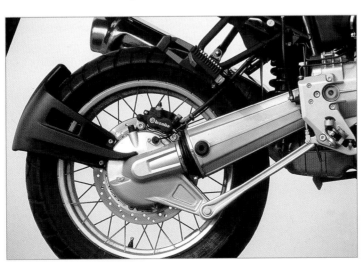

A rear preload adjustment (above), the R 1100 GS's Paralever swingarm (right), and the front spring strut preload (far right), which is adjusted with a spanner wrench.

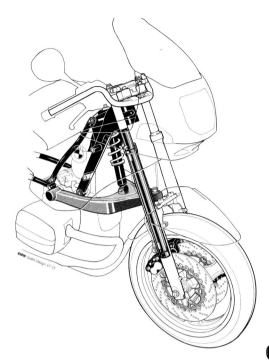

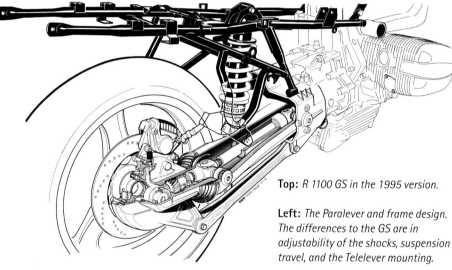

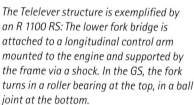

The Telelever structure is exemplified by an R 1100 RS: The lower fork bridge is attached to a longitudinal control arm mounted to the engine and supported by the frame via a shock. In the GS, the fork turns in a roller bearing at the top, in a ball joint at the bottom.

The rear suspension of BMW's four-valve GS models produced until 2004 conformed to a pattern familiar since the 1987 R 100 GS. Once again, we find the BMW Paralever system extensively discussed beginning on page 35. The 520-millimeter, light-alloy double-joint swingarm largely suppresses the Cardan drive's load alteration effects, thus providing reliable rear-wheel grip.

The four-valve boxer's Paralever displays some distinctive features: Here, the shock occupies a central, rather than lateral position. It features a helical compression spring and a single-tube gas damper. Right from the start, the four-valve GS's rebound damping and spring preload were continuously adjustable; for the preload, very conveniently so via hand wheel and hydraulics on the bike's left side. The R 1100 GS's rear suspension travel was an off-road and passenger-capable 200 millimeters.

For the frame, BMW also took an innovative approach: essentially, the four-valve boxer only features frame segments, which are bolted to the engine/transmission casing. The forward section is a sturdy and extremely lightweight permanent mold casting of

light alloy. At the front, it is attached to the engine casing and takes up the central shock and the upper ball joint. In the back, two tubular steel braces fix the forward frame section to the engine casing. The rear section frame is a tubular steel structure, anchored to the transmission and engine. A traverse between the frame's main tubes holds the upper shock eye.

▌ Tubular trellis frame, load-bearing engine, ABS

While the R 1100 RS features cast light-alloy wheels with a three-spoke design, the enduro is equipped with cross-spoke wheels like those first introduced in 1987 on the R 100 GS. The diameters of 19 and 17 inches, respectively, are enduro worthy; the tires, 110/80x19 and 150/70x17 (R 1100 GS), also well

adapted. However, because of high-speed requirements, the off-road capabilities of the standard GS tires were just average.

The R 1100 GS's triple-rotor brake system, by the Italian specialist Brembo, was only modified at the rear wheel. The front wheel featured the same dual-disc brake with a 305-millimeter rotor as the K and RS models. The rotor diameter in the rear was reduced from 285 to 276 millimeters. Braking safety could be even further improved with optional ABS II (disengageable off-road for the enduro). ABS II, developed in collaboration with FAG Kugelfischer and weighing only 6.9 kilograms, impressed with superior adjustment flexibility, high braking efficiency, even on reduced traction surfaces, and a low-maintenance self-diagnostic system.

Top: *R 1100 GS in the 1995 version.*

Left: *The Paralever and frame design. The differences to the GS are in adjustability of the shocks, suspension travel, and the Telelever mounting.*

Model upgrade: The new R 850 GS

With respect to the four-valve boxer, BMW had taken a two-pronged approach as early as 1994: Together with the newly introduced Roadster models, the Bavarians had added a free revving and sporty 850cc version of the 1,100cc powerplant already familiar from the RS and the then brand-new GS. This engine, whose sole difference was its bore, reduced from 99.0 to 87.8, developed 70 horsepower (52 kilowatts) at 7,000 rpm, and was thus the equal of the 1,100 powerplant in terms of output per liter (82.5 horsepower). It was only natural that its smaller pistons ran more smoothly over the entire speed range.

It took four years for a GS model with equally reduced displacement to arrive on the market: the R 850 GS. It had its premiere at the Munich Intermot in September 1998. The engine, taken over unaltered from the R 850 R, was available in an open 70-horsepower version or curbed to 34 horsepower. Apart from this, the cheaper R 850 GS was identical in technology, appearance, and equipment to the R 1100 GS.

In the course of model upgrading, BMW was constantly improving the GS in important details. The year 1995 saw better cylinder cover seals (rubber with metal insert). Also, the plastic tank was replaced by a steel part. In 1996, BMW modified the oil circuit with the addition of an oil thermometer and an air-release valve. The oil level was now easier to read. In case of excessive oil consumption, the factory occasionally replaced cylinders for free. In 1997, the smoothness of the originally hard shifting and clattering five-speed gearbox was improved with the insertion of O-rings between gears and shafts. A new side stand brought increased stability and anodizing gave the rims improved corrosion protection.

Altogether, the R 1100 GS, produced from 1994 to 1998, was one of BMW's most successful motorcycles, and the best-selling boxer from 1923 up to that point. Up to the summer of 1999, in only five years, 43,628 units were delivered.

A 1998 jubilee model, commemorating "75 Years of BMW Motorcycles," was quickly sold out. It cost 22,100 DM, including ABS, digital information system, heated grips, and luggage rack. Production of both models ceased upon the appearance of their successor, the R 1150 GS, in August 1999. While the ever-popular R 1100 GS was already sold out, there were remaining stocks of the R 850 GS; these went sold in 2000 for 18,950 DM apiece.

Above: The R 850 GS, available from 1998 to 2000, was 650 DM cheaper that the R 1100 GS. Only 1,954 units were produced. The boxer developed 70 horsepower and was also available in a version curbed to 34 horsepower.

Left: The 1998 R 1100 GS Jubilee model is painted a bright red and white and now has collector value.

Sportier, stronger, better-looking: The R 1150 GS from 1999

In our fast-paced world, in which not only computer firms but even some motorcycle manufactures renew their product range with every season, six years is a long time. By July 1999, with nearly 44,000 units sold, the very successful R 1100 GS, presented in 1993 and available from the spring of 1994, had finally reached the end of the road. Its worthy heir on the assembly line was the R 1150 GS. With its larger and stronger engine, a six-speed transmission, and revitalized design, the new model immediately shot to the top its category. After some initial tests, the trade press was full of praise: "The R 1150 GS is the most agile motorcycle in its class. Its looks are not quite as polarizing as they once were, and it's barely more expensive than its forerunner. A tailor-made redesign."

Relief had come in the nick of time. For the competition—led by Triumph and the improved Tiger 900 and Honda with its versatile and comfortable Varadero 1000—had powerfully rearmed with the avowed goal of challenging BMW in its big enduro hunting grounds. With the R 1150 GS, however, the Bavarians were able to brilliantly repulse the onslaught: at 4,370 new registrations for just the first semester of 2000, the new GS became Germany's best-selling motorcycle for all classes. There were 6,891 sold in the record-breaking year 2002, and 18,085 worldwide.

▌More power, more torque

That vast untapped reserves slumbered within the standard production four-valve boxer had long been demonstrated by the R 1100 S Sport Boxer and several racing versions, such as the then "Boxer Team's" 123-horsepower R 1100 RSR.

Thus, despite markedly higher output and torque values, the R 1150 GS's powerplant gave no hint of being overtaxed. Its extra power seemed to materialize at a mere snap of the fingers, imparting the 264 kilograms (with ABS) enduro at top speed of 195 kilometers per hour solo (data: *Motorrad*).

BMW had boosted output from 80 to 85 horsepower versus the old GS engine. Remarkably, now as before, peak output was reached at 6,750 rpm. Maximum torque had increased slightly from 97 Nm to 98 Nm at equally unchanged 5,250 rpm. All told, the engine felt even brawnier, primarily because the torque band had strengthened over the entire rev range, but above all between 3,000 and 5,000 rpm. And because more than 90 Nm was now always available between 3,000 and 6,500 rpm, the R 1150 thrilled the rider with outstanding acceleration: 6.2 seconds from 60 to 100 kilometers per hour and 7.9 seconds from 100 to 140 kilometers per hour.

How had the BMW engineers so impressively succeeded in optimizing power and torque band? They had simply taken the best from the entire four-valve model range and blended it anew for the GS: The cylinders came from the R 1200 C Cruiser (without the

Self-confident: With its dual headlight and aluminum-style cockpit, the R 1150 GS doesn't just look more sporty and modern than the R 1100 GS, it looks more aggressive.

engine fins grinding); cylinder heads and crankshaft came from the R 1100 S.

Accordingly, the bore was now 101 millimeters, as in the Cruiser, instead of 99 millimeters, and displacement reached 1,130cc versus 1,085cc. Like the Sport Boxer, the R 1150 GS (along with all boxers since 1999, incidentally) featured cylinder head covers of super-light magnesium. The GS's two overhead chain-driven camshafts located in the cylinder heads were special parts, specifically optimized with respect to the torque band.

▌Hydraulic clutch, six-speed transmission

The digital engine management system was state of the art. As in the Cruiser and the Sport Boxer, ignition and fuel injection were controlled by the upgraded Bosch Motronic MA 2.4 (previous GS: MA 2.2). With this model, emissions were, of course, processed by a closed-loop three-way catalytic converter. To handle the improved performance and correspondingly higher cooling requirements, the GS 1150 was equipped with the R 1100 RT's large oil cooler.

It's well known from racing that exhaust system configuration has a powerful overall influence on performance. Thus, 50 percent of the improvement in performance derived from the redesigned, chromed stainless-steel emissions control and muffler system. The light-alloy engine oil pan had to be slightly modified. While the old GS came equipped with a two-in-one exhaust system, the R 1150 GS, like the R 1100 S, had a two-pipe system in which the exhaust manifolds—their diameter now increased from 38 to 45 millimeters and connected by a crossover pipe—led directly to the pre-silencer. Clutch and gearbox also required a deep reach into the system parts bin: as in the Sport Boxer and the Cruiser, the four-valve GS's power was transmitted to the rear wheel by a single-plate dry clutch and a six-speed gearbox. The entire clutch, with its plate measuring only 165 millimeters (R 1100 GS: 180 millimeters), came from the R

1200 C. While the transmission ratios for the first five gears was identical to that of the R 1100, the sixth gear was set up as an overdrive. The result: lower rpm, reduced noise, less vibration, lower fuel consumption, hence: increased comfort and economy on the highway, where the "sixth" was primarily used.

Naturally, the R 1150 GS was also shaft driven. In *Tourenfahrer* magazine, Ulf Böhringer gave the bike good grades: "This 1150 is never worse and often better than the 1100, including off-road. Despite nominally higher horsepower, its power is far easier to modulate than was the case with

the 1100's engine. The R 1150 GS has improved more through this redesign than might have been expected. . . ." To save weight, the GS 1150's designers had given it the R 1100 S's light alternator along with its rather feeble 14 Ah battery. A more powerful 19-Ah battery and a large 700-watt generator were available at extra charge. However, machines with ABS and heated grips were equipped with the stronger electrical system ex-works.

The four-valve boxer series' frame and suspension design, in which engine and transmission casing functioned as weight-bearing components integrated to the forward and rear frame sections, remained unchanged. Yet almost every detail of the bike had undergone some modification. The rear frame section

A height-variable seat, adjustable shocks, and handlebars were all standard on the R 1150 GS. Pictured is a 1999 model in Titanium Silver.

was improved and mounted to the reinforced transmission case to provide maximum rigidity. Reconfigured footrest mounts offered added stability.

In keeping with the R 1100 S, the front wheel benefited from an improved and lighter version of the BMW Telelever fork. A special manufacturing process provided single-part outer tubes shaved a kilogram off the bike's weight. Wheelbase (115 millimeters) and rake angle (64 degrees) remained unchanged. Because unsprung weight had been reduced, the Telelever was more responsive than in the old GS. In the front, as before, we find the central shock with an unaltered 190 millimeters of travel, preload adjustable in five stages with a wrench from the onboard toolkit. The rear central shock with 200 millimeters of travel had also been adopted. It featured continuously adjustable spring preload via a finger adjuster and rebound damping adjustment with a set screw.

Once again, the Sport Boxer had been the model for the reworked Paralever rear swingarm. As the Paralever's mounting on the transmission case had been modified, swingarm length dropped from 520 to 506 millimeters.

Nevertheless, the wheelbase remained unaltered at 1,509 millimeters. The six-speed gearbox now took up the swingarm's missing 14 millimeters.

With respect to wheels and brakes, there were no changes, apart from an adjustment of the rear-wheel hub. Hence, the familiar cross-spoke wheels and the brake system were derived from the R 1100 GS. This meant that the front wheel was again equipped with a dual disc brake with four-piston fixed calipers and floating stainless steel rotors (diameter 305 millimeters). Mounted in the rear was the tried and tested single-rotor disc brake with dual-piston floating caliper and 276-millimeter rotor diameter. The organic pads on the front-wheel brake were now replaced by sintered metal pads. ABS II, which could be switched off in off-road use, was available at a 1,995-DM premium. With its maximum total weight unchanged at 450 kilograms, the R 1150 GS could take on up to 200 kilograms of payload, depending on equipment.

The old R 1100 GS had an unmistakable look, even if its rather odd front end with the clunky rectangular headlight did not suit everyone's taste. Its successor undoubtedly made a more pleasing impression, while retaining its originality. The new face of the four-valve GS from the summer of 1999, with its asymmetrically placed headlights, was more typically "bike-

like" and aggressive than the original, vaguely reminiscent of a Playmobil toy. The similarity to the R 1100 S was not coincidental: The new GS was meant to look sportier—and it did. The larger headlight had an "elipsoid" design with H7 bulb; it provided the low beam and guaranteed better road illumination than the old boxy light. A "free form surface" headlight with H1 bulb supplied the high beam.

▍ Sporty looks, flowing lines

Whereas the upper mudguard had heretofore rather resembled a duck's bill, the entirely reconfigured GS part was now more reminiscent of a bird of prey, especially when considered from the front and the sides. Transitions to the tank were flowing, the whole machine looked more agile and graceful. And functionality had not suffered: the mudguard continued to work as an additional splash guard, as an air conduit to the oil cooler, and as a spoiler providing downforce at higher speeds. The lower mudguard reached almost 20 centimeters farther ahead, thereby improving both appearance and protection.

The silver-colored cockpit cover above the double headlight was a flawless design solution. It perfectly matched a newly designed, aerodynamically improved windshield featuring three adjustment positions. The screen was now removable, which proved advantageous off-road.

The cockpit had become more sober. While in the old GS, the instruments individually rose from a display panel, all components, including speedometer and tachometer, were now integrated into a simple block. The indicator lights were located under the round instrument dials. The optional information display with digital clock along with gauges for fuel, engaged gear, and oil temperature had migrated from the right to left side.

With respect to handlebar controls, the GS 1150 was the third BMW boxer (after the R 1200 C and R 1100 S) to feature switches integrated into the grip units. The new controls had required widening the "tilting-disengagement" handlebars from 890 to 903 millimeters. Brake and clutch levers featured four-stage adjustment.

The 22-liter tank was unchanged in appearance. It now featured a racing derived so-called "rollover valve," which prevented fuel leakage

With a refined Telelever and sturdy Paralever, the R 1150 GS was equally convincing on- and off-road. At almost 58,000 units produced to 2003, the four-valve GS's second series was even more successful than the first. Both photos display the R 1150 GS from 1999 to 2000.

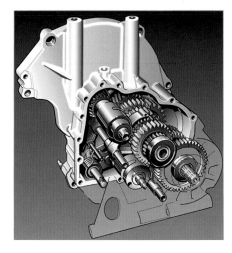

A cross-section of the six-speed gearbox.

Left: *The tank design was improved in the course of time. An R 1150 GS from 1999–2000.*

Below left: *The 2002 model with a new color scheme.*

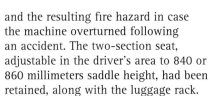

and the resulting fire hazard in case the machine overturned following an accident. The two-section seat, adjustable in the driver's area to 840 or 860 millimeters saddle height, had been retained, along with the luggage rack.

The first R 1150 GS series was available in three colors: Jet Black, Titanium Silver-Metallic, or Mandarin Yellow. From the start, the 1150 not only dominated the market in sales but also invariably came out on top in comparison tests. In May 2003, it was declared "Champion of the Alps" in *Motorrad* magazine's design comparison test featuring the KTM Adventure S, Aprilia RSV Tuono, Yamaha 900 TDM, and Ducati Multistrada. "Alpenmeister or King of the Hill, that's what they should have called this BMW," opined test-rider Stefan Kaschel. His colleague Rolf Henniges agreed: "The GS remains the Holy Grail on wheels: sovereign and faster than lightning. . . ."

Power was again transmitted to the 17-inch rear wheel via a Cardan shaft. Pictured: The frame and wheel suspension, engine, and transmission as load-bearing components.

A cross-section of the R 1150 GS's four-valve boxer. Power had increased from 80 to 85 horsepower. As before, valve actuation was via one overhead camshaft per cylinder.

Left and center: *The 1999–2000 R 1150 GS in various liveries. Extreme lean was possible on the road. Motorrad thus crowned the GS "King of the Alps."*

GS Adventure, model upgrading

The R 1150 GS "Adventure," presented in September 2001 and available from the spring of 2002, was BMW's reaction to the long-term trend to individualization and the boom in the travel accessories market. It stimulated a further quickening of demand. The Bavarians were no longer willing to leave the business entirely to the touring specialists. The Adventure made a decisive contribution to the continuing success of BMW's big enduros in the following years. Worldwide sales of the R 1150 GS reached 74,067 units by mid-2004, of which 16,233 were Adventures.

Technically, the 11,200-euro Adventure was a standard R 1150 S from which, with respect to looks and equipment, the BMW designers had hammered out the warlike long-haul motorcycle that many BMW fans had always dreamed of. Frame, suspension, tires, and standard equipment were consciously oriented to long-distance riding over challenging surfaces such as gravel tracks, sandy trails, and all manner of off-road terrain. Thus BMW had lengthened suspension travel by 20 millimeters to 210 millimeters front and 220 millimeters rear. In the rear, for the first time on a BMW, appeared a multi-adjustable shock (by White Power), which boosted damping in relation to increasing compression.

The front-wheel brake featured the caliper from the high-performance "EVO" brake introduced to several BMW models in spring 2001. At 305 millimeters, the front brake rotor diameter remained unchanged. Brake lines sheathed in steel mesh ("Steelflex") provided consistent pressure.

Disengageable ABS II was available at extra charge.

The powerplant derived unmodified from the R 1150 GS, though the engine could run on regular gasoline if necessary. An optional coded plug activated an ignition map in the "electro-box" for operation with regular 91 RON

A 2001 R 1150 GS Adventure with special accessories.

A standard 2002 R 1150 GS in Jet Black with its seat in Mandarin/Black.

A 2003 R 1150 GS and rider in a Rally 2 suite and Rally GS1 enduro boots.

(research octane number) gasoline. In contrast to the R 1150 GS, the sixth gear did not have a long (overdrive) but a short transmission ratio. An optional short first gear for improved startup in difficult terrain was also available.

The special one-piece seat allowed off-road seating positions and room for a passenger. A larger luggage rack offered expanded tie-down options. For enhanced wind and weather protection, BMW had enlarged the windshield in width by 12 centimeters at bottom and 5 centimeters at top, as well as by 13 centimeters in length. The forward

mudguard was longer and wider. Handlebar impact and hand protectors along with a reinforced solid aluminum sump guard (which had moved rearward) came standard on the Adventure. The cockpit featured an extra 12-volt socket to connect a reading light, GPS, or roadbook. The cylinder head covers were painted black; the aluminum rims were powder coated blue.

A wide assortment of specialized accessories was available. In place of the standard 22-liter gas tank, a client could order a 30-liter version. For the Adventure, BMW had developed a sturdy aluminum luggage holder with a carrier system, two side cases, and a topcase. The surfaces of the side case covers were level with the seat's rear section, thus offering an ideal base for larger pieces of luggage. There was also a large cylinder guard, a wire mesh screen for the main headlight, grills foglight, as well as special knobby tires, among other items.

▌ 2002: GPS navigation and dual ignition

From January 2002, the standard GS also featured the EVO brake with Steelflex brake lines. In March 2002,

BMW began offering a motorcycle GPS navigation system, developed in tandem with the American Garmin firm. The waterproof and anti-glare BMW Motorcycle Navigator for the R 1150 GS, produced until the end of 2003, and the Adventure, built until mid-2004, cost 1,980 euros. Its standard view was a roadmap with European basic data and a zoom function to 30-meter sections. It highlighted major waypoints. Among other functions, the integrated tripmaster calculated average speeds and projected arrival times. Tours could be planned on a standard PC, then transferred to the device's memory chip.

From November 2002, all four-valve boxers up to the R 1150 GS came equipped with twin plug ignition. This achieved improved exhaust emission values compliant with EU3 while retaining all running characteristics. A secondary effect was better efficiency at slightly lower consumption. Peak power and torque values remained unaltered. The second spark plug per cylinder was housed at the bottom of the combustion chamber. The engines with dual ignition were recognizable by a new spark-plug housing with the inscription "2 spark."

Top: *A dual plug cylinder head from late 2002.*

Middle: *Navigator GPS.*

Above: *The Navigator II from December 2003.*

Right: *A fully equipped 2002 Adventure in "White Aluminum."*

100 horsepower and 225 kilograms with a full tank: The R 1200 GS from January 2004

Rarely has a new BMW motorcycle model been praised in such glowing terms as the R 1200 GS, unveiled in South Africa in January 2004. "It's been a long time since any motorcycle redesign was as far reaching and successful. This new high end boxer makes its forerunner look outworn in every department," was Paul Steiger's judgment in *Motorrad News*. Whoever has ridden this new super-GS can wholeheartedly confirm BMW's own take of the boxer enduro (for details, see page 86) which sold for 11,762 euros at market launch.

If the R 1150 GS had already been a visionary travel motorcycle in its time, the R 1200 GS revealed itself from the outset as clearly superior in every respect. Buyers' experiences and reviewers' grades have unambiguously confirmed this. It's little wonder then that the 1200 once again shattered the sales records of precursor models: from January 2004 to December 2006, BMW sold 81,093 units of the 1200 GS (counting 10,058 R 1200 GS Adventures; see pages 99–101). This was the new record for this class. Whoever owns a late version GS can vouch for the following: the motorcycle is supremely self-assured, powerful, and comfortable, perfectly adapted to even the longest tours, yet maneuverable and agile. In addition, at 225 kilograms fully tanked, the GS is lighter than any other bike in its class, impresses with outstanding chassis and suspension characteristics, and finally, has an easy shifting gearbox. Still, this machine is no lightweight: The old R 80 G/S weighed a mere 191 kilograms.

▌ **New engine with 1,170cc and 100 horsepower**

In design, the R 1200 GS's dual-cylinder boxer engine elaborated upon past motors of the R 259 series. In detail, however, the engine had been reworked and improved and in some respects elaborately refined. Thanks to the most advanced calculation and simulation

methods, 3 kilograms were shaved off the machine's weight (about 8 percent) with increased displacement and additional functions (balancer shaft). Total width remained equal to that of the previous model. A new engine-management system and improved catalytic converter permitted yet another reduction in emissions.

Displacement increased to 1,170cc created the basis for an impressive peak performance of 100 horsepower/74 kilowatts (or 98 horsepower/72 kilowatts in Germany) at 7,000 rpm, a hefty maximum torque of 115 Nm at 5,500 rpm and majestic power development over a wide speed range: no slow coach!

"What a machine! Thirty kilograms lighter, 100 horsepower of power and so much new technology, it leaves you speechless."– Michael Pfeiffer, editor-in-chief, Motorrad.

85

R 1200 GS
principal features

- A new dimension in riding dynamics, agility, pleasure, and safety
- Outstanding off-road capability allied to enhanced road characteristics
- A 30-kilogram weight reduction, partly through the application of advanced lightweight construction and high-strength materials
- Redesigned boxer powerplant with 1,170cc and balancer shaft
- Torque and output increase of nearly 18 percent; fuel consumption reduction of 8 percent
- Newly developed BMS-K digital engine electronics and emissions control technology for reduced environmental impact
- Quiet exhaust system with rich sound; newly developed lightweight Paralever with reduced weight Cardan shaft drive
- New, lighter Telelever for even more precise front-wheel suspension
- Extremely rigid frame for the highest level of riding safety, tracking stability in a straight line up to top speed, thrilling handling, and exact cornering
- High-performance EVO brakes with disengageable ABS (optional)
- High-strength cast light-alloy wheels, optional cross-spoke wheels
- Use of electronics for reduced harness length
- Electronic immobilizer standard

The balancer shaft for elimination of disturbing vibrations was a significant development. Despite the inherent advantages of the opposed cylinder design, allowing the so-called free inertial forces (reciprocating connecting rods and pistons) to cancel each other out, boxer engines simply cannot run entirely without vibration. The cylinders' inevitable offset causes a "rotary mass moment" leading to spurious oscillations.

∎ Spur gear-driven balancer shaft
For the first time in the history of BMW engine design, a balancer shaft was built into the 1200 GS's engine. This shaft, counter rotating to the crankshaft, bears a couple of balancing weights offset at 180 degrees and dimensioned in such a way as to generate an opposite momentum. Through "superpositioning" with the crankshaft's mass moment, vibrations are reduced to residual

levels, entering into the dual-cylinder's vigorous basic character.

An elegant, space-saving solution was found for the balancer shaft layout. The shaft rotates on roller bearings within the previously mentioned intermediate shaft and is driven by the crankshaft via a spur gear system with a 1:1 transmission ratio. As in the older 1100 and 1150 engines, the intermediate shaft drives the two oil pumps along with both overhead camshafts in the cylinder heads via a couple of sprockets and chains (Hc principle). The intermediate shaft has a 2:1 reduction in relation to the crankshaft; it is powered via a roller chain.

Entirely redesigned for 2004, the R 1200 GS shown on both pages with a choice of spoke- or cast-alloy wheels, steel trellis frame, digital cockpit, Telelever, and Paralever II.

Piston design was only slightly modified in relation to the previous engine. Three-ring lightweight pistons were used; at 410 grams, these were again slighlty lighter than those of the previous engine (420 grams). The crankcase was also lightened. Through the use of cutting-edge casting technology, wall thickness, rigidity, and strength could be increased, saving another 1.4 kilograms in weight.

Effective solutions were also brought to bear on such details as crankcase ventilation; here, a reed valve was employed to reduce undesirable pressure pulses.

■ **Lighter redesigned cylinder heads**

The cylinder heads were modified, while their basic design remained unchanged. This is visually apparent in a modified contour with distinctive squarish valve covers. The typical BMW principle (not designed for highest rpm) of chain-driven camshafts "below" the valves and valve actuation via tappets and rocker arms was retained. But valve diameter was increased by 2 millimeters (inlet: from 34 to 36 millimeters; outlet: from 29 to 31 millimeters); for improved heat dissipation, the exhaust valves are sodium-filled.

Port configuration was adapted to the increased valve diameter; contours were hydrodynamically refined. Allied to the larger displacement, these measures contribute to the 18 percent increase in peak output and torque. At the same time, the cylinder heads were lightened by 15 percent. The R 259 engine's inner oil cooling of cylinder heads was adapted for higher performance.

The crankshaft is entirely redesigned. It is more compact for increased rigidity; the crank pins are now more closely spaced. This was partly achieved through narrower counterweights. At the same time, weight was cut by 1 kilogram despite increasing the stroke from 70.5 to 73. In order for crankshaft operation to achieve the required degree of compensation, part of the balancing masses were transferred to the balancer shaft flywheel and drive gear. As before, the flywheel carries the asbestos free single-plate dry clutch, whose diameter grew from 165 to 180 millimeters.

Paralever and Telelever suspension and steering for all to see—2004 spec. Simple in concept and thus competent and ultra-reliable in the field.

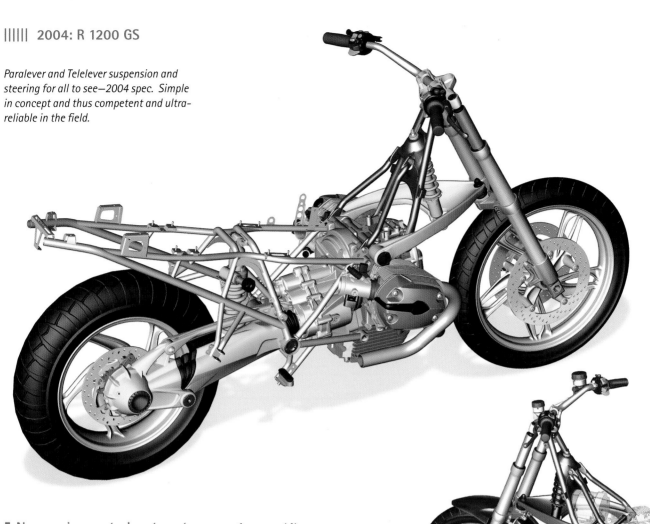

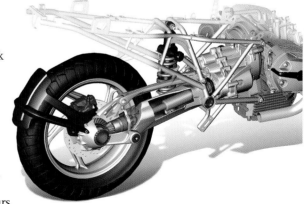

■ **New engine control system, two Lambda probes**

With the new R 1200 GS, BMW aimed to comfort its lead in engine management using its own BMS-K (BMW Engine Control) system, specifically designed for motorcycles. Fully sequential fuel injection, integrated knock control, accelerated processing of extensive sensor signals with cutting edge microelectronics, a compact layout, and low weight are its salient traits.

As before, basic parameters for motor operation are engine speed and throttle opening, as recorded by a sensor for each cylinder. Drawing on additional engine and environmental parameters (e.g., engine temperatures, air temperature, and air pressure), together with stored engine mappings, the engine control system calculates specifically matched values for fuel volume and ignition timing. Thus, fuel is individually injected into the inlet port precisely at the cylinder's intake stroke (full sequential injection).

Through the allocation of a Lambda probe to each cylinder, the air/gas mixture is selectively controlled for each cylinder. Both probes are located close to the engine within the corresponding exhaust manifold,

thus providing an even more precise recording of exhaust composition. BMS-K also includes an automatic idle speed control function as well as cold-start enrichment with a warm-up control unit. The required idle speed increase during warm up is automatic; it is controlled through so-called "idle steppers" (controlled bypass channels for extra air) integrated into the throttle valve housing.

Dual ignition, which has equipped all boxers (except 850cc engines) since 2003, was modified and improved for the R 1200 GS. The secondary spark plug is located at the cylinder's outer edge; ignition timing for both spark plugs can now be individually programmed, with a time offset adaptable to load and engine speed, thus further optimizing running charactistics, emissions control, and fuel consumption. This "phase shift" continuously occurs from part to full load.

The R 1200 GS introduces a knock control system, new to motorcycle engineering in this form. A structure-

The 1200 GS was thoroughly set-up for off-road use, yet rides great on the street. As with all BMW motorcycles since 1993, design is by American David Robb. The photos were taken in South Africa.

borne sound detector adapted to each cylinder handles the detection of knocking. The engine electronics react to corresponding signals with ignition timing (adjustment toward "late"), thus protecting the engine from possible damage. Temperature measurement combines with signal analysis to complete the protective system.

The knock control system allowed an increase of the compression ratio to 11.0:1, a considerable achievement for an air/oil-cooled engine of this displacement. The effects on fuel consumption are correspondingly positive. In the EU2 testing cycle, the R 1200 GS's fuel consumption was almost 8 percent lower than the previous model's. Set up for premium lead-free gasoline (RON 95), the engine can also run on regular gas (RON 91) or a similar quality fuel available in some countries without manual intervention thanks to the knock control system. A redesigned airbox with a capacity expanded to 9 liters and classic paper filter also figures among the improvements.

The exhaust system consists of two headers, a pre-silencer with catalytic converter and a muffler, and it is constructed entirely of stainless steel. It weighs 10.7 kilograms and thus 33 percent less than the old system. The exhaust path through both individual headers flows into a Y piece, which merges both gas currents. The Y piece connects to the pre-silencer, which holds the centrally placed catalytic converter. Close to the engine, a crossover pipe between the header provides pressure compensation, with positive effects on the torque band in the lower and middle speed range.

Another distinctive feature is a pressure-controlled valve integrated into the muffler. This provides further reduction of the noise level at middle to low rpm while retaining the rich sound motorcyclists so appreciate.

Generator (600 watts) and starter (1.1 kilowatts) were together lightened by 2.3 kilograms.

▌ New helical six-speed gearbox
The six-speed gearbox is a wholly new design with a weight now reduced to 13 kilograms. For the first time in a BMW, helical gears were used, providing low noise and smooth running. The overall gearing ratio was set up for emphatically dynamic riding characteristics. Accordingly, a sixth-gear overdrive was dispensed with; the last gear has a "short" transmission ratio.

The gear shafts are mounted in anti-friction bearings (ball-bearings); the gears (idlers) rotate with low friction on needle bearings. Ball-bearings run "clean," with seals preventing entry of even the smallest particles. This stretches maintenance intervals and reduces maintenance costs; gearbox oil changes are now only scheduled every 40,000 kilometers.

Shifting of gears occurs via a selector drum, shifter forks, and sliding sleeves (previously sliding gears). The hollow aluminium alloy selector drum is ball-bearing mounted. Detailed solutions in friction reduction for the

gear selector, selector shaft, and shifter forks further improve shifting and provide precise, secure engagement of individual gears.

▌ Lightweight Cardan shaft and a new Paralever
The new R 1200 GS could naturally not do without the traditional, maintenance-free Cardan drive to the rear wheel. With the R 1200 GS, the Paralever swingarm introduced on the 1987 R 100 GS was for the first time fundamentally altered along with the entire drivetrain. This results in a Cardan drive assembly which, together with the distinctly more rigid Paralever swingarm, weighs about 10 percent less.

The new design's main components are the final drive and the swingarm itself. The Paralever swingarm of high-strength cast-aluminum alloy could be constructed with the required lightness thanks to computerized calculation of layout and dimensions. The geometric configuration was altered; pitch compensation is now almost 100 percent.

▌ Swingarm now mounted on rear frame
The torque support for the rear-wheel-drive housing is now located above the swingarm. This provides improved ground clearance for this area while ensuring effective protection for the brace against damage from rocks and boulders in rough terrain. The brace itself is a two-section light-alloy part. Also new is the transfer of the swingarm mounting from the transmission to the rear frame section. The object here was again greater strength for extreme off-road applications.

The pivot for mounting of the final drive housing on the swingarm was moved downward, yielding increased rigidity. The mounting itself was reinforced. Through targeted kinematic configuration, the driveshaft is no longer subject to a geometry-related linear deformation; elimination of the uneeded slip joint saves yet more weight. The driveshaft is now one piece and runs dry (as before), that is without oil, within the swingarm.

All photos: *On the road—and off—the R 1200 GS amazes with its maneuverability and riding stability. The boxer, now with 100 horsepower, works up a mighty head of steam from as low as 1,500 rpm. Torque is abundant at all engine speeds.*

The differential housing was also redesigned. The crown wheel was recalibrated and lightened. To save weight, the wheel flange is now made of light alloy. Its increased diameter offers the wheel better support. The elegant and lightweight design is recognizable by its distinctive 50-millimeter end-to-end boring of the final drive housing axle tube. The final drive's lifetime oil fill makes oil changes unnecessary.

The signals for ABS and speedometer are directly picked up by a sensor from crown wheel quadrants, eliminating the need for the outer sensor wheel. The increased wheel flange pitch circle diameter allows the use of five light lug bolts.

New chassis, rigid tubular steel frame

BMW retained the basic principle of all boxer chassis produced since 1993. This includes a load-bearing engine transmission unit and the fixing of both front and rear suspensions to bolted frame sections. As before, the Telelever's longitudinal control arm is mounted on the engine casing. The R 1200 GS's frame consists of a front section for upper support and mounting of the Telelever and a rear section with the integrated swingarm mount. The engine transmission unit is bolted to the rear frame at five points and to the front frame at four. Together with the drive unit, this assembly provides the vehicle's support structure.

The R 1200 GS's two frame sections are lightweight structures engineered in a so-called pin-jointed design. The front section is a triangular construction of welded high-strength steel tubes. It offers increased solidity in off-road use over the previous cast-aluminum front frame section. The rear section also consists of straight welded steel tubes.

Refined Telelever with increased rigidity and a new shock

Through modification and geometric refinement, the properties of the R 1200 GS's Telelever were improved over its predecessor's. The longitudinal control arm is an entirely new, high-strength, and lightweight aluminum alloy forging. For better maneuverability, front-wheel caster was reduced by 5 millimeters to 110 millimeters. The 62.9-degree rake angle in normal position was retained. Its inherent high rigidity was further increased through enlargement of the inner tube diameter from 35 to 41 millimeters. A neat detail is the bore holes integrated into the lower fork crown, which elegantly distribute the braking pressure to the Steelflex brake lines for the right and left brake calipers without need for an additional connecting piece. Permanently lubricated ball joints and lifetime oil filling render the Telelever maintenance free.

For tougher off-road uses, the front gas pressure suspension shock preload has a nine-stage mechanical adjustment. Front travel is 190 millimeters. For the rear suspension there is a high-quality gas pressure shock with "path-dependent" damping (WAD), whose spring pre-load is continuously adjustable hydraulically

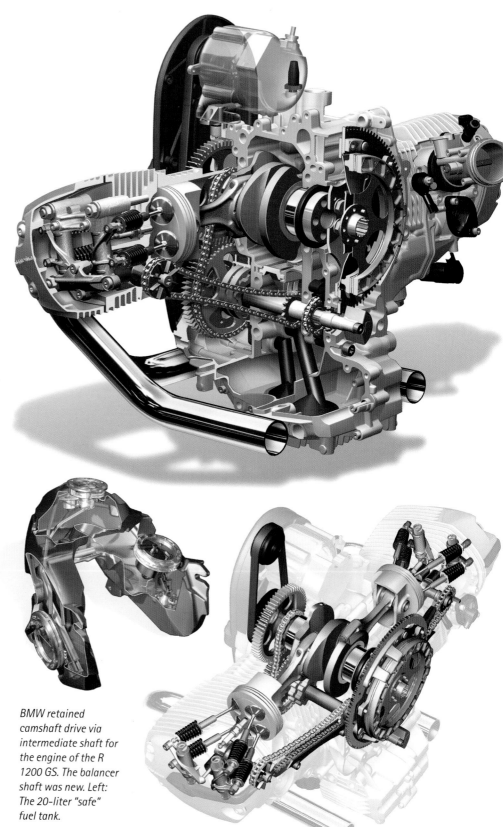

BMW retained camshaft drive via intermediate shaft for the engine of the R 1200 GS. The balancer shaft was new. Left: The 20-liter "safe" fuel tank.

via a hand wheel. Rebound damping is manually adjustable. The principle of path-dependent damping was first applied to a BMW motorcycle in 2002, with the R 1150 GS Adventure; it implies progressively increased damping dependent on spring compression. Rear spring travel is 200 millimeters. For

the wheels of the new R 1200 GS, the customer has a choice of high-strength cast light-alloy wheels or the familiar cross-spoke wheels. Dimensions are 2.50x19 inches, front, and 4.00x17 inches, rear (tires: 110/80x19 or 150/70x17). The new light-alloy rear wheel is 1.6 kilograms lighter than the spoked wheel.

■ EVO braking and integral ABS; innovative "single-wire" onboard electrical system

The R 1200 GS is equipped with the EVO brake system (known from the Adventure, among other machines), which provides maximum braking power at minimal hand pressure. The brake rotors have a diameter of 305 millimeters front (as previously) and 265 millimeters rear (new). The previously mentioned integral ABS system (disengageable for off-road use) is available as an option. The steel-sheathed brake lines provide an even more consistent pressure. An additional R 1200 GS feature is the newly laid out electrical system. The term "single wire system" denotes an innovative onboard network design employing electronics and the so-called CAN-bus technology (Controller Area Network). This network offers considerably expanded functions over conventional onboard networks, along with a reduction in cabling.

Its guiding principle is that all control devices, sensors, and loads are interconnected via a single common path into a network conveying all signals independently of their later function. All control devices are thus connected, can communicate with each other, and can exchange data bi-directionally.

Three control devices operate in the standard R 1200 GS (the instrument cluster functions as a control device). The control device of the digital engine electronics (BMS-K) not only governs the previously described engine control system, it also feeds all data to the central diagnostic unit. The central

The R 1200 GS in development, here still with the old cylinder covers.

chassis electronic unit (ZFE) controls non-engine electrical systems. The entire onboard network does without conventional fuses. In case of a short circuit or malfunction, the electronics simply shut down the concerned function. The problem can be quickly pinpointed through diagnosis. For optimal anti-theft protection, the R 1200 GS is equipped with an electronic immobilizer (EWS) ex-works. The anti-theft device, controlled through a transponder located in the ignition key, offers the highest level of security, on par with that of BMW automobiles. Up to this point, the electronics have mostly proven reliable, even under the harshest conditions.

So far, durability has also been satisfactory. In August 2006, BMW modified the central vehicle electronics system through installation of a new generation of control devices that optimize various functions.

■ Digital instrument cluster

The R 1200 GS's onboard electronics allow a wholly digital-based lightweight instrument cluster with speedometer, tachometer, and an information display known as the Info Flatscreen. Replacing the previous Rider Information Display (FID), it provides constant real time information on oil temperature, fuel tank level, remaining range, time, and engaged gear. Total and trip mileage

Left: *A prototype on an R 1150 GS base around 2002.* **Above:** *Together, the panniers and topcase offer 130 liters of stowage.*

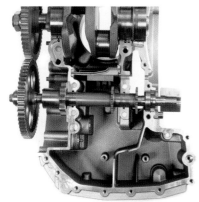

can also be displayed. Malfunctions are displayed via corresponding indicators. Switches and controls are also new, though they work according to the familiar BMW pattern.

The R 1200 GS's looks are intended to convey power, agility, and lightness allied to characteristic enduro ruggedness. All visible technical components are integrated into the design. Three basic colors (Ocean Blue Metallic, Red Sandstone, and Desert

Yellow), two seat colors (Light Gray and Black) along with two different colored tank sidecovers yield a total of 12 possible combinations and visual styles for the motorcycle.

Once again, the now distinctly more graceful front fairing with its forward extension constitutes the R 1200 GS's signature feature. This component also serves as an air conduit for cooling. The asymetrical double headlight with differing diameters for low and high beams is instantly recognized as new by its free-form reflector construction and clear glass covers. The reflectors' oval shape, with an expanded optical outlet surface, does a better job of lighting up the path ahead.

The windshield is tilt adjustable in five stages without tools. Thanks to quick releases, the plastic side covers to the left and right of the tank can be easily removed. The R 1200 GS's tank, now holding only 20 liters, is made of lightweight, impact-resistant plastic. Two lateral covers of thin aluminum and a painted top cover constitute its visible outer form. A new, dual-section double seat once again provides seating to driver and passenger in typical BMW comfort. For the driver, it is adjustable in two positions (840 millimeter and 860 millimeter). High (+30 millimeter) and low (-30 millimeter) seats with saddle heights between 810 and 890 millimeter are also available upon request. The R 1200 GS's luggage rack of lightweight, sturdy plastic has an entirely new design and offers adequate stowage surfaces for additional baggage, which can be conveniently secured through tie-down eyelets and thus securely transported. There is also the option of mounting a topcase. The plastic cover, configured as a supporting surface and located under the removable passenger seat, is yet another useful feature. It is level with the upper case edges. With mounted cases (special accessory), a generous area for securing additional luggage thus becomes available. Here also, integrated tie-down eyelets allow secure fixing.

The high-quality handlebars of thin-walled steel tube are capably designed and butted at the ends. For marginally higher weight, steel handlebars offer improved security over aluminum handlebars in case of falls (off-road use); they also allow emergency repairs. The clutch and brake levers are ergonomically optimized and adjustable for grip.

Above: *A cross-section of the 1.2-liter engine.*

Top: *The balancer shaft drive from the crankshaft via spur gears.*

Right: *The redesigned six-speed transmission.*

A 1200 engine prototype on the test-stand.

Left: *A preproduction model on a test bed at the Berlin factory.*

Below: *A production engine and Paralever.*

R 1200 GS: Model upgrading since 2005

March 2005—Operating logic modification: depress left blinker button for at least three seconds (elimination of unintented actuation)

April 2005—Windshield: modification of lower bearing bolts from plastic to metal (improved fixing, noise reduction)

August 2005—Two extra O-rings for lower bearing bolts (end play reduction)

August 2005—Compliance with EU3 emissions regulations with a new catalytic converter and adapted engine control software (also, new manifold holding the catalytic converter)

August 2005—Hazard warning lights: elimination of warning light button, activation through simultaneous depression of both blinker buttons (button remains for activation of other functions)

August 2005—Central vehicle electronics: a new generation of control devices optimized for various functions

August 2005—Front brake: new mounting of brake rotor to avoid squeaking

August 2005—Shocks: switch from WP to Showa

August 2005—Info display: switch from dot matrix to segment matrix (improved readability)

October 2005—Selector drum: installation of a selector drum with shortened travel for improved shifting

November 2005—Rear frame: simultaneous to R 1200 GS production launch, unifying modification (optimization) of rear frame and kickstand

December 2005—Engine protection: improvement of off-road characteristics (elimination of four bore holes in which foreign objects could become lodged)

February 2006—Battery: switch to a new type with reduced failure risk

February 2006—ABS sensor cable: new, more protected layout of front ABS sensor line

March 2006—Luggage rack: switch from a dual section to a single-piece rack

April 2006—Seat: reinforcement of lower edge areas (reduced damage risk)

August 2006—Mirror: redesigned clamp component

October 2006—Ignition coil: switch to a new ignition coil for all boxer models in connection with the introduction of ASC

November 2006—Topcase: new holding plate with bore hole

February 2007—Tank lateral parts: replacement of lower quick releases by screws (improved fixing)

A prototype in the wind tunnel.

"For all those who have always wondered that bike."—*Voices from the press launch*

At each previous revamping of the mother of all big enduros, you knew what was coming: boxer, driveshaft, more weight. Yet, with its 225 kilograms, on a full tank, the GS doesn't carry around more fat than the wiry KTM 950 Adventure or the original Africa Twin. And this even though it features the largest engine ever bolted to an enduro chassis. The prospectus promises a full 100 horsepower and an ample 115 Newton meters. . . .

And should you find only low-octane juice in place of the accustomed premium when you roll up to that end of the world gas station, the bike's electronics will automatically adapt as it does to ambient temperature. The GS now adjusts cold starts and warmup phase entirely without manual intervention. In the shadows, high-tech gnomes are hard at work: thanks to the single wire system and communicating control devices, the wiring harness manages with few lines and no fuses. A final relay supplies the starter. As with Hondas, the anti-theft protection (standard equipment) is deactived by a chip located in the ignition key, hence wilderness tourists should absolutely come up with a good stash for their reserve key.

A larger dry clutch connects the engine and six-speed gearbox in traditional style. It now also uses helical gearing for softer tooth mesh and smoother running, thus finally achieving the qualities that generations of BMW riders have longed for. Overdrive is so passé, the GS revs to the limit even in sixth gear. . . .

Ergonomic progress also for the sidestand, which can now actually be used from the front seat. The 20-liter tank's knee depressions are as effective in sitting position as they are standing in competitive off-road stances. The butted tubular steel handlebars quickly give you a sense of having it all under control. And that's saying something, because this boxer really puts out. Here, the 115 Newton meters are only half the story; 100 Nm already pour out at 3,500 rpm, only to be bested at the 7,000 rpm mark. For all those who have always wondered what true superiority feels like, the GS is the right bike.

—Paul Steiger, *Motorrad News*, February 2004

A dream enduro for dream touring in South Africa's left-hand traffic: the R 1200 GS.

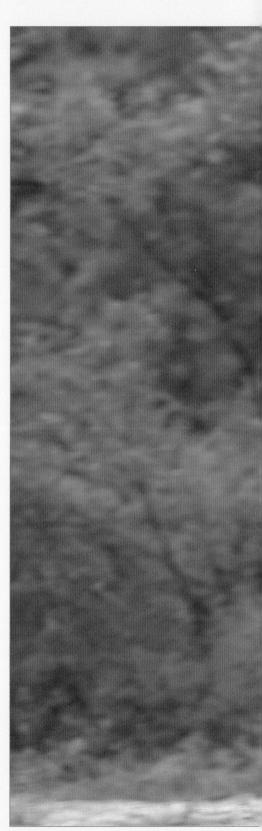

Right from top: *Cross-spoke wheels are an alternative to the new cast-alloy wheels, strong EVO brake. You will recognize it by its covers: Since 2004, the 1.2-liter boxer is more angular. This rear end can take punishment: solid tie-down eyelets, sturdy case mounts. Clever: Removal of the passenger seat creates a wide loading surface. Electronic helpers all 'round: digital cockpit and navigation system (at extra charge). More emphasis on the relation to the F 650 GS: the R 1200 GS front-end design.*

Everything about the R 1200 GS is genuinely new, from its engine, which finally no longer vibrates, to its gearbox, which finally no longer creaks, or its weight, now on a par with that of a KTM 950 Adventure, making the GS markedly more agile on and off the road. Bravo, BMW! ... When you consider the Bavarians' modular production concept, you can get set now for a whole new series of models with exciting qualities. For so much has been invested into the GS that a single model cannot do it justice even in 10 years.

    Michael Pfeiffer, *Motorrad*, March 2004

Despite all the innovation and improvement, this 1200 manages to elicit typical GS sensations: the narrow turning radius, the short first gear, the comfortable sitting position, the sense of balance, the certainty of always remaining in control. And that unique blend of all the above. ... Spectacular, the drivetrain: ... Refined

geometry provides nearly 100 percent compensation of driveshaft reactions. ... Simply unbelievable, everything this new GS has up its sleeve. The results are compelling. ... Well done, BMW.

    Ralf Schneider, *Motorrad*, March 2004

The competition already took a drubbing from the 1150; if the 1200 delivers on what it promises, Varadero et al. can pack their bags.

    mo, February 2004

It's good news that BMW has finally decided to slim down its four-valve enduro. But it's worth remembering that the R 1200 GS remains a heavyweight in comparison to the earlier 1980s models; the 1980 R 80 G/S tipped the scales at a mere 192 kilograms with a full tank. And the only thing electronic about the original G/S was the ignition.

    Der Syburger 2004

Take a trip around the world: R 1200 GS Adventure

In October 2005, BMW presented the R 1200 GS Adventure, the latest edition of the long-distance enduros, which, as with the R 1150 GS Adventure, had found 16,233 buyers worldwide between 2001 and 2004. The new model rolled to the start line with numerous improvements and considerably expanded standard equipment over its predecessor. Some examples: a 33-liter fuel tank, improved windshield, height adjustable seat, sturdy tank, engine, and valve cover safety guard, adjustable aluminum handlebars with hand protectors, along with wide driver footrests and adjustable shift and brake levers. Among the bike's distinctive technical features were longer suspension travel, cross-spoke wheels, and a stronger 720-watt alternator. The demand for the 1200 was enormous: to the end of 2006, that is. In only 15 months, 10,058 new Adventures were sold.

In its German version, as with the standard GS, the twin-cylinder boxer engine has an output of 98 horsepower at 7,000 rpm (rather than the full 100 horsepower) and reaches its peak torque of 115 Nm at 5,500 rpm. Its technology is identical to that of the standard model. Thanks to a lighter engine, transmission, and muffler parts along with reduced weight components such as the frame, suspension, and

wheels, weight was held within reasonable bounds despite considerably expanded standard equipment (256 kilograms vs. 225 kilograms for the standard model). With its six-speed transmission, modernized Paralever and Telelever designs, Info-Flatscreen digital instrumentation, CAN-bus technology onboard network, and electronic anti-theft device, the new Adventure is clearly superior to the old model. Thanks to the large tank, operating range could be extended to 750 kilometers.

Optional equipment and the accessories range match the machine's wide spectrum of applications. Available

ex-works, for example, are the BMW Motorrad Integral ABS (semi-integral, disengageable), special off-road tires, additional headlights, and onboard computer. An impressive aluminum luggage system and the motorcycle Navigator are also available as extras.

▌ Adjustable windshield and cylinder protectors

The details of the R 1200 GS Adventure's individual equipment merit closer inspection. The tilt-adjustable windshield, shaped in a wind tunnel, channels the airflow largely free of turbulence and away the driver, providing effective protection to the

Above: *A cockpit with GPS. The tank holds 33 liters.*

Right: *The fully equipped Adventure with top case (33 liters) and aluminum travel cases (79 liters for both).*

head and upper body, especially at high speeds. Moreover, specially shaped flaps mounted behind the windshield reduce the air current in the lower back area. The windshield's inclination adjustment offers riders of various heights excellent wind and weather protection. A sturdy and stable tubular stainless steel guard effectively protects tank and engine from the consequences of unintended contacts, whether off-road or on asphalt. High-grade aluminum covers protect the valve covers from damage during hard riding.

Sturdy yet practical fastening options for luggage are imperative for an enduro with globetrotting aspirations. Hence, the R 1200 GS Adventure features a large and rugged stainless steel luggage rack, which can also serve as a base for the optionally available aluminum top case. In order to provide optimal seating positions under a variety of conditions, the dual-section seat, markedly narrower at the front, is adjustable in two positions for the driver area. In raised position (saddle height: 915 millimeters), it offers the rider the comfort of a continuous seating surface without gradation, while allowing the necessary freedom of movement for off-road riding. The lowered position (895 millimeters) permits secure standing stops, for example, at traffic lights.

The high-quality butted handlebars of light alloy are equipped with a covered foam protector. The extra-wide driver footrests offer secure support, even in a standing position. The adjustable shift and brake levers also adapt to evolving demands. The height of the foot brake lever can be varied via a flap mechanism on the pedal surface; adjustment of the gearshift lever is via an eccentric.

The R 1200 GS Adventure's suspension holds up to even the toughest off-road riding. At 210 millimeters and 220 millimeters,

Top: *R 1200 GS Adventure basic version, including windshield, hand-protectors, adjustable footrests, and safety guard, among other equipment.*

Above: *The Adventure stripped of tank and seat; at center, the bulky air-filter box.*

Right: *For a curb weight of 256 kilograms (without cases), the payload totals 209 kilograms.*

respectively, an extra 20 millimeters of suspension travel over the standard GS are available front and rear. In front, we find the redesigned Telelever with a 41-millimeter inner tube diameter, in the rear the EVO-Paralever with center-mounted spring strut and path-dependent damping (WAD). The more the shock compresses, the stiffer the damping. (For additional suspension information, see the previous chapter on the R 1200 GS.)

▌ Tubular steel frame with pin-jointed design

The Adventure rides on 19- and 17-inch cross-spoke wheels that really show their stuff on challenging trails, at high off-road speeds, all under sustained stress. The tires (tubeless on demand) are adequately dimensioned at 110/80 R 19 TL and 150/70 R 17 TL. The spokes are individually replaceable.

The two-part tubular steel frame derives from the R 1200 GS; the rear section has been slightly modified in geometric configuration for center to side stand linkage. The frame's ultra-light pin-jointed structure integrates the engine as a weight-bearing component. To guarantee that additional electrical loads are reliably powered, the Adventure's alternator has an output of 720 watts, a full 120 watts more than in the standard GS. Like its four-valve engine, the six-speed constant mesh transmission with helical gears comes from the R 1200 GS.

High-grade materials and surfaces such as blast-treated stainless steel on the tank and engine guard as well as

the luggage rack, and powder-coated aluminum on rims and knee covers lend the machine a technical/functional elegance while highlighting its exacting quality standards. Two color combinations are available: Alpine White with red and black seat and black powder-coated knee covers, or White Aluminum Metallic matte with black-and-gray seat and olive-colored knee covers in magnesium powder-coated aluminum.

Top: *The Adventure has equally good off-road and street-riding characteristics. Top speed in solo is above 200 kilometers per hour; with cases mounted, it is limited to 180 kilometers an hour.*

Above: *Like the standard GS, the Adventure features the second-generation Paralever.*

Left: *The four-valve boxer is integrated into the dual-section tubular steel frame as a load-bearing component.*

Back to the source:
A minimalist sport enduro—the HP2

Motorcycles with a "pure" design have many devotees. In the days of the two-valve boxer, the type of customer who places more importance on technology than appearance was well catered for by BMW. The four-valve boxers on the market since 1993, among which the GS models of the 1100 and 1150 series, did not necessarily suit the taste of those for whom a BMW R 90 S, Ducati Monster, or Triumph Thunderbird were the measure of all things. In April 2005, however, when the Bavarians presented the HP2 Enduro, there was a buzz of excitement. They still knew how to do it: build motorcycles free of superfluous bric-a-brac, light, sporty, powerful, and with lots of character. And they could even reinvent themselves to the point of foregoing the much admired Telelever and returning to a conventional fork.

The fact that the 16,000-euro HP2 immediately ran into stiff competition in the shape of a KTM 950 Super Enduro R that sold for a whopping 4,500 euro less did nothing to dampen business. From market launch in the fall of 2005 to the end of the same year, the HP2 already found 1,967 buyers; 932 joined them in 2006. BMW was entirely comfortable with these figures; the company had never expected the market for an off-road machine of this caliber and price class to be any larger.

As expected, the trade press had a field day with the newcomer. *Motorrad* didn't miss the chance to send the two magnum dual cylinders back to back: "You don't see this every day. Four hundred pounds, over 100 horsepower and prices that'll pay for a nice compact (car), with the HP2 Enduro and the 950 Super Enduro R, BMW and KTM have pulled out all the stops in the enduro world."

As far as BMW was concerned, the HP2 was simply "a boxer designed for

off-road loving riders and the world's most challenging trails. Pure, yet noble and endowed with fine, thought through details, the HP2 is perfectly equipped for thorough off-road enjoyment and is a sound basis for amateur enduro racing." From the outset, as if to underline its point, BMW Motorcycles provided service and material to a private racing team that entered the factory-furnished HP2 at various enduro competitions, such as the German Cross Country Championship (GCC). The Finn Simo Kirssi, winner of the competition's 2004 series, was signed as a rider for the GCC. The HP2 went international at the Baja 500 and Baja 1000, along with the Erzberg Race prologue in Austria (for photos and information see page 152.)

Far left: *"A symbiosis of high-tech and fine craftsmanship": The HP2.*

Left: *A strictly functional cockpit without tachometer.*

Below: *The HP2 front and side; a solo brake rotor, front, round headlight, and graceful frame*

Opposite: *the HP2 off-road.*

▌ One guiding principle: Less is more

Technologically, the HP2 naturally elaborates upon the R 1200 GS. Yet in detail there are significant departures. These range from its elegant looks, with features such as the classic round headlight, to the largely redesigned lightweight frame and suspension with upside-down telescopic fork and pneumatic spring/damper system for the rear wheel, culminating in the lightened four-valve boxer with an output boosted to 105 horsepower. The drivetrain is especially configured for off-road. With lightweight construction applied throughout and omission of the comfort-enhancing components typical of production BMWs, the machine's curb weight was held under 200 kilograms (DIN curb weight: 195 kilograms). Dry weight is 175 kilograms. All this improved handling and control in difficult terrain over the R 1200 GS. The boxer design's low center of gravity diplays its strengths over tricky and slow sections. On fast off-road sections, the boxer enduro's outstanding performances and riding stability were already well established, not least by the Paris-Dakar victories of the 1980s.

For this machine, BMW had come up with a new label: "HP" stands for "High Performance", the "2" refers to the twin-cylinder boxer engine. In keeping with BMW's auto business, where "M" designates especially sporty models, its motorcycle division would now also identify particularly competitive and

Top: BMW also offers many accessories for the HP2.

Above: Boxers don't come any narrower.

Right: Frame and load-bearing engine.

performing machines through a special symbol. Motorcycle media chief Jurgen Stoffregen: "HP represents the expert tuning of all individual components to a single, convincing totality. It is a byword for perfection down to the smallest details, for superior riding characteristics and unadulterated riding pleasure. And HP naturally also stands for the prestige of an especially high grade machine." Supposedly, there are people who buy rare items like the HP2 just to add them to their private collections.

BMW is considering bestowing the HP label to additional high-performance models, primarily on a boxer basis. "HP motorcycles utilize production machines as a technological basis, yet are distinguished by an uncompromising adaptation to their respective application, their clear and thorough going sport orientation, and their exclusive product features."

Not unlike the M auto models by BMW M GmbH, these special motorcycles are developed by small teams of specialists. In this process, the developers' individual skills and "feel" are key. At the same time, the engineers have access to the most advanced simulation tools and technical resources that BMW has to offer.

On closer examination, it's quickly apparent that, apart from the powerplant (though modified) and the onboard network, nearly all components are new or at least thoroughly

redesigned. Weight reduction, consistent configuration to the demands of off-road riding, but also durability stood at the very top of the developers' list of priorities. Testing of the HP2 was correspondingly thorough. The machine was spared no tribulation: punishing enduro use on the trails of Spain and South Africa, endless full throttle runs on German Autobahns, trials under freezing winter conditions, and brutal desert heat, riding in tropical downpours, and mixed use in regions with extreme climates. All this rounded out by extensive test bench evaluation. Participation in the "Baja California" desert race under the direction of one-time Paris-Dakar racer Jimmy Lewis also formed part of the overall vehicle and component testing cycle.

■ **105-horsepower four-valve boxer without balancer shaft**

The output of the R 1200 GS's twin-cylinder boxer engine was boosted through special configuration of the engine control system; using Superplus grade fuel (RON 98), it reaches 105 horsepower at an unchanged 7,000 rpm. Maximum torque remains 115 Nm at 5,500 rpm. Jolt-free slow riding without resort to the clutch is made possible in large part through the refined electronic engine management system with automatic idle speed control of the post-2004 boxer generation. This is a real advantage in difficult spots and on soft surfaces.

Above and below: BMW: "The pricing results from superb overall characteristics, distinctly more complex product design, and the comparatively low number of units produced." The drawings depict the frame and suspension design, specifically modified for the HP2.

The pneumatic spring/damper system developed by Continental, whose primary function is to prevent bottoming.

It's worth noting that a balancer shaft was left out to reduce weight. The air intake is slightly modified and features a deflector to guard against direct water spray entry, always a possibility in street use. The exhaust headers were taken over as is; the muffler, on the other hand, is a new design weighing almost 2 kilograms less. Exhaust system weight reduction is achieved largely through elimination of the casing duct and a shorter design. This works out because there are no provisions for travel cases on the HP2. The standard GS requires a certain minimum damper length in order to avoid excessive heating of the cases by hot exhaust gases. The six-speed transmission's intermediate shaft bearings were reinforced. Gear ratios and other technology are similar to those of the standard R 1200 GS.

The Paralever swingarm and the Cardan shaft are entirely redesigned; the latter features a rubber damper of differing hardness and is adapted to the modified swingarm length. The Cardan drive's secondary tranmission ratio, however, remains unchanged at 2.82:1. The entire drivetrain is powder coated a magnesium gray.

▌ Fully independent chassis

In geometry and overall chassis configuration, the challenge was to pull off the balancing act between satisfactory road characteristics with high tracking stability on the highway on one hand and excellent off-road qualities with light handling and great agility on the other. BMW devoted considerable resources to achieving this. Thus, the frame layout was based on insights garnered from the R 900 R racing machines deployed by the factory from 1999 to 2001 at the Paris-Dakar Rally and other international desert races. It was a tubular steel trellis frame with optimal, very evenly distributed rigidity.

On the HP2, the front suspension, unlike with the Telelever GS, has a conventional Marzocchi upside-down telescopic fork with a whopping 270-millimeter of travel (GS: 190 millimeter). This would not have been possible with a Telelever. One special fork feature is path-dependent damping; spring rebound and compression are individually adjustable in many stages. To prevent bottoming, the hydraulic system is also adjustable. What's unusual about this system is

that the compression stage damping remains largely unaffected by the anti-bottoming adjustment.

The fork achieves the required rigidity with an inner tube diameter of 45 millimeters. The inner tubes feature an extremely hard special coating that is even more wear resistant than standard titanium nitride surfaces.

For the rear suspension, the engineers once again relied on the Paralever swingarm design, which was completely reworked as a lightweight design for the post 2004 boxer generation. Although now hardly to be improved upon in effectiveness, the Paralever for the HP2 was reconfigured and above all lengthened by 30 millimeters. While the GS's Paralever is cast, the HP part is a welded construction of high strength, forged light-alloy "shells" that will stand up to even the toughest demands of competitive enduro riding.

For the rear shock, BMW Motorcycles once again created a sensation by introducing a world premiere in motorcycle suspensions. In collaboration with the German manufacturer Continental Automotive Systems, it had developed a spring/damper system operating entirely on air. This 2.3-kilogram pneumatic spring/damper system, which is approximately 2 kilograms lighter than conventional designs, does retain some resemblance in structure and operation to the latter. In the air shock, a piston also travels along a damping chamber. But instead

of hydraulic fluid, here it's air that's displaced and transferred to a second chamber via plate valves. Leakage can be compensated by pumping air into a valve. Even saddle height can be adjusted through air addition or release. Adaptation to varying loads also occurs simply via inflation pressure. A nifty detail: The motorcycle's normal position can be determined with the small bubble tube mounted on the rear frame section. For pumping on the go, a hand-operated high-pressure pump with manometer is included in the standard delivery; this is also useful for re-inflating the tires after an off-road pressure loss.

One unique feature of the pneumatic spring/damper system is the option of frequency selective damping enabled by targeted tuning of the inner flow circuit to the split dampers (for details, see page 140). Basic damping characteristics can additionally be adapted in two stages either to a comfort-oriented street setting or a stiff off-road setting via hand wheel, which releases a bypass opening in the damper (see box on page 109).

In keeping with its pronounced off-road design, the HP2 rides on sturdy cross-spoke wheels. The front wheel has dimensions of 1.85x21 for high ground clearance and optimal suspension. The rear-wheel dimensions are 2.5x17. High-performance tubeless off-road tires (90/90x21 front, 140/80x17 rear) are mounted standard; these were especially developed for the HP2 by

Bred for off-road racing: the HP2. BMW provides specialized training courses and offers customized off-road tours.

Metzeler under the designation "Karoo." Motocross tires (also a collaborative effort with Metzler) are optionally available. The rear wheel features a second valve opening (capped while not in use) for the use of clamps when riding with lowered tire pressure.

The brake system is also something out of the ordinary. The front wheel features a single disc brake with floating caliper. The "semi-floating" rotor has

a diameter of 305 millimeters and a thickness of only 4.5 millimeters to save weight. In the rear, we find the R 1200 GS's fixed-caliper single-disc brake with a rotor diameter of 265 millimeters. The brake lines are only steel sheathed in the front. For a softer pressure point, a conventional "rubber fabric" brake line was employed for the rear brake. There were no initial plans for ABS.

The configuration of tank, seat, and controls was guided by the ergonomic demands of enduro riding, with its frequent upright position. The completely new fuel tank of impact

resistant, semi-transparent plastic (high-density polyethylene) is overlaid with a light plastic cover. The tank, with a capacity of only 13 liters, is lodged between the upper frame tubes. Innovatively, the fill level is visible from the outside through an opening in the cover; the volume can be judged with sufficient accuracy through a couple of scale lines. In the event of off-road filling from canisters, this type of outside reading proves more practical than an electrical display. A reserve warning light is also part of the standard equipment.

An exterior sign of the elaborate new Paralever construction: magnesium-tinted powder coating.

Above: *With appropriate tires, the Enduro can also go fast on asphalt.*

Right: *The HP2 is an all-round off-road machine that shrinks from no obstacle. High ground clearance and a large front wheel strongly contribute to off-road capability.*

this patented BMW mechanism does not modify the brake lever's position in relation to the brake cylinder, so the necessary and correct "test-play" remains in spite of the adjustment possibilities.

The electric onboard network with CAN-bus technology was taken over unaltered from the R 1200 GS. Reduced cabling versus conventional onboard networks, the absence of ordinary fuses, and full diagnostic capability are special advantages for enduro riding. The integrated electronic anti-theft system (EWS) comes standard. The instrument cluster, with speedometer and Info Flatscreen, focuses on essentials, omitting a tachometer. Operating hours can also be displayed; these are important for air filter replacement intervals when riding dusty trails.

The HP's design is extremely Spartan and oriented to component functionality. Especially with regard to bodywork, this stripping down to essentials represents a deliberate stylistic approach. Only the tank cover and part of the mudguard are painted. Plastic components in areas vulnerable to falls, such as tank parts and the front mudguard, are constructed of unpainted, tinted, grained plastic that hardly reveals scratches. The HP2's color scheme is distinctive: Indigo Blue and Metallic Alaska Gray.

The headlight mounting is extremely sturdy and can thus also serve as a conveniently placed "salvage yoke." Recessed grips are also found in the rear section under the seat; these are located to be well protected from dirt thrown up by the rear wheel. License plate holder and blinkers are easily removed with five screws; their cables are disconnected via plug and socket connector.

Each HP2 is delivered standard with a set of additional protective parts for subsequent installation. This protection package includes hand protectors with an open configuration, a large surface plastic engine guard, and a transparent plastic plate for mounting before the headlight for protection against breakage of the glass headlight lens (this is not authorized on Germany's public roads). There is also a guard for the differential housing against damage from striking rocks, along with a short steel cable in the foot brake lever area to prevent stones, branches, or other objects from lodging between the lever and the engine and bending, blocking,

To guarantee optimal control even in standing position, narrow vehicle contours are emphasized in the transitional area from the tank to the seat. The two-tone seat is especially narrow in the forward section up to the tank. Driver saddle height is 920 millimeters, or 900 millimeters, for the optional lower seat.

Handlebar clamps with asymmetrical bore holes allow individual positioning of the wide handlebars in two different positions. If the clamps are rotated 180 degrees, the handlebars' longitudinal position is shifted by 20 millimeters. The handlebars proper are of aluminum

with butted ends. Special attention was given to a tight turning circle. This amounts to 42 degrees both left and right, increasing maneuverability, and allowing secure vehicle control even at exceedingly slow speeds.

The rustproof stainless steel footrests are wide for secure footing in the greatest variety of foot positions. The highlight here is a folding spacer at the brake foot lever with which the lever position can be quickly and simply modified in relation to the foot, without tools. Thus, whether riding upright or seated, the brake lever is always perfectly accessible. Incidentally, or even actuating the former, thus causing unintended braking.

All in all, the HP2 is an off-road boxer that those of us traveling the Alps and the Pyrenees in the early 1980s on the first R 80 G/S could only have dreamed of. BMW has learned much in the intervening 25 years; with the HP2 it has created a Super Enduro that beats the old Monolever mules in every department and looks better in the bargain. That it also costs four times as much just has to be taken in stride by whoever really wants one.

Real innovation

A real innovation: the pneumatic spring/damper system for the HP2's rear wheel, developed in conjunction with the Continental tire company. Damping is achieved through throttling of the airflow. As it is subject to compression, the enclosed air can assume the damping function, thereby replacing the customary steel spring. Air is a medium with ideal properties for a spring/damper system and offers multiple advantages: resistance to overheating (no temperature related decrease in damping under high loads, e.g., on washboard trails); a "naturally" progressive spring rate (rising pressure in the system) and damping (air viscosity increases along with temperature) under high stress; elevated bottoming protection (the gas law: pressure rises along with temperature); frequency dependent, selective damping with "automatic" adaptation to load; simple adjustment to load conditions and saddle height.

Proportionally reduced unsprung masses improve the suspension's responsiveness and rear-wheel traction. The design of the pneumatic suspension strut features three successive air chambers interconnected through air ducts. An aluminum cylinder forms the two upper chambers, which are separated by a piston. The enclosed air is compressed through the longitudinal movement of the piston, thus acting as a spring. Simultaneously, a defined air volume moves into the next chamber via plate valves (split dampers) and dampens the wheel movement through throttling. The lower air chamber is formed by a gas-tight air bellows made of rubber fabric. It allows the stroke movement and seals the strut against the outside, eliminating the need for a friction-increasing piston rod seal. Resistance from the rubber bellows rolling over a specially formed cone increases the system's progressiveness.

High-grade firecracker: The HP2 Megamoto

"She's a real looker, loads of fun, and a worthy representative of BMW's new, dynamic direction. Those who dreamed of a spirited, racy boxer equally at home in the city and the wilds have found the answer to their wish with this downright inspired HP2 Megamoto. As long as they manage to pay for it."

Stefan Kaschel, a reviewer at *Motorrad* magazine, was full of praise after putting this special, supermoto-style boxer, first presented in October 2006, through its paces (the test appeared in the November 2007 issue): "The new HP2 Megamoto is something like BMW's spearhead in the quest for a sportier future. Here, we leave the old-fashioned comforts of yesterday far behind." What particularly impressed the reviewer was that the megamoto sacrificed everything, but really everything, that customarily made up a BMW's rather staid character. No luggage rack here, no heated grips, not even ABS. As in the HP2 Enduro, there was a Marzocchi telescopic fork instead of a Telelever, lightweight construction all over the place, small 13-liter tank, the whole thing in a look "flooded with air and light." And performance galore: 114 horsepower at 7,800 rpm, a top speed of 215 kilometers per hour, perfectly stepped six-speed transmission, jaw-dropping corner clearance and handling.

It was only at 216 kilometers per hour (speedometer: 230 kilometers per hour) that the tested boxer's rev limiter finally kicked in, at 8,000 recorded rpm and 8,300 rpm displayed. Unheard of in a boxer: the maximum torque of 120 Nm at 6,300 rpm, reminiscences of BMW's high rpm car design. (The men from Munich raised the bar even further

Light, powerful, aggressive: The HP2 Megamoto with 113-horsepower four-valve boxer and small front wheel.

Left: *Prior to his bout with Henry Maske on March 31, 2007, the American boxer Virgil Hill checked out the Megamoto boxer.*

Below: *The HP2 Megamoto from the side, front, and rider's perspective.*

at the 24 Hours of Le Mans in April 2007 with a 140-horsepower racing engine, their first factory involvement with a circuit race in 50 years.)

The Megamoto signals BMW's unequivocal commitment to more "passionate motorcycle design," leaving the beaten path in a quest to attract younger but affluent clients. An HP2 Megamoto will set you back 17,330 euros, excluding fees and accessories. Technically, the machine is based on the previously described HP2 Enduro. At 202 kilograms with a full tank, it is almost 20 kilograms lighter than an R 100 S with two-valve boxer

from the late 1970s, this with much more elaborate suspension and engine technology and double the power. Super lightweight construction and special materials make it all possible.

The Megamoto is designed for sporty riding on country roads but also for runs on the racetrack. The suspension was set up in consequence, with taut adjustment and pronounced lowering. The fully adjustable upside-down fork provides the requisite stiffness, with 45-millimeter-diameter inner tubes; its mere 160 millimeters of travel are a full 110 millimeters less than on the Enduro version. Instead of the complex pneumatic spring/damper system, the rear end is equipped with an Öhlins suspension shock featuring 180 millimeters of travel. It is also adjustable in preload and rebound damping. However, testing revealed a lack of responsiveness of the fork along with a tendency to judder when riding over road irregularities in a full lean.

Naturally, rims and tires (Michelin Pilot Power) also reinforce the machine's special character: In the front, a 120/70 ZR 17 tire is mounted on a 3.5-inch rim,

while the back has a 180/55 ZR 17 tire on a 5.5-inch rim. Unlike the Enduro, the Megamoto features a front brake with a second 320-millimeter (instead of 305-millimeter) diameter rotor and a four-piston caliper. The rear-wheel brake has a 265-millimeter rotor. Equally distinctive are the cockpit, headlight, and tank, along with the aggressively styled, minimalist, and part carbon fairing components.

The custom double-flow Akrapovic exhaust system produces a rich sound. The 1.2-liter boxer powerplant, rated at 113 horsepower, was primarily set up for instant throttle response and maximum torque. And the four-valve boxer is economical in the bargain: in the test, a mere 4.6 liter/100 kilometer (highway) shot through the Megamoto's injectors. "An uncompromising riding machine: light, powerful, agile and, above all, highly exclusive." It's hard to disagree with BMW's press release.

Munich's single-cylinders: The historical precursors to the modern BMW F and G models

The year 1948: After the nightmare of World War II and the misery of the immediate postwar period, this was the first year to offer a new glimmer of hope, despite the Soviet blockade of Berlin on June 24 and the forced division of the old German capital by the Communists operating in the "Eastern Zone." The currency reform, brilliantly planned by a certain Professor Ludwig Erhard (future chancellor of the Republic of Germany), laid the foundations for the rebirth of the West German economy. In Bonn, for the first time in many years, parliament went into session. On August 8, Nuremberg became the first German soccer champions since the end of the war after a 2 to1 nail-biter against Kaiserslautern.

▌Cooking pots of aircraft-grade aluminum

At BMW, primarily involved in the production of military equipment during the war years, there was renewed hope as well after the catastrophe of 1945. The production facilities had been largely destroyed, whatever was left seized and hauled off by the occupying armies. The loss of the Eisenach factory was particularly painful. It became all the more important to get things moving again in Berlin and Munich. "Roll up your sleeves, there's work to be done!" was the slogan of the day here as everywhere else in a country reduced to smoldering ruins.

Already in the first year after the war, at the plant north of Munich and at the Berlin-Spandau factory (which had produced aircraft engines to the bitter end) the Bavarians did their best to restart production with the few means at their disposal. From whatever raw materials remained (primarily aluminum from aircraft parts production), the surviving BMW workers fashioned such useful items as cooking pots, bakery equipment, and agricultural machinery.

This hardly provided an adequate economic foundation for the long term. Workers and designers wanted

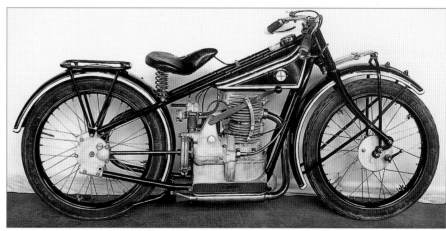

With 247cc, 6.5 horsepower at 4,000 rpm, ohv cylinder head, and 100 kilometers per hour at top speed, the 1925 R 39 (both photos) was not just BMW's first single-cylinder motorcycle, it instantly won the German championship.

111

to build motorcycles again, just like before the war; they wanted to save up for their own BMW on an employee discount. And in the population at large, the demand for motorcycles was stirring once more, for a variety of reasons. Nothing even approximating public transportation was yet operating in the bombed-out cities. Only a few dilapidated streetcars clanked about, hopelessly overcrowded. Passenger cars were rare and exorbitantly priced, even when worn out and bullet ridden. On the other hand, whoever owned a motorcycle ruled the road, arrived on time at the office or factory, could even go on a country picnic at the weekend.

BMW's decision to restart motorcycle production with a single-cylinder machine was the right one: hardly anyone as yet could afford a big boxer; speed was no pressing concern on pothole-strewn cobbled streets. What was needed was a motorcycle for the common man: economical, sturdy, low maintenance, sidecar capable, and cheap to service in the bargain. And so, at the end of 1948, the R 24, BMW's first postwar motor vehicle, rolled off the assembly line. This elegant machine, which could be economically produced in vast numbers, was something like a two-wheeled answer to the Volkswagen (not yet referred to then as the Beetle, but simply as the "VW").

Exempt of tax and driver's license: the 1931 R 2 (right, first series; below, second series). The 398cc R 4 also featured a pressed-steel frame and front leaf spring.

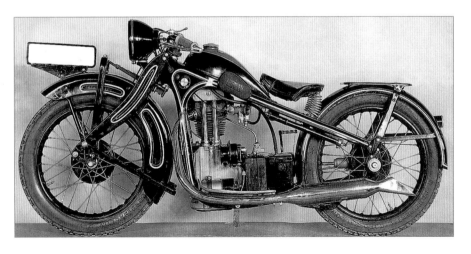

A *photo of the first series, from 1932. At the time, the license plate holder was on the front mudguard.*

1948: Halting first steps with the R 24

From a technical standpoint, the first 250cc BMW of the postwar period was anything but a sensation. It came along as a purely utilitarian article devoid of the slightest ornamentation, available, like Henry Ford's Tin Lizzie in its own time, only in a sober black. The machine's sole concession to luxury were the white, finely arched pinstripes lovingly brushed by hand on the tank and mudguards. The rider sat on a rubber-covered hinged saddle with coil springs; there was no rear-wheel suspension whatsoever. Still, the feeble front-wheel suspension already operated on the telescopic fork principle, featuring long helical springs and a simple hydraulic system to dampen the worst road surface outrages.

Available at extra charge were a passenger saddle with separate springing, additional footrests, and an air pump for the road. The 19-inch spoke wheels with narrow drum brakes were interchangeable; in this way, the tire profiles, which naturally tended to wear more in the rear, could be alternately scraped off to the last millimeter. The motto then was save, save, and save some more, for the average worker made 42 cents an hour, only bringing home about 80 DM a month. The price of a motorcycle like the R 24, which cost 1,750 DM, was thus equivalent to 22 months of salary. The "average Joe" had to plug away seven times longer for a motorcycle than today's autoworker for a brand-new VW Golf.

The R 24's chassis, comprising only the minimum tubes and braces, came unmodified from the pre-war R 20 and R 23 models. However, what distinguished the R 24 from other motorcycles of its class was the Cardan shaft (introduced by BMW as early as 1923), leading to the rear-wheel drive via a creaking Hardy disc and crudely encapsulated universal joint. The chain was gone, no need to dirty one's hands anymore tightening, oiling, and replacing a chain. In this respect, the classic BMW single-cylinder was one up on today's F 650.

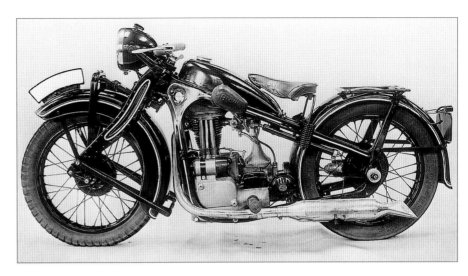

▌ Sturdy single-cylinder technology for many miles

For the R 24, the engineers had thoroughly revamped the ohv single-cylinder, that "half a boxer." Output had been boosted from 10 to 12 horsepower. There were separate valve covers and an improved electrical system. Control and setting of valve clearance, ignition, and carburetor were really no problem, unless you had two left hands. With a little practice, the tank, engine, and transmission could be dismantled in half an hour. The massive dry clutch, which operated like that of a car, lasted forever and could be replaced in a flash, if necessary.

Entirely new on the R 24 was the four-speed transmission with short first gear and an extra hand gear shift. Both features were designed for the then popular sidecar operation. As early as 1949, the thousandth R 24 left the Munich assembly line. Around the same time, the first postwar boxer was launched: the 24-horsepower R 51/2.

▌ The 1920s: BMW luxury boxers

BMW's successful singles got off to an early start in 1925, merely two years after the launch of the first BMW ever, the legendary twin-cylinder R 32. The initial situation was anything but favorable: in the early 20th century, dozens of small and medium-size manufacturers from all over Europe vied for the business of customers sown very thin on the ground. Money was tight in an era of social turmoil and galloping inflation. Millions of unemployed beat the pavement in search of jobs, the rest largely living from hand to mouth. German society and politics were in complete upheaval. Whoever could afford a motorcycle almost belonged to the "upper crust."

A BMW boxer was a pipe dream beyond the reach of the average earner. So there was a compelling logic to the idea of the single: to bring out a cheap "people's edition" of the boxer design

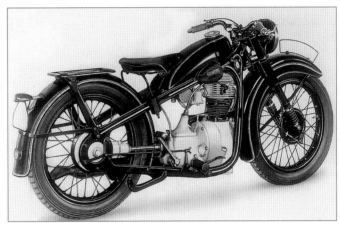

With reduced bore, the R 3 (top), which was only produced in 1936, had a displacement of 305cc. **Left and bottom:** *From 1937, the R 35 was the first BMW single to feature a telescopic fork. Ordered in large numbers by the German army, it sold a considerable 15,386 units.*

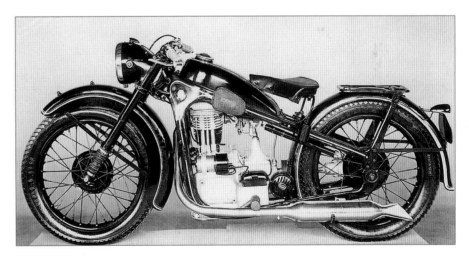

without sacrificing such a defining attribute as the Cardan drive. In a way, the singles already had a head start on the twin cylinders: while until the war and without exception, BMW offered side-valve engines in parallel to its ohv sport models, the single-cylinder models exclusively featured overhead valves. More advanced ohv designs, originally introduced in 1925 with the twin-cylinder R 37, allowed higher rpm and more efficient combustion.

▌ 1925: BMW's first single-cylinder, the R 39

The first single-cylinder BMW, the R 39, came out in 1925. It had a displacement of 250cc and an output of 6.5 horsepower at 4,000 rpm. The valves in the light-alloy cylinder head were actuated via a lateral overhead camshaft, relatively short pushrods, and rocker arms with accessible set screws. The principle would remain unchanged until 1966, the year in which the last

R 27 rolled off the line. BMW's two-valve boxers continued to operate with this mechanism until 1996 (see R 80 GS Basic, pages 54 and 55).

The R 39's top engine cover and cylinder were a light-alloy single component; the liner was pressed in. The ohv cylinder head was inherited from the R 37. A three-speed transmission and rigid Cardan shaft transmitted power to the rear wheel equipped with an all-weather tire. You shifted using a kind of pump handle that projected ominously from the gearbox. The speedometer sat on top of the tank; the front wheel was "guided" by a tubular swingarm and was simply suspended by a longitudinal leaf spring.

There was no real muffler or even brakes in any genuine sense of the word: In the front a puny drum brake wasn't much more than an alibi, and in the rear a Cardan shaft brake did little to break the momentum. The most effective way to slow down was with the engine by double clutching. In order to avoid getting thrown by the bone shakers of the time, you had to know something about both riding and mechanics.

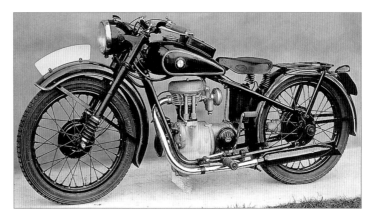

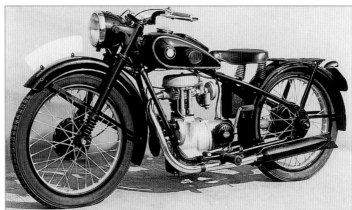

Left: *Weighing only 130 kilograms and with 8 horsepower, there were 5,000 192cc R 20s built in 1937. With its 247cc, the technically identical R 23 of 1938, with tubular frame and telescopic fork (middle), was the precursor to all BMW singles until 1966. It sold 9,021 units.*

The first postwar model, the R 24, is assembled in Munich, 1949.

The narrow clincher tires with mountain bike dimensions of 27x5 were anything but puncture resistant, if only because of all the horseshoe nails strewn about the Weimar Republic's gravel roads. Still, at 1,870 marks, this first BMW single was more than 1,000 DM cheaper than the ohv boxer. At extra charge, BMW also delivered a "Sport Model" with enticingly narrow mudguards. To 1927, the R 39 sold at 855 units; nowadays, at such low figures, one might be moved to speak of an exclusive special edition.

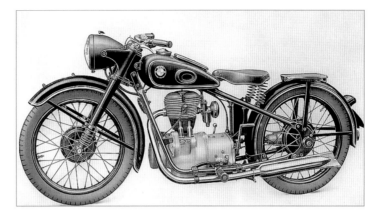

With 12,020 units sold, the Spartan R 24, built from 1948 to 1950, was a genuine success.

▮ 1931: Breakthrough with the low-cost R 2

The R 2, introduced in 1931 and produced in several series until 1936, set sales figures of a completely different order. BMW managed to sell 15,207 units of its new entry-level model; this was a real success for those times (or even these). There were a good many reasons for this. First, the R 2 was precisely the right bike at the right time. Since 1925, Germany groaned under the weight of the worldwide Depression, money was scarce; many thousands of motorists had had to take their cars off the road, simply because they could no longer afford the taxes, gas, and repairs.

The under 200cc R 2, however, was tax exempt under a 1928 law; in fact, you didn't even need a driver's license to operate this type of motorcycle. The fact that at 975 DM the R 2 cost half as much as the R 39 matched the economic realities of the time. Another reason for the motorcycle's brisk sales was that the BMW brand had gained immensely in popularity. In 1929, the racer Ernst Henne had set a new world record with a boxer on the Ingolstadt Highway: 216.75 kilometers per hour. It was only natural that the motorcycle riding public, keen on capturing something of this reflected glory, displayed a marked preference for the blue-and-white brand.

Technically, the R 2 was in many ways an economy version of the sporty R 16 boxer. Especially noteworthy was its newly developed pressed-steel frame. As in auto production, individual components could be rationally produced in batches of requisite volume; what's more, sheet metal construction saved weight, the original R 2 weighed only 110 kilograms. The fact that the cylinder head possessed no cover also fit in with low-cost production: valve springs and rocker

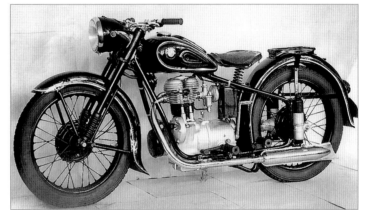

The 1950–1951 R 25 was the first single-cylinder BMW with a rear-wheel suspension. It found almost twice as many buyers as the preceding model.

The R 25/2 in a rare 1953 off-road version with raised exhaust mounted on the right.

arms enjoyed the great outdoors.

In 1932, however, the cylinder head was once again decently packaged, and a pressure oil riser was set between the pushrod sleeves. Initially, the 198cc ohv single developed 6 horsepower at 3,500 rpm. Eventually this rose to 8 horsepower at 4,500 rpm. Along the way, a shock absorber joined the leaf spring at the fork. The dry clutch, three-speed transmission with ball and socket shifting, and Cardan drive remained

unchanged. Still, for the first time there were drum brakes front and rear.

The R 4, which was launched in 1932 and went through 15,295 units in various versions until 1937, also became a legend. This success was due in no small measure to the army and police, who ordered considerable numbers of the machine in an off-road version featuring camouflage paint and linen panniers. Where all this would lead to is sufficiently well known.

We had a chance to ascertain just how hard boiled the R 4 was (and remains) on the occasion of a classics event. What immediately impressed us was the primaeval power of the 398cc, 12 to 14 horsepower (according to series) engine. Speeds of around 100 kilometers per hour are no problem. Yet at full throttle, one had better hang on for dear life: The prehistoric vehicle meted out some wicked blows with its unsprung rear end, the vibrations were brutal, the noise considerable, and the two mini drum brakes only provided the illusion of braking. Roadability was only as good as the road.

■ R 4 from 1932: A successful model with 400cc

Back to our story: In 1932, the BMW fan had to plop down 1,150 DM for this exercise machine. In 1933, the rather absurd three-speed gearshift with the enormous automobile shift lever yielded to a modern four-speed transmission. The III Series won admirers with a gas tank expanded to 12.5 liters, a generator now enclosed by the engine housing, and a reworked cylinder head, which boosted output to 14 horsepower. The generator later found its way outside again, now driven by a v-belt, the early anticipation of a solution also applied to the four-valve boxer. There really is (almost) nothing new under the sun.

The R 3's appearance in the year 1936 proved short lived. In practice, it was little more than an R 4 with bore reduced to 305cc. Other than its modified cylinder head, the machine was identical to the R 4. It only remained in the program for a year, a mere 740 units being sold. Meanwhile, Ernst Henne had almost flown off the track during a renewed record-breaking attempt: his BMW Kompressor with streamlined fairing began lurching from side to side at 270 kilometers per hour; evidently a problem with the aerodynamics. But in 1937, it finally all paid off: The instruments indicated 279.5 kilometers per hour.

■ 1937: R 35—first single with telescopic fork

Speeds the likes of which single-cylinder riders had only dreamed of: the R 35, launched in 1937 to replace the R 4, easily reached 100 kilometers per hour. A 995 marks, it was relatively inexpensive while it introduced a technical innovation that had already arrived for the boxer series in 1935, a hydraulic telescopic suspension fork (which admittedly still operated without damping).

While the boxers already featured a modern tubular frame, the single-cylinders still displayed the pressed-steel chassis, now as obsolete in technology as in appearance. Apart from the telescopic fork and the cylinder, the R 35 was identical to the R 4. Displacement had decreased to 342cc, though the engine put out 14 horsepower at 4,500 rpm. Not least because of its popularity with the military, the R 35 achieved sales on par with its predecessor: 15,386 units left the Munich plant.

■ Lightweight construction: R 20 with the graceful tubular frame

Modern times came to small single-cylinder chassis construction at the end of the 1930s. The 8-horsepower R 20, replacing the R 2 in 1937, not only featured the advanced telescopic fork but also a graceful, boxer-style tubular frame. The engine had also been completely redesigned and improved. With its timeless, clear lines the R 20 already displayed all the typical features of the single-cylinder models of the 1950s and 1960s: teardrop tank, compact engine crankcase with integrated generator directly above the crankshaft, foot-shifted (three-speed) transmission, coil sprung hinged saddle. While the 19-inch front wheel was guided by the R 35's undamped telescopic fork, the rear wheel remained unsprung. Those 5,000 customers who acquired an R 20 between 1937 and

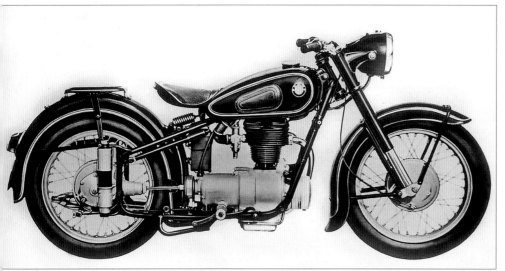

The 250cc BMW models of the 1950s were among the most successful motorcycles of the time. The R 25/2, produced from 1951 to 1953, enjoyed sales of 38,651 units. Between 1953 and 1956, the R 25/3 even made it to 47,700 units. **Top:** *The author purchased this 1952 R 25/2 in 1975 as a regular used vehicle, before restoring it at a later date.* **Above:** *An R 25/3 with a modern telescopic fork and larger tank.*

Above: *There were 30,236 units of the R 26 with full swingarm chassis produced between 1956 and 1960.*

Right: *An outstandingly restored stock R 25/2 from 1951 belonging to a collector from Braunschweig.*

1938 were 725 DM lighter, but in no way poorer, for they had acquired a genuine BMW, if at a subsidized rate.

An upgrade came two years later: The R 20 became the R 23. It now featured a tool compartment in the top part of the tank, reducing its volume from 12 to 9.5 liters. But the most important modification remained unseen, though hardly unfelt. Bored out, displacement had risen to 247cc and output by 25 percent to 10 horsepower at a lively 5,400 rpm. The reason: The Nazis had raised the motorcycle tax exemption threshold from 200 to 250cc. That is how BMW's famous singles came about their displacement for the following era.

For almost 30 years, nothing could budge those meager 247cc. Still, 9,021 R 23 sales contracts were signed in 1940, when BMW went over to wartime arms production, along with rest of German industry.

▌ Postwar 250s and the road to success

We've already touched upon the course of events at war's end. The R 24, with an improved engine brought up to 12 horsepower, turned out a real success despite its relatively high price of 1,750 DM. There were 12,020 machines of this type sold between 1948 and 1950.

Its successor, the R 25, arrived with important modifications and an engine thoroughly improved. Its most obvious innovation was the plunger-type suspension, which, though it still had to do without damping, considerably enhanced riding comfort in conjunction with a new hinged saddle and somewhat wider 19-inch tires. The double-loop tubular frame was no longer bolted together but welded; the front mudguard had taken on wider contours. At an unchanged price, BMW managed to double its singles sales within two years to 23,400 units.

The R 25/2 appeared in 1951. It differed from the R 25 through its modified front mudguard and a reworked cylinder head. Up to 1953, 38,651 were sold at a unit price of 1,990 marks. This was also the era when BMW, moving with the times, began developing a scooter that hid the R 25/2's drivetrain (including Cardan shaft) under its skirts. Though additional scooter prototypes were tested, none ever went into production. The final model of the R 25 series, the 1953 R 25/3, already had something of the large boxers' flair. A new front fork, featuring chromed outer tubes and hydraulic damping together with extended rear travel, improved riding comfort.

▌ Top-selling BMW: The R 25/3 from 1953

The 19-inch steel wheels of forerunner types were replaced by 18-inch wheels with aluminum rims and wide aluminum full-hub brakes. A markedly expanded tank extended the range. The 250cc engine now developed 13 horsepower at 5,800 rpm, thanks in part to a better air intake with a wet air filter. With 47,700 units sold in 1956 at 2,060 DM *per exemplar*, the beautiful and solid R 25/3 held the record of BMW's best-selling bike until 2000. Moreover, from 1954 its engine found wide employment in BMW's egg-shaped bubble car for the masses, which became famous as the Isetta.

By 1955, a whole new generation of BMWs had the motorcycling world abuzz: These were the famous models with full swingarm chassis. They were to set the tone until 1969 and offered fabulous riding comfort. But you can't please everyone: Discontented sport-oriented riders soon coined the unflattering term "rubber cow" to designate the new comfort BMW.

▌ 1956: Full swingarm model R 26

It took another year following presentation of the swingarm boxer for the new technology to surface in the BMW singles. As with the larger machines, the suspension was quite elaborate, not to say complex. The frame also was completely redesigned. The 18-inch front wheel was now steered by a leading link "swingarm" with separate hydraulically damped shocks pivoted behind the axle.

For the first time, the rear wheel was fixed to a taper roller bearing mounted tubular steel swingarm. The separately hinged rising spring shocks reacted to the slightest irregularities in road surface. Another novelty was that the Cardan shaft no longer rotated in the open but, now well protected from dust, was integrated into the right swingarm shaft. The large 15-liter tank matched the bike's impressive appearance. An optional nicely upholstered double seat was available in place of the hinged saddle.

Though by now an old friend, the 250cc engine had undergone numerous improvements in detail. Among these were a carburetor with a bore increased to 26 millimeters, and an extended air intake with wet air filter that fit into a large box under the seat. Peak performance climbed to a perfectly respectable (for the time) 15 horsepower at 6,400 rpm, enough to propel the 158-kilogram motorcycle at a top speed of 128 kilometers per hour. The R 26 sold for 2,150 marks. Quite a bit of cash for the time. Still, at 5,000 marks, a VW Beetle cost more than twice as much, and so no fewer than 30,236 buyers went for the small BMW.

▌ 1960 to 1966: R 27, last of the 250 machines

In 1960, a heavily optimized successor rolled off the line. With 18 horsepower at 7,400 rpm, the pushrod single was coming up against its limits. To absorb vibrations primarily arising at high rpm the engineers had mounted the new model's engine on rubber wherever possible. Still, there was no denying that the aging engine design was overtaxed; cylinders that occasionally "tore" at the base caused much dismay and did little for the prestigious manufacturer's image.

At first glance, the R 27 differed from its predecessor by its blinkers at the handlebar ends and the large round taillight assembly, derived from BMW's V-8 luxury sedan. Headlight flasher

R 27 Touren-Sport 250 ccm 18 PS
mit »Schwebemotor«

Vollschwingrahmen. Leistungsstarker Einzylinder-Viertakt-Schwebemotor. Vierganggetriebe, Fußschaltung. Vorder- und Hinterradschwinge mit Federbeinen und Öldruckstoßdämpfern. Hochglanzpolierte 18" Leichtmetallfelgen. Leichtmetall-Vollnabenbremsen. Verschließbarer Werkzeugbehälter. Schwingsattel oder Sitzbank.

Lichtanlage: 6 V/60-90 W
Tankinhalt: 15 Liter
Reifengröße: 3,25 x 18
Gewicht fahrfertig: 162 kg
Normverbrauch: 3,9 Liter (DIN 70030)
Höchstgeschwindigkeit: 130 km/h

Above: *Single-cylinder production ceased in 1966 with the 18-horsepower R 27, built from 1960, after sales had declined to 15,364, half the number of the R 26 that sold.*

Right: *In the heyday of the German economic miracle, with the winner of the 200,000th postwar motorcycle and then-BMW chief Kalkert (right).*

and maintenance-free "Micronic" dry air filter also figured among the innovations.

In spite of these improvements, the 2,430 DM R 27 could not repeat the success of preceding models. In the early 1960s, the motorcycle industry underwent its worst crisis ever, and by 1960, BMW, because of a failed automobile model strategy, was on the brink of ruin. By the time the last R 27 rolled off the line in 1966 with only 15,364 units produced, the company had managed to right itself, but by then motorcycles were considered old hat in Germany, and the fate of BMW's motorcycle production appeared to be sealed.

The explosion in sales that soon followed was above all a product of the counter culture and protest movement. Motorcycle riding suddenly became a form of protest against middle class values and social injustice. BMW reacted just in time, bringing the /5 boxer series to market. The good times were back.

In 1956, Sebastian Nachtmann became the German off-road champion on a specially prepared factory R 26.

In October 1964, 250 machines of the R 27 type were delivered to the police. Standard equipment: signaling disk and luggage.

From 1993 chain-driven not shaft-driven: The F 650 and F 650 ST

In November 1993, when BMW introduced the F 650, its first single-cylinder in 27 years, the experts were skeptical. How would this experiment turn out after such a long hiatus? Would boxer pampered riders accept a single, especially if it radically broke with hallowed BMW traditions?

In retrospect, it's clear that BMW won its bet with the F 650. In 1999, it sold almost 54,000 units of the standard model and of the more street-oriented versions, thus renewing with old single-cylinder sales records. No one had predicted it. The F 650 not only quickly became the best-selling bike of the BMW model range, but also an overall top seller in many countries. The sturdy, nimble, many-sided single-cylinder "Funduro" appealed particularly to novice and returning riders, along with people switching from other brands. From the outset, the little BMW was the first choice for female riders.

The decision to revive the single-cylinder tradition was already taken at the end of the 1980s. **Pictured:** *Two design drawings from 1991.*

▌ F 650: First motorcyle produced in a collaboration of European manufacturers

The F 650 was also a milestone as the first motorcycle to be built with European collaboration. It was developed by Aprilia according to BMW design, quality, and styling guidelines and assembled at the Italian firm's modern production facilities. The engine, modified by BMW, was provided by the Austrian specialist Bombardier-Rotax.

That the F 650 was the first BMW with chain rather than shaft drive was only initially controversial. By now, the lightweight power transmission system, standard elsewhere, had gained general acceptance. The F 650 had little in common with the clattering single-cylinders of BMW's earlier years, of which 230,000 were produced from 1925 to 1966. Instead of an air-cooled ohv engine, like BMW's four-cylinder K models, it featured an up-to-date liquid-cooled motor with a couple of overhead chain-driven camshafts and four valves.

▌ Well adapted to everyday riding and long trips

The new single-cylinder motorcycle's frame and suspension were largely identical to the chassis of the Aprilia Pegaso. This didn't prevent the F 650 from meeting the Bavarian brand's high standards of quality, performance, and comfort, along with everyday and touring qualities. Though its design could not provide the traditional BMW riding experience, it won the client over simply by being a good and solid motorcycle and beyond this a single-cylinder enduro that hardly any bike of whatever make could hold a candle to on the street. In 1993, the basic model sold for 11,400 DM. By 1999 the price had only risen to 12,200 DM (including fees). The F 650 ST "fun bike," strictly for the street, was added to the model range in 1996. It was 250 DM cheaper. It differed with the standard F mainly through an 18-inch instead of a 19-inch front wheel, rear suspension travel reduced from 165 to 120 millimeters, and a saddle height lowered to 785 millimeters.

It didn't hurt sales that the Funduro from Noale, Italy, had a feel and ride reminiscent of certain Japanese or Italian competitors. With regard to everyday qualities and riding characteristics, the F 650 was a full-blown BMW. Though a little chubby in appearance, the bike was original, solid, and imposing. Like the boxer models, it impressed with excellent long-distance comfort. Driver and passenger sat comfortably on the wide and plushly upholstered seat; knee and arm angles afforded many hours of fatigue-free riding; average speeds of 140 kilometers per hour on the highway were painless. The aerodynamically well designed wind deflector did a good job of controlling the airflow.

From the beginning, one of the F models' strengths was its above-

As especially maneuverable and uncomplicated motorcycles, for a time, every other F 650 was being purchased by women. The pictures show the first F 650 from 1993.

Top: *together with the classic Cardan R 27 from 1966 (247cc, 18 horsepower).*
Right: *The F 650's cockpit was exemplary in its clarity.*

average range. While conventional enduros of the time often had to head for the nearest service station after 150 kilometers, the F 650, its 17.5-liter plastic tank hidden under a cover, could go 360 kilometers. That was the record for this class, highlighting the F 650's touring capability. In brisk riding on country roads, it managed 4.8 liters/100 kilometers. This surely also had something to do with the dual ignition and the two lean-running CV carburetors. In our test, we were unable to raise consumption above 6.3 liters, even blasting full throttle with no let up on the freeway. In normal city/highway riding, our test F 650 consumed 5.0 to 5.5 liters of premium to 100 kilometers.

▍Wear-resistant motor technology

The initial F models were already relatively environmentally friendly: Since 1995, the euro bike was equipped with an open-loop catalytic converter, initially as an option (250 DM), then standard in Germany, Austria, Switzerland, and the United States. The super quiet, rather bulky exhaust system was constructed of stainless steel; plastic components could be easily recycled. Overall workmanship was satisfactory and improved continuously over time.

The F 650 had a long service life: The endurance tests conducted by several motorcycle magazines gave nothing but good news at 30,000 kilometers and over. Nearly every component of the Rotax engine showed zero wear after disassembly. Some points were even better than on the boxers, the blinker switch, choke, high beam, and horn actuation, for example. This all conformed to high Japanese standards, with optimal placement and foolproof reset.

The H4 headlight, derived from the (now discontinued) K 75, provided excellent high- and low-beam illumination. The speedometer and tachometer featured outstanding readability night and day, thanks largely to the high-contrast instrument faces: black center, white border with clear numbers, and symbols. A coolant thermometer was also part of the standard instrumentation, though it wasn't terribly accurate.

Another F 650 quality was that it turned over instantly, even after a cold night. A centrifugal decompression mechanism in the exhaust camshaft facilitated startup. An 0.9- kilowatts

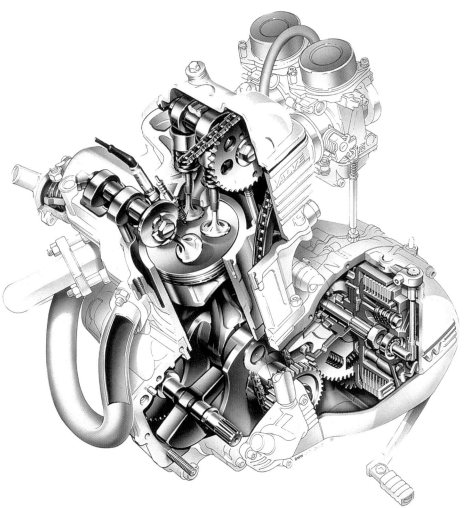

Top: A basic F 650 from 1995–96 in Black and Orange.

Above: The Rotax four-valve engine featured a balancer shaft, two overhead camshafts and four valves, for an output of 48 horsepower.

Right: A view of the Aprilia assembly area in Noale with complete F 650 chassis, 1993.

Below right: The frame, swingarm, and chain drive were entirely new; the frame contained the oil tank for the dry-sump lubrication.

electric starter came standard; a kick starter, as in classic BMW's, was lacking, however.

On the open road, it quickly became apparent that the Rotax four-valve single, developed according to BMW guidelines, required a certain rpm level to come into its own. Down in the basement, it really didn't work up much steam, only really coming to life above 2,800 rpm. When rpm sank below 2,500, for example in city traffic, downshifting was in order.

▌ Open-loop catalytic converter, balancer shaft

Whoever held the 652cc single burner between 4,000 and 6,000 rpm, however, was rewarded with good torque, prompt throttle reaction, and thrilling acceleration, all this largely free of vibrations. A gear-driven balancer shaft, plain bearings on the crankshaft, and conrods provided excellent running characteristics. What's more, the drive wheel on the balancer shaft was configured as a tensioned gear; this compensated for tooth backlash while reducing mechanical noise.

All in all, the BMW single performed its job in rather more leisurely style than the five-valve Aprilia Pegaso, from which it was derived. While the Pegaso managed 0 to 100 kilometers per hour in 5.2 seconds solo, the F 650 took 6.3 seconds. This was nothing more than average. We managed a top speed of 161 kilometers per hour (in an uncomfortably flat riding position); the speedometer displayed 170 kilometers per hour. Real Pegaso top speed: 163 kilometers per hour.

The fact that even over full throttle stretches the engine never went into the red in fifth gear was also a plus for the engine. Peak 48 horsepower (35 kilowatts) output is reached at 6,500 rpm, also maximum rpm at full throttle on the freeway. Both versions of the F 650 were optionally available in a beginner-friendly 34 horsepower version.

The BMW single-cylinder's frame was a typical mass-production item. It was composed of sheet metal parts,

square tubes, and bolted tubular main beams. The engine was load-bearing. The engineers had integrated the elaborate dry sump lubrication's 1.5-liter oil reservoir into the frame's upper section. A suction and a high-pressure pump provided oil circulation.

▌ Liquid cooling, electronic dual ignition

A centrifugal pump, balancer shaft driven by gears, was at the heart of the system. A wax-type thermostat valve released full coolant flow at 75 degrees C. At temperatures above 95 degrees C, the auxiliary electric fan located behind the finned radiator kicked in.

The air gas mixture came from a couple of Mikuni VV carburetors (type BST 33) with venturi of 33 millimeters each. The identical carburetors featured idle and bypass as well as a main and cold start systems. A three-phase alternator with permanent magnet rotor and 280 watts generated the current. The non-contacting high-tension capacitor ignition was map controlled and possessed an electronic ignition backfire control, i.e., the engine could not backfire on startup. A magnetic pickup created a pulse around the generator rotor, the microprocessor then took over this pulse, setting ignition dependent on rpm. Two spark plugs shortened the spark paths, thereby reducing the advance, improving combustion under partial load, and providing better emissions control.

The F 650 with a high windshield from late 1996.

It was highly rigid, insensitive to all manner of road surface irregularities, resilient, and comfortable in the bargain. Unpleasant wobbling on the highway was unknown on the F 650. The disc brake system (two perforated stainless steel rotors, 300-millimeter diameter and dual-piston floating caliper, front; 240 millimeters and single piston, rear) gave full satisfaction, even under wet conditions. The brakes could be well modulated and did not require much pressure. From the fall of 1995, all models received two standard features: an open-loop catalytic converter and a convenient center stand.

F 650 and F 650 ST model upgrades

■ Five-speed transmission, wet clutch, all round chassis with limited off-road capability

The dual-shaft five-speed transmission was integrated into the double section, vertically divided light-alloy engine casing. The clutch consisted of a basket, hub, seven steel and friction discs, pressure plate, compression springs, release bearing, clutch release shaft, and release lever. Service intervals for the single-cylinder were 10,000 kilometers, as in the four-valve boxers and the K models.

The suspension was up to international standards and largely identical to that of the Pegaso: a conventional telescopic fork with 41-millimeter stanchions and light deltabox rear swingarm. The fork and central shock came from the Japanese manufacturer Showa, as was generally the case with BMW since the early 1990s. Spring preload was continuously adjustable hydraulically via an accessible hand wheel, even on the move. Damper rebound could be adjusted via a slotted screw at the lower shock mounting.

With proper maintenance, the O-ring chain (employed here for the first time on a BMW bike) achieved a satisfactory service life thanks to permanent lubrication. As everywhere in this class, the rear-wheel sprocket featured a sturdy rubber cush drive.

With its medium suspension travel (170/165 millimeters) and large wheels (19/17-inch with tire dimensions of 100/90x19 S and 130/80x17 S) the high-riding standard F could also take a jaunt off-road. On fast gravel tracks, the 189-kilogram (full tank) F 650 kept up with other enduros of the time. Superior handling banished all stress. It was only on difficult, deep, or slippery surfaces that the design showed its limitations.

All in all, the F models' simple and solid chassis made a good impression.

The F 650 ST, built from 1996 and sold until 2000, has a smaller front wheel and features oriented to street riding.

The F 650 remained unchanged for three years until the fall of 1996, when the bike underwent a facelift. From the 1996–97 model year, the fairing in the cockpit area came up to the instrument level. The cooler opening and the fairing front section were narrowed, the blinkers no longer sat on the fairing but on short arms. Cooler and cylinder covers were integrated into a reconfigured part, which took the shape of a spoiler in the cooler opening area. The new, distinctly higher and transparent windshield offered enhanced wind and weather protection.

Replacing the rather imprecise coolant temperature display in the cockpit was an analog clock. There was now only a warning lamp to signal excessive water temperature. From the fall of 1996, the previously removable tank cover was now mounted so that it could be popped up from the filler neck.

Saddle height (at 810 millimeters, already low for this type of motorcycle) could be lowered by an extra 10 millimeters in the driver section of a reconfigured seat. With a lowering kit available for subsequent installation, the F 650's saddle height could be decreased by a further 50 millimeters to

750 millimeters. The side stand finally no longer folded up automatically but could easily be turned back with the foot by the sitting rider. A contact breaker prevented riding off with extended side stand.

▮ From fall 1996: F 650 ST, parallel street model

With the F 650 ST variant, available from 1996 to 2000, the Bavarians were aiming at riders, both male and female, with sportier expectations from the single-cylinder BMW and looking for more fun on the road. The distinction between both F 650 models essentially lay in differing chassis configurations and in modified equipment and appearance (F 650 values in parentheses).

With its smaller 18-inch front wheel (19-inch), the F 650 ST's chassis was even more maneuverable and sporty than the standard F 650's chassis. The tires were also for the road, just as the slightly modified chassis geometry with a shortened wheelbase of 1,465 millimeters (previously 1,480 millimeters) and reduced caster of 110 millimeters (116 millimeters), along with the rear shock modified in damping and featuring travel of 120 millimeters

Top: *This photo highlights the differences between the F 650 and F 650 ST in 1996.*
Above: *The F 650 ST looks especially compact.*

This is what the last versions looked like before production stopped in fall 1999.

Left : *The F 650 with a large windshield.*

Below: *The ST continued to be sold from stock well into 2000.*

(165 millimeters). However, the ST's front fork spring travel remained at 170 millimeters, as in the standard model.

The lowered chassis necessarily led to a reduced saddle height of 785 millimeters (800 millimeters). With the lowering kit also available for the ST, a reduction of saddle height to 735 millimeters was even possible. The F 650 ST's curb weight stood unchanged at 191 kilograms. Because of their durability, thousands of F 650s from the 1990s continue to ply today's roads.

▌ A BMW tradition since 1982: Street models derived from enduros

The narrower ST handlebars were specially configured. Instead of 800 millimeters, they featured a grip width of only 760 millimeters, were cranked farther forward, and omitted the enduro typical cross brace. The result was a sitting position with a clear street orientation, improved agility, and great handling. The ST's sporty orientation was reflected in its looks. Thus, in place of the F 650's higher transparent windshield, it featured a small cockpit fairing, like the original standard version. The instruments had reworked faces, with backlit numbers.

While the F 650's radiator and cylinder barrel were painted matte black, they were silver on the ST. The engine's black matte gravel shield had yielded to an aerodynamic, silver-colored engine spoiler. The front mudguard was narrower; the fork outer leg covers were history. A special paint

job also distinguishes the ST from the basic model.

In keeping with BMW's tried and tested modular system, the customer could also order his or her F 650 ST with the higher, transparent windshield and hand protectors. Matching handelbars were also available. All components were offered together as a "touring set."

▌ Special models and production end in 1999

In the spring of 1999, BMW brought out another special model on an F Model base; this was equipped ex-works with heated grips, touring handlebars, high windshield, topcase, luggage holders,

and open-loop catalytic converter. In fall 1999, shortly before the end of the series, three special F 650 ST models with different paint jobs came out: Jet Black with a black seat, Ocean Green with a light gray seat, and Blue Metallic with a black seat.

BMW halted production of the standard F series in March 2000, upon the appearance of the F 650 GS and F 650 GS Dakar successor models. Production of the ST also ceased, although it remained available for some time because the units assembled by Aprilia until 1999 had to be sold off. All told, the Italians produced 43,535 units of the basic model and 10,083 of the F 650 ST for BMW.

F 650 and F 650 ST: Used bike sales

■ **F 650 and F 650 ST as second-hand bikes: Getting on an enduro for relatively little coin**

Buying a used F 650 or F 650 ST can be a good value, as the four-valve Funduro with the modern design is technically brilliant. Riding fun and everyday practicality are guaranteed, service costs are reasonable, and maintenance is easy.

Of course, BMW's single-cylinder is not entirely free of defects. Beyond 10,000 kilometers, the initial models often had porous intake nozzles. Some welds in the exhaust system initially did not hold up to the large displacement engine's vibrations and had to be reinforced.

■ **Chain drive: Pre-programmed wear**

The original drive chain with two sprockets had a service life of about 15,000 kilometers. One reason for this relatively rapid wear was the single's distinct jerking up to 3,000 rpm. The clutch springs aren't particularly durable either. On more than one F 650, they had to be replaced after 30,000 kilometers.

Even with low mileage, machines that have been frequently ridden off-road often display pronounced wear of suspension (worn dampers, damaged swingarm bearings, and Silentblock bushings), brakes (scores on rotors or drums), and even of the engine v(diminished compression and high oil consumption).

Leaky telescopic fork seals are often seen on high mileage bikes. The steering head bearing is sturdy, but should display no play on a jacked-up bike with an unsupported front wheel. The rear swingarm must also show no play. A brake system in perfect condition is of vital importance. The brake fluid reservoir sight glass reveals the state of the hygroscopic solution: the darker, the worse. The brake fluid level should never sink below the minimum mark; otherwise air can be sucked in when leaning over and the brakes fail. If the pressure point moves toward the rider after several squeezes of the brake lever, this indicates air in the hydraulic system and inadequate brake maintenance.

As second-hand bikes, the F 650 and F 650 ST are good choices.

■ **Sturdy technology that still requires attention**

The brake rotors must be free of score marks and display a minimum thickness of 4.5 millimeters. Light, ring-shaped grinding marks, however, are normal. Two millimeters of remaining pad thickness (minus backing plate) is the service limit. On the F 650, as elsewhere, porous, bent, or torn brake lines are a grave security risk.

When inspecting a used F 650, the seat should also be removed. In what condition are the battery and electrical system? Are the onboard toolkit and the owner's manual present? Corroded battery terminals and insufficient acid are indications that the previous owner was not concerned with maintaining his BMW. After checking the oil level, with choke pulled, the engine should start right up and immediately run smoothly. The clutch should disengage cleanly and the gears engage easily.

Minor defects in finish are typical of this euro BMW. The handlebar controls are often loose and can only be fastened with difficulty. Misfires or strong voltage drops, to the extent that the engine dies, may be due to cables corroded or completely disconnected by vibration in the voltage regulator area.

■ **Misfires through cables disconnected by vibrations**

If the dual carburetor is constantly flooding and fuel consumption is thus too high, the cause is generally a disconnected or clogged overflow line. But apart from these minor irritants, the F 650 is a real trooper. Another advantage is the above-mentioned lowering (or raising) option, along with 34-horsepower or 48-horsepower versions. What makes the F 650 particularly attractive is that it can be maintained and repaired with a modicum of mechanical knowledge. Even work on the engine and transmission is not excessively complex, as detailed throughout the 132 pages of the service manual.

Fascination in BMW's GS single-cylinders: The F 650 GS

In 1993, when BMW presented the F 650, it was at most a half-hearted step in the enduro direction and not in any "GS" direction, in the sense of "off-road sport." For this single-cylinder motorcycle, the first chain-driven BMW on the market, was more suited to street than to off-road riding, earning it the well-deserved moniker of "Funduro," that is, a machine meant for harmless fun.

Six years later, the harmless fun came to an end: The looks of the original F 650 generation now seemed dated, the technology was no longer cutting edge in every respect, and the market called for thoroughbreds. That's exactly what it got, in the shape of the F 650 GS and the especially off-roadworthy F 650 GS Dakar. "Fascination BMW GS" now finally also applied with respect to what had been rather plain single-cylinder models.

The Bavarians let the cat out of the bag in January 2000, at a point that could not have been better chosen. For the second time, Frenchman Richard Sainct had just won the most spectacular desert race in the world, the Paris-Dakar, on the BMW factory single-cylinder.

The BMW engineers had now provided the original F 650's successor

types a design, which bore a strong resemblance to the R 1150 GS boxer model only released half a year earlier. Initial tests soon revealed that the resemblance was not merely visual, but that the little GS also exhibited off-road and travel capabilities. The thoroughly redesigned motorcycle certainly deserved to bear the legendary "GS" seal.

▌ F 650 GS: First production single-cylinder with closed loop catalytic converter

This alone would have been reason enough to include the F 650 GS in this book, but there was another reason: The elaborate single undoubtedly represented a milestone of motorcycle technology. When BMW spoke of the F 650 GS setting "new standards in its class," this was no mere figure of speech. It really did. For here was the first production motorcyle equipped with a digital engine management system and closed-loop, three-way catalytic converter, which was standard. ABS was optional. In environmental and safety technology, the revamped single was thus on a par with BMW's modern two- and four-cylinder models. The new GS's market reception was enthusiastic. With 3,073 new registrations in the first

semester of 2000, just for Germany, it became the best-selling single-cylinder enduro, taking fourth place in the overall motorcycle hit parade, behind the R 1150 GS and a couple of Suzuki street models. And it held on to this top position in the following years.

▌ Production transferred from Noale to Berlin

In contrast to the precursor models, the F 650 GS was now no longer produced in Noale, Italy, but like the the two- and four-cylinder models at BMW's motorcycle plant in Berlin-Spandau. It's doubtful whether the Italians were happy with this, given that the F 650 had represented a sizable share of the Italian factory's workload.

But Aprilia owner Ivano Beggio soon took up the slack: In the spring of 2000, the Italian acquired the ailing and highly leveraged traditional maker Moto Guzzi. Beggio wanted to compete with BMW with modernized Moto Guzzi models: "I can envision Guzzi being close to BMW again in the future," the Italian mused in an interview with *Motorrad* magazine. And the relationship could indeed have been reestablished, though on a completely altered basis. Today, this statement seems quaint.

The F 650's styling was of a piece and was strongly derivative of the twin-cylinder GS. The 17.5-liter fuel tank was under the seat; note the filler cap.

The F 650 GS was the first single-cylinder motorcycle with ABS. BMW had reinforced the telescopic fork primarily for ABS installation. The disc-brake system came from the previous model.

BMW set up an entirely new assembly line at the Berlin plant to produce the F 650 GS, creating 60 new jobs in the process. The new F 650 was not built from the ground up in Berlin, however. Unlike the two- and four-cylinders, it was merely assembled there. Altogether, 35 mostly European companies delivered the components to the banks of the Spree. The only parts produced at the plant were the camshafts. These were manufactured at the central production facility for automobile and motorcycle camshafts, machined, then shipped to the Bombardier-Rotax engine factory in Gunskirchen, Austria. The complete powerplant was subsequently sent back to Berlin for final motorcycle assembly.

Naturally, the F 650 GS's engine was not an entirely novel development but an improvement of the proven Rotax design. The main intent had been to make the engine more powerful, refined, and environmentally friendly. The liquid-cooled four-valver with an unchanged displacement of 652cc now developed 50 horsepower (an increase of 2 horsepower), once again at 6,500 rpm. Maximum torque had risen from 57 Nm to 60 Nm, at rpm down to 5,000 rpm from 5,200 rpm. Important for good acceleration: between 3,000 to 6,500 rpm more than 50 Nm were now always available. At last, the bike could accelerate jolt-free from a low 2,000 rpm. Whoever drew on full performances quickly registered the increased revving ability. In Germany and Italy, the F 650 GS was also available with 34 horsepower at 6,000 rpm and peak torque of 51 Nm at 3,750 rpm. Curbing was via a reduced throttle aperture angle.

The bike featured the first ever single-cylinder motorcycle engine with a digital engine electronics system, named BMS, also installed in the BMW C 1 scooter. The system regulated the ignition and injection fuel supply.

The result: Exceptionally low fuel consumption and emissions. Indeed, in *Motorrad*'s enduro comparison test (October 2000), the new F 650 GS revealed itself the most economical, at only 4.9 liters/100 kilometers. At a steady 140 kilometers per hour, consumption was 5.8 liters/100 kilometers; the carburetor-equipped Aprilia Pegaso went through 6.9 liters/100 kilometers, over a liter more.

By its very principle, a single-cylinder simply can't run quite as smoothly as a four-cylinder engine. In order to improve running characteristics, however, BMW designers

Right: *The refined four-valve Rotax single; fuel-injection, central spark-plug, and the eight clutch discs were new.*

Below left: *The BMS electronic system operated with numerous sensors.*

Below right: *The closed-loop catalytic converter was located in the right muffler.*

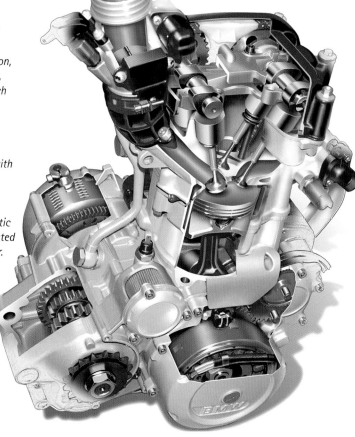

reached deep into their bag of tricks to come up with BMS.

As a so-called "alpha" control, BMS continually monitored engine rpm, throttle aperture angle, and Lambda values, along with general parameters such as air temperature, air pressure, and coolant temperature.

Because BMS began regulating idle speed immediately after startup and during the warm-up phase via an air volume control, the customary choke system with lever and cable could be dispensed with. Last but not least, BMS Lambda regulation allowed use of a three-way closed-loop catalytic converter.

BMS electronic engine management

But *Motorrad*'s measurements revealed that the emissions control system evidently only functioned up to par when the engine ran on a strictly controlled test cycle compliant with the Euro 1 standard. At full throttle, however, it emitted more pollutants than comparable engines without a catalytic converter. It was suspected that the emissions control electronically switched off at full load. Be that as it may, the bike achieved a respectable top speed of 168 kilometers per hour.

It's a known fact that BMW motorcycle engines exhibit a number of similarities to automobile motors, at least to BMW automobile motors. Thus, the F 650 GS's powerplant benefited from the blue-and-white brand's accrued knowhow. For example, the newly redesigned cylinder head was directly derived from the high-performance engine in BMW's M3 sport sedan. Computer-assisted detail work yielded useful modifications. The throttle was mounted in the downdraft close to the inlet valves; the inlet tract and combustion chamber were configured so hydrodynamically that optimal cylinder charge was guaranteed at all times.

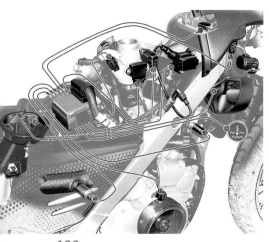

DOHC and dry sump lubrication

Whereas the old F 650 had featured dual spark plugs, with the new GS, the engineers went back to a centrally placed spark plug. Electronic engine management allowed an increase of the compression ratio from 9.7:1 to a beefy 11.5:1. The goal was high-performance output for limited consumption. The charge exchange process was controlled via a couple of chain-driven overhead camshafts carefully optimized for rpm. The cams actuated four valves via rocker arms.

As before, a suction pump and a high-pressure pump handled the oil feed. The proven dry sump lubrication without oil pan was also taken over. The oil circuit held a total of 2.3 liters (0.2 liters more than previously). While in the original F Model the frame functioned as an oil reservoir, the GS had a separate oil receptacle of die-cast aluminum located on the left part of the frame, next to the steering head bearing. Whereas the oil level previously had to be checked with a dipstick, it could now be easily gauged through a spy glass.

The cooling system had also been reworked. A more efficient coolant pump, allied to reduced flow resistance and a smaller cooling jacket, now shortened engine warm up; this reduced both wear and emissions.

In order to satisfy the increased power demand for BMS and optional ABS, the F 650 GS received a larger alternator with a 400-watt output (previously 280 watts). The wet clutch was reinforced with an eighth steel friction disc.

Also, BMW had come up with a completely new exhaust system. Once again, it was made of stainless steel and rather than one, it now featured two mufflers that were connected by a pipe and rakishly let out left and right of the tail. Heated Lambda probes and the three-way catalytic converter, which was integrated in the exhaust system directly in front of the left muffler, were standard. The five-speed transmission was taken over unaltered from the previous model. Even the gear reduction and secondary transmission ratio remained unchanged.

New, highly rigid tubular bridge frame

The crankshaft drive and balancer shaft were also unaltered. Power transmission to the rear wheel was again through an O-ring chain now with improved cush drive between sprocket and rear-wheel hub. As with all BMW motorcycles, service intervals for the F 650 GS were 10,000 kilometers.

The F Models' chassis, on the other hand, had been entirely redesigned.

Whereas the original version had a relatively crude single cradle frame of square tubes and sheet metal parts, the new F 650 GS featured a modern tubular bridge frame of square steel tubes, strong main beam, and a bolt-on rear frame section. A cross brace before the cylinder head reinforced the structure. The frame beam was firmly bolted to the main frame, enclosing the engine in a protective segmented tubular steel structure. The forked main frame, which descended in a straight line from the steering head to the swingarm mounting, offered the rigidity expected of a 12,950-DM (or 13,950 DM for the Dakar version) machine.

The 19-inch spoked front wheel was again guided by a Showa telescopic fork with 41-millimeter inner tubes and an unchanged 170 millimeters of travel. The additional stabilizer was new. Its function was to absorb the stresses on both fork legs with installed ABS.

Reinforced telescopic fork, steel square swingarm

The unchanged 17-inch rear wheel was suspended by a steel dual square swingarm that had been strengthened and slightly modified over the previous model. To achieve the necessary

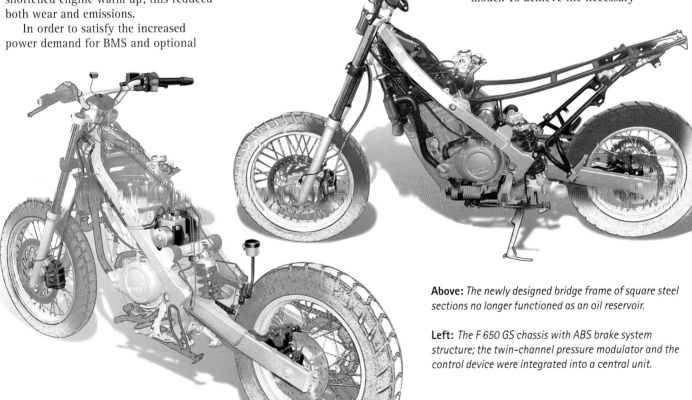

Above: *The newly designed bridge frame of square steel sections no longer functioned as an oil reservoir.*

Left: *The F 650 GS chassis with ABS brake system structure; the twin-channel pressure modulator and the control device were integrated into a central unit.*

in one important respect: Pressure adjustment was digitally controlled via a valve system (as opposed to ABS II, introduced in 1993, which operated with plungers on an analog basis). The rider noticed the difference in the pulsating hand and foot brake levers. As with the GS models of the boxer series, the F 650 GS's ABS could be disengaged in off-road use. A red lamp blinked while the ABS was turned off.

In shaping the F 650 GS's looks, the designers had been influenced by the R 1150 GS boxer model on one hand and by the successful racing model F 650 RR on the other. In typical BMW style, the fairing and seat were configured in such as way as to allow the rider's legs to have continuous contact with the motorcycle. The design of technical components was crisp and functional, largely eschewing embellishments. While chassis and engine components displayed plain aluminum surfaces or were painted silver, parts such as footrests, brake and shift levers, center and side stand, and chain guard were painted a sober matte black.

▌ Design deriving from the boxer GS

From the front, the F 650 GS displayed no more similarity to the previous model. It was more aggressive, dynamic, and elegant. The narrow front end's main feature was the headlight with fashionable new edge design. Whoever took the trouble to adjust the hydraulic spring preload via the hand wheel to the load also thereby secured correct headlight leveling. A black plastic housing, which also functioned

progression, the central shock was connected to the rear swingarm at the lower mounting eye via a system of levers. As previously, the shock could be continuously adjusted in spring preload and rebound damping. Travel was an unchanged 165 millimeters.

There was little to improve upon in the tried and tested braking system. Thus, the F 650 GS featured a front single-disc brake (rotor diameter: 300 millimeters) with dual-piston floating caliper and sintered metal pads. The rear wheel had a single-disc brake (rotor: 240 millimeters) with single-piston floating caliper.

▌ First single-cylinder motorcycle with ABS

Single-cylinder bikes with ABS? Before 2000, there weren't any. The F 650 GS was the first motorcycle of its class that could be equipped with this safety technology at an additional 980 DM. Once again, BMW's modular production system was useful. The F's especially light (2.1 kilograms) and compact ABS, developed in tandem by BMW and Bosch Braking Systems, was also installed on the C 1 scooter.

The F 650 GS ABS's mode of operation deviated from that of the two- and four-cylinder ABS II

All photos: *The 2000 model F 650 GS in the two most popular color schemes. The cockpit was exemplary in design and equipment (including digital displays). Distinctive: the engine guard and mudguard.*

The F 650 GS is equally at home on winding country roads as on dusty trails. Pictured, the 2000 model, initially at 12,950 DM.

as a cockpit fairing, enclosed the headlight. The rear section featured some interesting details. Because the mufflers were located below the seat, rear end width could be reduced by a considerable 12 centimeters versus the previous model. One result was that now a couple of equal-sized touring cases could be attached.

▌ Large fuel tank under the seat

What looked like the little GS's tank was in fact nothing more than nicely shaped plastic. And what appeared to be left and right side covers was in fact the tank. This was located in the frame triangle, under the seat, visually integrated with seat and side covers; it was made of impact-resistant plastic and had a volume of 17.5 liters. The tank filler nozzle had a user-friendly location at the right of the seat. This offered better weight distribution, a lowered center of gravity, and improved handling.

Where conventional motorcycles have theirs, the F 650 GS featured a cover with the appearance of a tank and characteristic air intakes. Underneath were the air filter housing, cooling water expansion tank, oil reservoir, electrical box, and battery. Saddle height had been lowered by 20 millimeters to 780 millimeters.

Modern times had also arrived with respect to cockpit and controls. The rally-style silver aluminum, fully redesigned cockpit featured asymetrically located speedometer and tachometer. Total and trip mileage were digitally displayed, toggled via switch. Located between both electronic instruments were the indicators for blinkers, high beam, neutral, coolant temperature, oil pressure, and ABS. When tank fuel volume sank under 4 liters, a warning lamp came on.

▌ Rally cockpit, digital mileage indicator

A digital clock indicated the time. One advanced control feature was that the switches were integrated with both grip units and configured so that they could be operated without risk of mixup even by a rider wearing heavy winter gloves. Standard equipment comprised a center and side stand along with an aluminum

engine guard. The F 650 GS's 2000 first edition came in three color variants for the fairing parts and in two seat colors: Titanium Blue combined with a yellow seat, Red with yellow seat, and Mandarin Yellow with yellow seat.

Like the older model, the new F was available ex-works with a lowering kit that diminished saddle height from 780 millimeters to 750 millimeters. Unlike with the more simply designed standard F 650 of 1993, however, retrofitting was expensive. The lowering was achieved via a different shock, a modified fork as well as shortened center and side stand. Retrofitting was correspondingly complex in the opposite direction.

A new item in the accessories range was the more heavily upholstered seat for large riders, with which saddle height could be raised to 820

millimeters. Extra thick upholstery also improved long-distance riding comfort. As usual, BMW offered heated grips. The beginner-oriented and cheaper to insure version was curbed to 34 horsepower.

The new travel case system was innovative: both (equal-sized) touring cases could be varied in depth via an adjustment mechanism, offering either 20 or 34 liters of storage space per case, according to need. The motorcycle's overall width thus decreased along with a reduced carrying requirement. There were also matching waterproof inner bags. Also available: a 31-liter topcase, single key for motorcycle and luggage system, hand protectors, handlebar impact protectors, high windshield, engine protection frame, onboard computer, and 12-volt power socket.

F 650 GS: More upgrades

In 2004, all single-cylinder series models were redesigned. Technologically significant was the reintroduction of dual ignition in tandem with the new BMS-C II engine management system for lowered emissions, improved throttle response, and lower fuel consumption. In this, BMW was renewing with the original design, for the engine of the original F 650, built from 1993 to 1999, had already featured two spark plugs. Output remained unchanged at 50 horsepower; peak torque of 60 Nm, however, was now already achieved at 4,800 rpm. A muffler with a new inner construction and an optimized catalytic converter rounded out the package.

A revamped front end with a mudguard suggestive of the "big GS," the new license plate holder, the windshield providing improved aerodynamics in the helmet area, as well as a larger headlight, all contributed to improve the F 650 GS's looks. The windshield was removable for off-road use.

The luggage rack was reconfigured. It was now possible to mount the topcase without an intermediate plate. The new headlight possessed an expanded illumination area, providing more consistent lighting of the roadway, especially on the nearside. A more angular instrument cluster cover and gray dials created a high-tech feel. An ergonomically improved clutch lever completed the package.

From 2004, warning blinker and alarm systems also became available for the single-cylinder models. There was also an onboard electric socket, which, among other things, allowed charging of the battery without having to remove it. Already designed by the author for BMW motorcycles at the beginning of the 1990s and now available ex-works: an "emergency start point" with positive terminal located under the seat and negative terminal on the transmission cover. The basic colors were also new (Yellow, Iceberg Silver Metallic, and Jet Black), as were the seat colors (Black or Terracotta Orange). In August 2005, the yellow color of fixed parts was replaced by red, while the orange seat was discarded.

Because of sustained demand, as of mid-2007, the F 650 GS and F 650 Dakar remained in the model range. Why indeed should anyone want to retire these models? At 76,579 units sold by the end of 2006, the F 650 GS (minus the Dakar) was BMW's most successful motorcyle of all times.

Top and above: *the F 650 GS, available from March 2004, and (again) with dual ignition and slightly altered design. New (among other items): double front mudguard, windshield.* **Right:** *2002 F 650 GS.*

For the love of sport: The F 650 GS Dakar

After BMW victories at the 1999 Granada-Dakar and 2000 Dakar-Cairo rallies, what could have been more natural than to release an F 650 GS Dakar special model inspired by the F 650 RR racing version? Back in the 1980s, BMW had already learned to successfully market its Paris-Dakar victories with a special boxer model. Though the Dakar version was anything but a hard core enduro, it demonstrated genuine aptitude for light to medium off-road terrain as well as long-distance travel on bad roads. The front-wheel had a diameter of 19 instead of 21 inches; suspension travel had increased by 40 millimeters, from 170 millimeters to 210 millimeters. The telescopic fork had been adapted to the tougher requirements.

Suspension travel for the unchanged 17-inch rear wheel had also increased by 45 millimeters to 210 millimeters. The side stand had been lenghtened to fit the higher frame and suspension, which now offered an extra 50-millimeter clearance. A special front mudguard also matched the larger front wheel.

The high seat was standard, increasing the Dakar version's saddle height to an impressive 870 millimeters. The F 650 RR's hand protectors and distinctive windshield were also included in the standard equipment of this special model (1,000 DM extra),

initially available only in white. A lengthened centerstand was available at extra cost. Because of the altered frame and suspension geometry, the ABS had to be retuned and only became available for the Dakar as of the summer of 2001. Beginning in February 2001, the F 650 Dakar was exclusively available in the colors of Andrea Mayer's 2001 Paris-Dakar bike: Desert Blue/White Aura.

From 2004, the windshield of the F 650 GS Dakar, now also with dual ignition and the above mentioned improvements, was larger and (as before) tinted. There were also new colors: Metallic Blue, White Aluminum, and Metallic Matte. In addition to the more than 76,000 units of the basic GS, BMW managed to sell another 20,544 "Dakar" units—a roaring success.

Below: *The 2001 model in the colors of the BMW Rally Team of the time: Desert Blue and Aura White.* Bottom left: *F 650 GS Dakar in Aura White, 2000 model.* Bottom right: *2004 model, with a distinctly larger windshield and new color scheme.*

F 650 CS "Scarver": Radically different with single-sided swingarm and belt drive

"It seems something like official BMW policy: never to build motorcycles like everyone else," wrote Loic Le Blainvaux in France's largest-circulation daily, *Ouest-France*, upon presentation of a machine that flouted Bavarian tradition with particular thoroughness: the F650 CS "Scarver." The "Star Wars" design shocked the BMW community. The belt-driven rear wheel was admittedly far removed from the much-loved Cardan shaft, already abandoned in the chain-driven forerunner models to the 1993 F generation.

The single-cylinder motorcycle presented in September 2001 at the International Automobile Exhibition in Frankfurt and at the Milano Auto Show was hailed by BMW as a "city bike and curve handling star with elevated fun factor," destined above all for commuting and city riding, yet also admirably suited to sporty riding on twisting country roads. A stowage compartment integrated in the central cover offered multiple opportunities to accommodate everyday items. The low

Technically tops, visually bold—and successful: the 2001–2002 F 650. Very enduro: the cockpit.

780-millimeter saddle height, optionally even 750 millimeters, made the CS attractive to smaller riders.

BMW was innovative with a self-developed softbag luggage system; for the first time, the touring cases, a fixture of BMW motorcycles, were omitted. Single-cylinder engine and five-speed transmission derived from the F 650 GS, along with the digital engine controller and closed-loop catalytic converter. However, because of the modified airbox and new exhaust system, the charge exchange process had to be retuned. The result was a minor change in performance characteristics: peak performance of 50 horsepower (37 kilowatts) was only achieved at 6,800 rpm (F 650

GS: at 6,500 rpm); maximum torque had grown from 60 Nm to 62 Nm, accessible, by contrast, already at 5,500 rpm (6,000 rpm). In Germany, the F 650 CS was also available in a version curbed to 34 horsepower, aimed at the tiered driver's license system.

To make space for the stowage compartment before the rider, BMW had eliminated the separate oil tank, as in the first F 650, in favor of a motorcycle frame functioning as engine oil reservoir. Both of the bridge frame's main tubes were connected at the bottom at a right angle and took up the 2.5 liters of engine oil. The Japanese had already produced similar designs in the mid-1970s (Yamaha XT 500 and succeeding models). As with the F 650 GS, the fuel tank was located under the seat. The exhaust system was an entirely new design configured for optimal aesthetic appeal. To save space, a three-way catalytic converter and lambda probes were integrated into a muffler of polished stainless steel, thus making a pre-silencer unnecessary.

▌ Cutting-edge BMW for city streets

A glance at the rear wheel's right side immediately revealed the technologically salient traits: single-sided swingarm and belt drive, surely a "world premiere in motorcycle engineering" in this particular combination, yet nothing terribly fresh when taken separately. With its R 80 G/S, BMW had introduced the Monolever swingarm for mass production as early as 1980. Belt-driven rear wheels have come standard on Harley-Davidsons since 1979 (Sturgis model).

For bikes like the F 650 CS, which ordinarily stick to the roads, belt drive offers a sound alternative to driveshaft and chain. It runs quietly, requires no lubrication, is clean and low maintenance to operate, and its service life is at least twice that of a chain.

The F 650 CS's 26-millimeter wide-drive belt featured a special pitch (11

The Scarver, with the American design, was a rather unconventional BMW with futuristic details and belt drive; pictured: the 2002 model.

millimeters) and profile. The rear-wheel belt sprocket was a cold formed precision stainless steel part; the corresponding gear on the transmission output was of sintered metal. The F 650 CS's aesthetically pleasing single-sided swingarm of highly rigid aluminum alloy was unique in the Scarver's market segment, contributing to chassis stability and to the bike's agile and precise handling with its torsional stiffness.

As on the F 650 GS, it featured a central rear progressive shock. Progression and shock settings (spring travel 120 millimeters) were configured in such a way as to render further adjustments unnecessary. All in all, the CS suspension was rather stiff; comfort was not its strong suit, especially at the full 181-kilogram payload.

As with the F 650 GS, the F 650 CS's backbone consisted of a bridge frame of square steel tubes. Because of their additional function as an engine oil reservoir, these had an increased size, which in turn enhanced rigidity. The panels covering the lateral profiles were not merely cosmetic, they also protected the rider's legs from the engine oil's radiated heat.

As on the F 650 GS and forerunners (F 650, F 650 ST), front suspension was handled by a conventional telescopic fork, only distinguished from the GS part by its shorter travel of 125 millimeters and special street tuning.

The redesigned, silver-colored 17-inch cast light-alloy wheels with three-spoke design stood out. The rear wheel's curved shape from hub to rim was a surprise; this was conditioned by the location of the brake rotor and belt sprocket on the right side.

Like the F 650 GS, the F 650 CS was equipped at the front with a single-disc brake (300-millimeter diameter) featuring a dual-piston floating caliper and sintered metal brake pads. Installed at the rear was a single-disc brake (diameter 240 millimeters) with a single-piston floating caliper. ABS developed for the single-cylinder series was optionally available.

The F 650 CS was initially offered in three attractive colors: Sky Blue Metallic, Gold Orange Metallic, and Beluga Blue. Two colors were available for the seat and the interchangeable central fairing covers: Dark Blue or

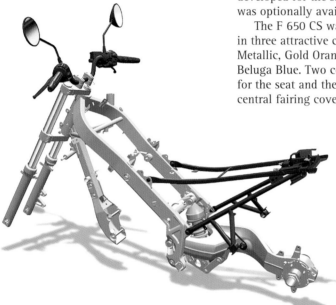

A frame of square tubes with an integrated oil reservoir, rear outrigger, telescopic fork, and single-sided swingarm.

Sepia vs. White Aluminum or Golden Orange. In the front, worlds apart from the usual BMW design, the F 650 CS displayed a character more reminiscent of some futuristic Far Eastern experiment, with a blue-gray windshield, translucent windshield mounting, and lowered double headlights. This was the mark of U.S. designer David Robb (as in all other BMW motorcycles since 1993).

The low beam featured the latest ellipsoid technology; the high beam illuminated the roadway at an especially wide angle. A small parking light was centrally located beneath both headlights. The cockpit's main feature was an instrument panel essentially derived from the F 650 GS. Speedometer and tachometer now featured the new graphic design seen in modern timepieces, highlighting the motorcycle's advanced appearance.

The silver-painted handlebars featured a grip width of 745 millimeters; rearview mirrors and handlebar controls came from the F 650 GS. As with the GS model, the 15-liter tank fit into the frame triangle under the seat, promoting a low center of gravity and enhanced handling. The tank filler nozzle was located to the right of the seat, which precluded filling while the rider sat on the machine. Two sturdy light-alloy

The single-sided swingarm with maintenance-free belt drive.

The 2002 dohc four-valve single with single ignition and toothed belt pinion.

passenger holds were integrated into the slender luggage rack.

Visually, the F 650 CS's most prominent feature was the fuel tank mock-up, referred to by BMW as the "central cover." It contained a basin-like depression configured as a stowage compartment. This featured an "attachment rail" to secure the "softbags" included in the standard equipment via quick-release rubber tensioners. In place of the standard series 12-liter softbags (which were not always watertight) a higher quality "front bag" was also available. A plastic hard case (volume: near 10 liters) could also be attached. At a sizeable extra charge, an audio system with two integrated loudspeakers and stereo amplifier featuring manual and speed-dependent volume control was available for installation in the hard case housing. Signal sources for the audio system were portable CD, MC, and MD players.

Additional accessories supported the continuing trend to individualization and upgrading: engine spoiler, chrome finish kit, onboard computer, onboard power socket, anti-theft system, even a work stand and a bike cover. Oddly enough, though, a center stand was not available.

The response to the 7,950 euro was positive. Its handling was praised, along with its economy and low maintenance requirements, all traditional BMW virtues. However, control ergonomics and the sometimes careless workmanship, in relation to expectations and price, didn't get as good a reception.

The Scarver could accelerate jolt-free in fifth gear from 2,500 rpm (65 kilometers per hour), but its running

characteristics at low rpm left something to be desired. The French criticized the large effort required to work the non-adjustable hand levers. "They are made for the hands of stranglers," noted Loic Le Blainvaux, who concluded: "The CS has a place in the market. There's a dearth of motorcycles outside the norm, and few manufacturers really have the nerve to build something like this. Let's support those who do. BMW's image takes care of the rest!"

From 2004, the F 650 CS was also equipped with dual ignition, otherwise going into the new model year largely unchanged. New points were an

On winding roads, the Scarver impressed with its handling. **Above and lower left:** *The 2002 model.* **Lower right:** *The 2004 version with dual ignition. Production ended in 2005.*

adjustable clutch lever, modified blinker control, and the now standard onboard power socket. The windshield holder, luggage rail, and luggage rack were no longer translucent in 2004 but consisted of black plastic. The new colors: Midnight Blue Metallic, Juniper Yellow Metallic, Titanium Silver Metallic, and Stone Gray. To the end of production in the summer of 2005, BMW sold 20,845 units of the CS.

BMW changes its stripes: The G 650 X series

That BMW no longer entertained any taboos concerning series development and model policy had already become plain in 2005 with the introduction of the K 1200 R, which, with its transversally mounted and restricted inline-four, appealed more to Japanese than Bavarian traditions. With the fully independent G 650 X single-cylinder series presented at the 2006 Intermot show, BMW once again demonstrated that it was in no way beholden to outworn patterns. Already on the first modern BMW single, the 1993 F 650, the driveshaft had yielded to a chain. With the F 650 CS, it was even a belt that drove the rear wheel.

Now, as far as looks and technology were concerned, the new G models might as well have been designed in Hamamatsu or Iwata. But this should not be understood in a negative sense. Rather, BMW, having recognized the sign of the times, committed itself to cutting-edge, lightweight construction allied to conventional, though sophisticated, technology.

■ **Aggressive marketing contrasts with past safety and environmental policy**

Old BMW hands might well be irritated by the aggressive ad campaign that the company used to market the new line, and which stood in stark contrast to everything Munich had advocated for decades. "Live for the drift" screams the bold lettering on double-page ads in the motorcycle press, displaying an Xmoto as it leans into a turn at an extreme angle, its rider dragging his left foot along the asphalt for added stability.

We, who have ridden BMWs since the 1970s, not merely following the brand's unremitting safety and environmental campaigns but actively affirming them, could not believe our own eyes. We were reminded of that 1973 ad for the 2002 Turbo, shown chasing other vehicles from the fast lane, under the mirror image of the "Turbo" inscription. (The slogan was "The best thing to do with exhaust. . . .") At the time (with the energy crisis looming) the Bavarians had taken a mighty drubbing from

the media and politicians and quickly pulled the offending ad. Let's wait and see whether something similar happens to the Xmoto campaign. I tend to doubt it when I see how *Motorrad* built up its "master bike test" in the November 2007 issue (headline: "10 years at full throttle") with a photo of six supersport machines raising a curtain of acrid smoke with their fierce burnouts. Climate change, CO_2, Kyoto, don't we have a slight problem there?

So, rather than "coming on" to the reader, we shall limit ourselves here to technical, practical concerns, describing the engineering work that conjured the G Series into existence. At the outset, it's apparent that once again the people in Munich remained

When compared to other BMW models, the G types come off as unusually nimble. **Below:** *Xcountry.* **Bottom:** *Xmoto.* **Opposite:** *Xchallenge.*

true to their inspired modular system. Three motorcycles of widely differing characters were born of a common fundamental design with broad similarity in engine, frame, and basic equipment parts: the G 650 Xcountry Scrambler, the hard-core enduro G 650 Xchallenge, and the streetmoto G 650 Xmoto. The model designations, in vintage "Gerglish," will hardly raise an eyebrow anymore these days.

It's also noteworthy that the new G models do not replace, but merely complete, the successful G 650 GS and F 650 GS Dakar types (for now). In the words of Jurgen Stoffregen, formerly an engineer in motorcycle development and since 2003 chief of public relations at BMW's motorcycle division, "Both models remain very good sellers, so that we'll still be producing them in 2007 for sure. And it certainly looks like the F 650 GS will still be available in 2008." With regard to price, the F single-cylinders (assembled at BMW's Berlin plant), which for a long time

From top: *Xmoto, Xchallenge, Xcountry cockpits.*

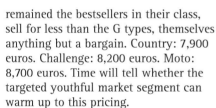

Same base, different configuration.

Opposite top left: *The G 650 Xcountry.* **Below:** *Xchallenge.* **Above and right:** *The Xmoto.*

remained the bestsellers in their class, sell for less than the G types, themselves anything but a bargain. Country: 7,900 euros. Challenge: 8,200 euros. Moto: 8,700 euros. Time will tell whether the targeted youthful market segment can warm up to this pricing.

BMW doesn't wish the G single-cylinders to be perceived as beginner models in the ordinary sense: "Our new hard enduro, the G 650 Xchallenge, will thrill people who actually want to take advantage of their machine's enormous off-road potential. With the agile G 650 Xmoto supermoto, the pilot will experience a new dimension in riding pleasure." Finally, the G 650 Xcountry Scrambler stands for fleet-footed riding on and off-road. With curb weights from 156 to 160 kilograms (DIN weight at 90 percent fueled), or dry weights ranging from 144 kilograms to 148 kilograms, the G models are also considerably lighter than the F 650 GS, which, after all, tips the scales at 191 kilograms.

The new single-cylinder models were developed in collaboration between BMW Motorcycles and Aprilia SpA. of Noale, Italy (acquired in the interim by the Piaggio Group). Unlike the Berlin-built F, they are assembled by Aprilia in its northern Italian Scorzè plant according to BMW quality standards, in a setup reminiscent of the arrangement for the first F models from 1993.

The engine for all three models was the liquid-cooled, four-stroke single-cylinder powerplant originally developed in Austria by Bombardier-Rotax for the F 650 and optimized in performance and weight for the G. The reworked engine for the G 650 X models now develops 53 horsepower (versus 50 horsepower) at 7,000 horsepower rotating a maximum torque of 60 Nm at 5,250. It's quickly obvious that power development is more dynamic, as a result of a lightened crank and a few other modifications.

An O-ring chain transmits the power to the rear wheel. All three models feature a newly developed tubular steel bridge frame with cast-aluminum lateral parts and bolt-on light-alloy rear frame section along with a matte-finished cast light-alloy rear swingarm. The differing model personalities and riding characteristics result from adaptations in tuning and design of the upside-down telescopic fork,

chassis technology (wheel travel, wheel dimensions, and modified front-wheel mountings), as well as attached parts and lighting components specifically styled for each type. What primarily varies are handlebar mountings, seats, headlights along with wheels, tires, brakes, rear-wheel spring struts, and final transmission ratios.

The Xchallenge features the elaborate Air Damping System (as does the HP2), while the Xcountry possesses a length-adjustable shock. The wheels and their dimensions are tailored to each application: 17-inch light alloy cast wheels for the streetmoto, 19/17-inch spoke wheels for the scrambler, and 21/18-inch wheels for the enduro. The brake systems also vary. The single-disc brake for the front wheel has a 300-millimeter diameter on the Xcountry and Xchallenge and comes equipped with a dual-piston caliper, while the Xmoto features a four-piston caliper and a 320-millimeter rotor. Like the F 650 GS, the G models can also be delivered with ABS. It should be noted that this is the latest generation, lightweight and compact dual-channel ABS, disengageable for off-road riding.

▍ Modified single-cylinder from the F Series

The tried and tested single-cylinder motor from the BMW F 650 series constitutes the basis for the powerplants of the G 650 X models. A few parts were modified in order to bring down the weight by about 2 kilograms, increase revving ability, and boost engine power by 3 horsepower. The lighter alternator reduces the gyrating mass of the crankshaft drive supported in babbitt bearings, thereby increasing the single-cylinder's responsiveness. The balancer shaft was retained for improved running characteristics. The new starter and magnesium generator cover contribute in no small part to weight reduction. The four-valve cylinder head redesign was primarily aimed at optimal integration of the engine as a load-bearing element in the chassis.

Engine management is handled by the BMS-C II electronic motor control system, which, besides the multi-point injection, also regulates

The G 650 Xcountry is a street single-cylinder with off-road capabilities, a multifaceted street scrambler—agile, economical, and powerful. "Riding an Xcountry means unfettered motorcycling from the very first few feet. It whips around corners... light as a feather... wholly uninhibited." (Motorrad, June 2007)

BMW provides an optional navigation device for all models.

The G series offers three designs on a unified base. **Opposite top:** The Xmoto is at home on twisting roads. **Below:** Even large off-road leaps are possible on the Xchallenge.

G 250 X Series: Essential characteristics

- Sporty lightweight design
- High-revving single-cylinder engine with 53 horsepower at 7,000 rpm and 60 Nm at 5,250 rpm
- Crankshaft supported in babbitt bearings with light alternator, thus reduced gyrating mass
- DOHC valvetrain, tappets, four valves
- Liquid cooling with aluminum radiator
- BMS-C II electronic engine management for multi-point injection and dual ignition
- Stainless steel exhaust system with three-way catalytic converter and Lambda probe
- Dry sump lubrication with center of gravity enhancing oil tank location
- Close ratio five-speed transmission with secondary chain drive
- High-quality suspension components, powder-coated aluminum mounting parts
- Torsion-resistant tubular bridge frame with bolt-on light-alloy rear frame section
- Sturdy upside-down telescopic fork, inner tube diameter of 45 millimeters
- Lightweight extremely stable dual swingarm of cast light alloy
- High grade rear spring struts
- Limited dry weight between 150 kilograms and 160 kilograms
- Butted tubular aluminum handlebars
- Foot brake and clutch levers of forged light alloy
- Fuel tank located in optimal center of gravity position under the seat, with accessible filling nozzle
- High-performance brake system, optionally available with disengageable ABS
- Specific and complete accessories range

the dual ignition. It relies on vehicle specific mappings that take the varying motorcycle designs into account. Thanks to the wholly redesigned, raised stainless steel exhaust system with Lambda probe and three-way catalytic converter allied to precise tuning, the short-stroke engine operates distinctly below EU3 emissions standards. The proven valvetrain with timing chain, twin overhead cams and tappets, along with the aluminum radiator, remained unaltered. As did the transmission.

Differences between the individual models crop up in the final chain drive transmission ratio, which, with a 15-tooth gearbox sprocket and 47-tooth drive sprocket, works out shorter in the G 650 Xchallenge than in the other two models, with their longer ratio of 16 to 47. However, differing rear-wheel rolling circumferences also affect riding dynamics.

Newly developed parts for the G type include the dry sump oil tank, located behind the cylinder at the left (thus contributing to concentration of masses in the center of gravity, which in turn improves handling). With service intervals of 10,000 kilometers, quite long for this type of machine, maintenance requirements remain low.

▌ Lightweight steel and aluminum frame

The exceptionally light vehicle frame is identical in all three models of the G 650 X series and consists of five highly rigid assemblies: 1. the welded main frame of steel sections, 2. the cast-aluminum parts, bolted to the main frame in the swingarm mounting area, 3. the light-alloy main beam, which supports the engine, 4. the forged light-

The chassis as seen on a pre-production Xchallenge with special brakes.

G 650 X frame details.

A standard rear shock (Xcountry, Xmoto) and multi-adjustable high-tech pneumatic version (Xchallenge).

alloy auxiliary frame, which absorbs the shock forces, and 5. the bolt-on light-alloy rear frame section. This lightweight construction design is largely responsible for lowering curb weights to 156 kilograms (Xchallenge) and 160 kilograms (Xcountry). In the swingarm area, where contact with the rider's boots is unavoidable, aluminum parts are powder coated, so that the former leave no unsightly traces. The swingarm mounting followed a different design from the F 650 GS. Rather than on the engine casing, the swingarm is now exclusively mounted on the main frame, relatively close to the pinion. This not only reduces drive reactions but also slack, thus also play, in the drive chain.

The rear frame section is bolted on; it can be easily and cheaply replaced if damaged. So that the rear frame holds up to the highest stresses, high-strength forged light-alloy parts are welded at the ends of the powder-coated aluminum frame tubes for optimal bolting to the main frame. This characteristic is replicated in the connection of the main beam to the forward engine mounting.

The extremely rugged dual-shaft swingarm features high-grade powder-coated surfaces. The cast part is heat treated during manufacture, yielding a more uniform structure with high rigidity. In all G 650 X models, rear suspension occurs directly via a shock hinged above to a light-alloy forged part. This part guarantees homogenous distribution and transmission of forces as it features a dual anchorage to the lateral frame components and to the cylinder head in immediate proximity to the latter's sturdy fixture to the frame.

Another common chassis component is the upside-down telescopic fork. Adaptation to the differing vehicle characteristics occurs by way of suspension travel, along with differences in tuning and configuration of wheel mounting. In the Xmoto and Xchallenge, rebound and compression stage damping are also adjustable. With its 45-millimeter inner tube diameter, forged light-alloy fork bridges and 20-millimeter wheel axle diameter, the telescopic fork displays extreme torsional stiffness and provides for optimal tracking.

The concept of the center of gravity–lowering fuel tank located in the frame triangle under the seat was taken over from the F 650 GS. The 9.5-liter plastic tank is filled from the right via a locking cap. The limited tank capacity allows a range of only 160 to 180 kilometers, even though the electronically managed

Far left: *The structure of a wet multi-disc clutch and clutch basket.*

Left: *The cooling circuit of the four-valve engine.*

Below left: *A cut-away of the Bombardier-Rotax 652cc four-stroke engine with two overhead camshafts, four valves, and 53 horsepower at 7,000 rpm.*

Below: *The circuit of the dry-sump lubrication with oil tank (right) and oil-spray cooling under the piston.*

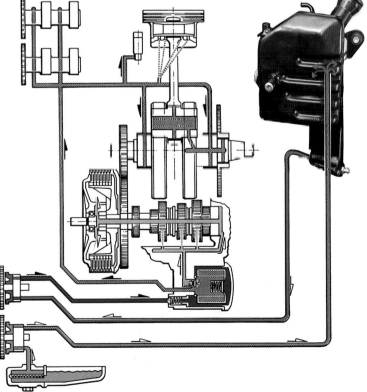

single-cylinder proves extremely economical in fuel consumption.

As previously mentioned, the G 650 X models are optionally available with a new dual-channel Bosch ABS.

The same ABS generation is found on F 800 S/ST and R 1200 S models. At 1.5 kilograms, it is compact, light, and extremely effective. The pressure modulator regulates the optimal brake pressure in the control range via linear adjustable inlet valves, generating fast

and fine control intervals. The modern valves with continuously adjustable variable cross-section openings also ensure that the rider only experiences a weak pulsation of the brake levers. In order to provide an optimal and constant pressure point, the braking system is equipped with steel encased brake lines, even in the absence of an ABS system. Off-road, and in especially hard riding, either cross-country or on closed courses, the ABS can be switched off.

The G 650 Xchallenge is perhaps the most interesting model of the G trio. "Off-road, the enduro handles even better than the scale might have led one to believe. Because of this superb handling, the BMW does not lose in the comparison to a 640 KTM enduro. . . . It's got the stuff to bring back a lot of excitement to the single-cylinder hard-enduro segment." (Motorrad, June 2007) With the standard all-weather tires, it's extremely stable on asphalt, but the range is severely limited by the small 9.5-liter tank located under the seat.

▌ Lightweight construction also for the equipment

The ABS version equipment includes a 12-volt power socket. A lightweight design is systematically applied to the high-quality mounted parts. Foot brake and gearshift levers are of forged, high-strength light alloy. The gearshift is equipped with a folding spring-loaded arm. With its anti-friction mounting, the foot brake lever allows for especially fine modulation of the rear-wheel brake. This reveals itself as particularly advantageous in the streetmoto, when initiating drift (on the race course). The side stands of Xchallenge and Xmoto are also constructed of forged light alloy. The license plate holder and blinker can be quickly removed for racing over a closed course. Wide serrated footrests provide secure footing.

The high-strength light-alloy tubular handlebars have a conical cross-section, thus offering a large surface at the clamping points for minimal weight. The handlebar clamps with different heights for all three models are mounted to the forged fork crown on rubber bushings. This dampens unpleasant vibrations.

The rider looks at a minimalist cockpit providing data for speed, time, and mileage. Flicking a switch displays a couple of travel mileage indicators. In addition, the cockpit indicates battery tension. The taillight features modern

LED technology. It provides a long service life and high luminosity. The blinkers are equipped with white lenses, standard. Electrical power supply and cabling use conventional technology. The battery is readily accessible behind the steering head, under the cover, and to the right.

Above: *Rear suspension with chain drive and rear disc-brake on an Xmoto.* **Right:** *Simple, narrow, light—the all-round talent Xcountry.*

Below *(from the left): Xcountry 19-inch front wheel; Xmoto with 17-inchers; Xchallenge with 21-inch front wheel and raised mudguard.*

▌ G 650 Xchallenge: BMW's hard enduro

The G 650 Xchallenge is an uncompromising, radically weight-optimized off-road motorcycle with long suspension travel. Its design, featuring a high sideline, sitting position, and front mudguard along with a narrow rear end, is archetypically enduro. The lightweight and tough fairing components are impact resistant and made of elastic plastic (primarily polypropylene). The asymmetrical headlight features a freeform surface reflector with an off-center parking light.

With its 270 millimeters of travel, front and rear, this lightweight enduro shies from no obstacle. The

45-millimeter stanchion diameter imparts the upside-down telescopic fork enormous rigidity. Springing and, individually adjustable damping (rebound and compression stage) are tuned to hard off-road riding. The 20-millimeter front axle is hollowed out to save weight.

The rear suspension is a technical gem. Like the HP2 boxer, the G 650 Xchallenge features the (somewhat lighter) "BMW Motorcycle Air Damping System." Within the damping chamber, a piston operates in a manner similar to that of a conventional shock. But instead of hydraulic fluid, here it's air that's displaced and transferred to a second chamber via plate valves. Damping is achieved through throttling of the airflow. As gases are compressible, the trapped air functions as a damping agent thus replacing the usual steel spring. The box at right lists the system's advantages and describes its functions. Basic damping characteristics can be adjusted via a set screw, acting upon a bypass bore in the damper, in two stages between a comfort-oriented street setting and a stiff off-road position.

Naturally, wheels and tires are configured for off-road use. The high-quality wheels feature hollow cast light-alloy wheel hubs, which are laced to the powder-coated light-alloy rims by high-strength wire spokes. The front wheel features the classic 21-inch diameter and is mounted with a 90/90x21 tire. The rear has an 18-inch wheel with a 140/80x18 tire. Mounting of special off-road tires is possible.

The brake system is designed for high demands, with an impressive rotor diameter of 300 millimeters front and

Air damping system: Advantages and functions

- "Natural" spring rate progression under elevated stress (system pressure increases)
- High bottoming protection (gas law: pressure rises along with temperature) through "natural" spring rate adaptation and frequency selective damping
- "Natural" damping progression under high demands (air viscosity increases along with temperature)
- Frequency dependent and selective damping through targeted tuning of the inner flow circuit together with split dampers; result: a considerable improvement in rear-wheel traction and ground adherence over undulating surfaces, better propulsion under hard acceleration, and increased braking security
- Resistance to overheating (no temperature-dependent decrease in damping under high stress)
- Simplified adaptability to payload conditions
- Low part weight
- Individualized chassis adjustment and adaptation to rider weight and payload with the aid of a bubble tube (displays normal position of motorcycle)
- Improved suspension responsiveness and rear-wheel traction through proportional reduction of unsprung masses
- Air-tight seal of shock to the outside, hence improved protection against soiling
- Compensation of leakage through air addition in valve
- Simple adaptation to varying payloads via system air pressure; for inflation on the road, the Xchallenge's standard equipment includes a high-pressure hand pump, located under the seat

240 millimeters rear. Besides reduced weight, the Xchallenge's perforated wave rotors feature a higher self-cleaning capacity than conventional rotors. While the front is equipped with a dual-piston floating caliper, the rear-wheel rotor is acted upon by a single-piston floating caliper. As already mentioned, the G 650 Xchallenge's final drive, with its 15-tooth gearbox and 47-tooth drive sprocket, has a shorter ratio than in the other G models. This ensures better acceleration on loose surfaces.

Technology made visible: The Xcountry's chocolate side. Emphasis: The stainless-steel muffler.

G 650 Xmoto: BMW's curve-loving machine

Even on its stand, it's obvious that the streetmoto version is designed for pure riding pleasure on asphalt. The small 17-inch wheels, aluminum handlebars fixed via shortened clamps, the front mudguard mounted close to the wheel, the brightly colored outer leg protectors, and the two-tone (Graphitan Metallic and Red) headlight housing lend the G 650 Xmoto a more compact appearance. And this although many fairing components and the asymmetrical headlight are identical to those on the enduro.

It's above all in chassis configuration that the streetmoto clearly distinguishes itself. First, the smaller 17-inch tires of cast light alloy with their 3.5- and 4.5-inch wide rims and especially adherent sport tires enhance the bike's handling characteristics, with obvious advantages in city riding. Typical of its class are the machine's generous tire dimensions of 120/70 front and 160/60 rear. Besides reduced front-wheel gyroscopic forces, the shorter caster also has a positive effect on handling. On twisting roads, the forward sitting position proves a clear advantage, while appreciable running stability is available for straight-aways.

To achieve optimal chassis geometry, the front-wheel axle-mount bore hole

was set back. Springing and damping are specially tuned. Though the upside-down telescopic fork offers 270 millimeters of travel, like the enduro, it generally displays stiffer characteristics at compression and rebound. Damping is continuously adjustable in rebound and compression. The rear suspension has a stiffer and, with 245 millimeters of travel, shorter setup.

Of the G 650 X trio, the streetmoto has the strongest brakes. The front features a four-piston fixed caliper on a floating 320-millimeter rotor, a setup, which, in conjunction with particularly sticky radial tires, provides exceptional braking power. The especially high rigidity of the USD telescopic fork, with its 45-millimeter stanchions, also plays a part in this. With its 240-millimeter rotor and floating caliper, the rear-wheel brake is identical to what is found on both other models. At 16 to 47 teeth, the Xmoto's final drive ratio is somewhat longer than the enduro variant.

G 650 Xcountry: BMW's scrambler

In the 1950s and 1960s, scrambler was the name given to street bikes that after a few technical modifications could also be ridden off-road. This versatility also defines the G 650, which unites the

best of both worlds: outstanding street capabilities allied to typical enduro off-road capacities. The Xcountry clearly departs from its sister models in both appearance and technology. With its round headlight, unfaired cockpit, dual-level seat, and wheel-hugging mudguard supported by a sturdy tubular frame, the machine clearly renews with the classic "street scrambler" look. The effect is intensified by the raised exhaust along with the two-tone paint

job in Jet Black and White Aluminum Matte Metallic.

The G 650 Xcountry shows technical originality: A relatively long-stroke telescopic fork with 240 millimeters of spring comfort along with adequate off-road capability. The rear gas pressure suspension offers 210 millimeters of travel and is fully adjustable. Special feature: The rear shock features a longitudinal adjustment allowing saddle height settings between 840 and 870 millimeters. In conjunction with the high aluminum handlebars equipped with vibration damping weights, this allows an always relaxed riding position.

It goes without saying that to keep with tradition a scrambler must ride on wire spoke wheels. Here again, the light-alloy hubs are hollow cast, the powder-coated rims fashioned of light alloy. The typical scrambler 19-inch front wheel and 17-inch rear-wheel rotate on hollow axles. With their profile structure and dimensions of 100/90 front and 130/80 rear, the tires do justice to the machine's broad spectrum of application. Braking is handled by a system with a 300-millimeter rotor diameter front and 240-millimeter rotor rear. The rotors are floating; the front caliper has dual pistons. The final drive ratio with 16-tooth gearbox sprocket and 47-tooth drive sprocket is similar to the streetmoto's secondary transmission ratio.

▌ Wide assortment: The accessories range

Typically BMW: the wide accessories product range. The aluminum under guard is included in the standard G 650 Xchallenge equipment and can be subsequently installed on both its sister models. The G 650 Xcountry has a small under guard of impact resistant plastic, which is also offered as an accessory for the G 650 Xmoto.

Certain accessory parts are fashioned of light alloy; these can replace standard plastic parts such as the chain guard and sprocket cover. For hard enduro riding, a frame protector preserves surfaces from scuffs caused by enduro boots while offering protection to the rear main brake cylinder. All G versions are approved for two riders and can be equipped with a passenger kit with high-quality footrests.

Something new: 450 Sport Enduro

The most radical sign of BMW's new thinking has to be the 450cc Sport Enduro, whose prototype made its surprising first appearances in off-road races at the beginning of 2007. More than 50 years after Sebastian Nachtmann became German off-road champion on the single-cylinder R 26 (see page 118), BMW tested a novel single-cylinder design in the shape of a slender, entirely new mini-GS. From the start, the Bavarians raised the bar as high as possible, choosing the enduro world championship as the venue for their efforts.

▌ Showing the flag in international competition

On April 28 and 29, 2007, the single-cylinder enduro started in both heats of the E2 class in the Enduro world championship (450cc four-strokes and 250cc two-strokes) in the Spanish town of Puerto Lumbreras. As riders, BMW had signed five-time motocross world champion Joel Smets and two-time German enduro champion Sascha Eckert.

On the first day, Smets took 13th place. On the second, he dropped out because of an electrical short circuit. Still, Eckert finished the premiere with positions 15th and 18th in the overall ranking. There followed 14 more entries in 2007, including world championship events in France and Italy, the Erzberg race in Austria, along with 7 runs in the German Cross Country Cup. Even indoor enduro events were planned for the BMW 450 in Barcelona and the United States.

Officially, BMW was only taking part in the contests "for testing and optimization purposes," but behind this cautious involvement lay the focused ambition of a time-honored manufacturer now trying with all its might to escape its tradition-bound confines, having recognized that the motorcycle market eventually collapses if it can no longer attract younger buyers.

From way back, the way to attract the youth's attention is with racing victories. Hence BMW's renewed involvement, after a half century absence, in endurance races such as the 24 Hours of Le Mans with the boxer.

▌DOHC single-cylinder, innovative chassis

The 450 Sport Enduro exhibits interesting, sometimes patented, details. For example, the rear swingarm bearing axis coincides with the chain drive sprocket's axis of rotation. Advantage: no more chain-length alterations between full spring compression and rebound. Moreover, a swingarm with an extra 30 millimeters can be installed at an unchanged wheelbase. What's more, the engine can be positioned farther back, with a more inclined cylinder, thus creating space for straight, long induction tracts with ideal positioning of injection nozzles and the double-throttle system. This, in turn, provides the basis for compliance with the EU3 emissions standard. The design was realized under the direction of Markus Theobald, a BMW development engineer with solid off-road riding experience and one of the fathers of the HP2 Enduro.

The four-valve, liquid-cooled single-cylinder engine features two overhead camshafts, dry sump lubrication, fuel injection, a Lambda-controlled catalytic converter, and an electric starter. In keeping with the F and G series, the fuel tank is located under the seat. The clutch sits directly atop the crankshaft. The stainless steel frame tubes with welded in diagonal bracing run in a perfectly straight line from the swingarm

Right: *Sascha Eckert on the 450 GS.*

Below: *The machine's highlight: Coaxial mounting of the swingarm and drive pinion. The frame tubes are stainless steel. In front, a Marzocchi upside-down fork with 300 millimeters of travel. Rear-wheel damping is accomplished with a progressive Öhlins shock with 320 millimeters of travel. Because the drive chain length hardly changes, there is no need for a tensioning device.*

mounting to the steering head. The rear frame section consists of square light-alloy tubes bolted to the main frame. The pivot axle mounted on the frame leads through the hollowed out transmission output shaft, which bears the drive sprocket. To replace the sprocket, the motorcycle is jacked up, the pivot axle extracted, and the swingarm folded back with the wheel mounted. An experienced mechanic requires about 15 minutes for this. The conventional Marzocchi upside-down fork features 300 millimeters of travel.

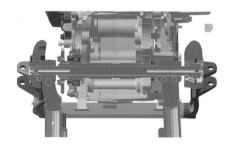

The GS in rallies before 1992: Four Paris-Dakar victories

At the end of the 1970s and the beginning of the 1980s, the motorcycles in international off-road racing were becoming ever lighter. As a result, at some point, despite all the tuning tricks, the twin-cylinder BMW's setup for off-road racing simply could no longer keep up. But as luck would have it, with the great rallies a new field of application soon opened up for the brawny boxer. Amid desert sands, they would once again demonstrate their stamina.

A specially prepared swingarm BMW with an 800cc boxer, 55 horsepower, and Maico fork already competed in the first Paris-Dakar Rally, from December 23, 1978, to January 14, 1979. Its rider was a Frenchman, Jean-Claude Morellet. Among desert rats, the journalist and writer was better known under his pseudonym of "Fenouil" (Fennel). Some years earlier, he had been among the first to cross Africa on a motorcycle. Though provided by BMW France,

Fenouil's machine was prepared by Herbert Schek. The French importer had initially inquired directly at the factory, but was directed to the specialist for lack of rally competence. The finished Dakar GS weighed only 150 kilograms.

On Scheck's desert racer, Fenouil managed to battle his way to third place. It quickly became clear, however, that because of the short rear-end suspension travel the rims took more knocks than they could tolerate. Frequent wheel replacements cost precious time. What's more, after Bamako (Mali) the engine began running rough, burning out one spark plug after another. By the end, it was only running on one cylinder before finally giving up the ghost, almost within sight of the Atlantic.

In the first years of the desert extravaganza, BMW still underestimated the value of such events for product testing and marketing purposes. This

Frenchman Hubert Auriol won the Paris-Dakar Rally twice. **Above:** *The photo shows him with the winning 1981 machine.* **Left:** *Auriol, with the 1000 GS on the path to victory in 1983. Wheels, suspension and brakes were special components; the frame was largely production.*

explains Munich's renewed hesitant reaction to the French partner's second inquiry, in 1979 and only giving the green light a couple of months before the start of the 1980 Paris-Dakar.

Years later, Dietmar Beinhauer, who at the time had already assumed responsibility for the entire motorcycle racing program, described those hectic weeks: "After some back and forth, we finally got approval for two machines; they would be ridden by Fenouil and Hubert Auriol. The factory was providing the machines and equipment. In our preparations, we had to rely entirely on experiences gained at the European championship and the Six Days during the 1970s." From the beginning, BMW France attached great importance to the rally, pushing for professional preparation. Besides PR for the French market, the men in Paris counted on boosting their far from negligible business with government agencies.

Beinhauer, who managed the BMW rally team until 1986, was from 1980

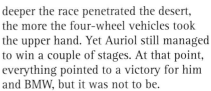

responsible for team coordination and services on location, a team that was nevertheless sponsored by the French importer and its dealerships. In 1980, besides Fenouil, BMW France chose the then 27-year-old Auriol. The machines were again prepared by Schek. As previously, the 800 boxer developed 55 horsepower and provided muscular torque. Its backbone was the standard production frame, but suspension travel had been considerably lengthened, building on the hard lessons of 1978–79.

▌ 1980: Hard luck for Auriol in Upper Volta

Auriol's start in Paris was promising. At the first stage, he was originally in eighth place, behind the previous year's and premier edition winner, Cyril Neveu, riding one of the race's 44 (!) Yamaha XT 500s. But then he, along with Fenouil, took penalty points and lost precious time stuck behind an opening drawbridge. Yet already in Algeria, both Frenchmen had made up for lost time: Auriol held second place behind Neveu, far ahead of any cars. But the

deeper the race penetrated the desert, the more the four-wheel vehicles took the upper hand. Yet Auriol still managed to win a couple of stages. At that point, everything pointed to a victory for him and BMW, but it was not to be.

In Upper Volta (now Burkina Faso) a transmission problem brought the Frenchman's ride to an abrupt end. Now Auriol committed a fatal mistake: Instead of waiting around for Beinhauer's service team, he innocently loaded his racing enduro onto a taxi-truck and, exhausted by the extremely arduous stage, lay down for a little rest. Inspectors soon discovered Auriol and immediately pulled him out of the ranking. Still, BMW rider Fenouil landed in fifth place, behind four of the single-cylinder Yamaha XT 500s, with their paltry 40 horsepower.

▌ 1981: First victory for Auriol and BMW

Then, in 1981, the two desert specialist friends, now increasingly rivals with the growing pressure for success, pulled it off. Auriol, born in Ethiopia and raised in Africa, lived up to his nickname ("the African ") by triumphing on the GS boxer with a three hour lead over Yamaha rider Serge Bacou. Fenouil moved up to fourth place on his third Paris-Dakar, while Bernard Neimer, a French policeman, took seventh. The BMW machines had been prepared by HPN.

Alongside the factory team, Herbert Schek also went to the start on a BMW; he had formed an independent team with the truck driver Karl Friedrich Capito. Yet after an encouraging start, the rally-loving German sadly drove his 100,000-DM budget into the sand: the 47-year-old suffered a serious fall and had to abandon the race with a broken hip.

Both photos depict the Rally-GS 1000 prepared for the 1984 Baja California race. With a different cockpit and single headlight, this model was also deployed for the Paris-Dakar Rally. Note the asymmetrically mounted rear shock.

1982: Abandonment after a series of transmission failures

In 1982, everything pointed to another BMW victory in the world's toughest rally. Up to the sixth day Auriol was in the lead, now supported by Fenouil and yet another cop, Raymond Loizeaux. Then the collapse: after two transmission failures, Auriol rode into the fourth stage finish now only in 40th place. A couple of days later, when the title holder lost yet more ground because of orientation and renewed transmission problems, an early end to the BMW involvement already hung in the air. After additional breakdowns, expedition boss Beinhauer had no choice but to let the undertaking, which had cost BMW 600,000 DM, run out there and then into the desert sands.

1983: Second Auriol Dakar victory

Yet, the BMW rally team was rewarded in the following year and not only by hat tricks at the Pharaohs Rally, which Auriol won once and Rahier twice. The GS boxers again blazed the way to Dakar: Already in 1983, Auriol snatched the victory for BMW.

In 1983, besides the official BMW team (Auriol, Fenouil, Loizeaux, and Schek), the Belgian Gaston Rahier rode a boxer GS into the desert. While Auriol, who initially held back, constantly moved toward the front of the race, pulling his compatriots in his train, Rahier, in first place, had to quit with a shattered oil pan. Schek, who had tuned the engines, was also left behind in the Sahara after a fall resulting in a dislocated shoulder. In the rocky desert beyond the Tenere, Auriol ended up with tire damage twice in a row. It was only because team member Loizeaux helped him with his rear wheel that in the end Auriol rode into Dakar as victor. Fenouil took ninth place, Loizeaux, fourteenth.

BMW could not have hoped for a more brilliant success on the 60th anniversary of the boxer design. And there would be one more victory, one with important consequences above all for the company's U.S. business: Auriol won the famous Baja California race (see photos page 155) on a special 1000 BMW with 75 horsepower and 145 kilograms dry weight.

Meanwhile, BMW had also signed Rahier to the rally team. Together with Auriol and Loizeaux, the three-time 125cc motocross world champion (1975–1977) would bring the title back to Munich. Once again, Schek had prepared the machines, which featured more advanced technology, such as 45-liter Kevlar tanks or cellular rubber tire cores.

Little big man: The Belgian Gaston Rahier won the Paris–Dakar Rally in 1984 and 1985.
Left and below: *The photos are from 1985.*

▌ 1984: Gaston Rahier on the trail to victory

Gaston Rahier's BMW was the only one to feature an electric starter, as the 5-foot, 4-inch cross-country powerhouse had trouble turning over the 1-liter engine by kick starter. Getting on and off his machine with 310 millimeters and 280 millimeters of suspension travel front and rear also proved no easy task. In pure cowboy style, he usually only jumped on once the bike was running and already in motion.

Yet BMW had undoubtedly made a smart move in signing the diminutive Belgian as a second Paris-Dakar contestant. In downright astonishing style, Rahier demonstrated that small size was no obstacle to winning the world's toughest rally on a monster of a bike. The veteran motocross rider rolled into Dakar as victor, with 20 minutes on Auriol.

But behind this spectacular double victory lay a number of harrowing days in the course of which the teammates had increasingly become rivals. That Auriol, the "White African," who had to yield to the Belgian had a number of problems: oil loss, scarcity of fuel, along with a number of close encounters with African cattle. Yet he won seven special stages and managed to pull up to Rahier once more.

In the meantime, two service vehicles had broken down. Not knowing that one of these was his, Rahier complained of inadequate support by the remaining BMW technicians, at one point even reportedly threatening to quit the

The light and powerful BMW special racer reached speeds of up to 185 kilometers an hour on the rallies.

Above: *Gaston Rahier on his way to victory in 1984.*

Left: *The BMW Rally Team for the 1986 Paris-Dakar; left to right: Raymond Loizeaux, Eddy Hau, and Gaston Rahier. The GS had 1,040cc of displacement and an output of 70 horsepower; the tank held 60 liters. Fully loaded, the machine weighed 230 kilograms.*

race. Yet despite all the squabbling, he managed to hold on to his lead even through the extreme stages in Guinea, down to the finish. BMW used the sensational double victory, which had all but burned up its 700,000-DM budget, to rush to market with the R 80 G/S Paris-Dakar, a mainly visually modified version of the standard G/S for the common man. But Munich continued to leave construction of the rally machines to the specialized shops.

HPN assumed responsibility for the 1985 generation of Paris-Dakar racers. As in 1981, the specialist trio settled on the full-liter displacement, from which the boxer drew a hefty 70 horsepower at a reduced compression

ratio. Sophisticated chassis technology helped the riders achieve top speeds of 170 kilometers per hour. For example, the GS rear wheel was suspended by a dual swingarm with White Power shocks. The front wheel featured a special Marzocchi telescopic fork. HPN's quality work already paid off at the dress rehearsal in Egypt: Rahier won the third Pharaohs Rally, in front of his new teammate Eddy Hau.

▌ 1985: Success amid gigantic difficulties

The 1985 edition of the Paris-Dakar would be Rahier's toughest race. Even before the crossing to Africa, the Belgian had bent his machine almost beyond serviceability in a collision with a French passenger vehicle. After emergency repairs by the Beinhauer service team (which this time included

Left: *Eddy Hau (left) became a marathon winner in 1988 on the BMW 1000 (80 horsepower) and 12th in the overall motorcycle ranking. Next to him, Richard Schalber (25).*

Below and below left: *Four-time Dakar contestant Raymond Loizeaux, 1984. Middle: Rahier, 1987 (third place, behind Cyril Neveu and Edi Orioli on Honda).*

HPN engineer Alfred Halbfeld), Rahier started into the desert; yet here again, he seemed dogged by bad luck. Blown tires and a broken front wheel threw him back to 30th place. After falls, Loizeaux and Hau had had to throw in the towel early in the game.

Then, after Ténéré, Rahier suddenly had only Yamaha rider Franco Picco in front of him; three days before Dakar, however, he followed the Italian down the wrong track, losing two valuable hours in the process. This now brought Auriol (who in the interim had gone over to Cagiva) dangerously close. But engine failure on Auriol's machine ended the duel to the little Belgian's advantage even before it had really started.

Rahier then dispatched Picco with a rather wicked trick: following his involuntary excursion in company of the leader, he convinced the latter of the necessity of gassing up. Picco had to wait 15 minutes to get 10 liters of gas from the BMW tanker and Rahier had gained valuable time. Feeling victory at his grasp, he now covered the next murderous special stage with an hour over the utterly exhausted Picco, thus handing BMW its fourth Paris-Dakar victory in five years in the face of overwhelming Japanese competition.

1986: A disastrous year for the Paris-Dakar

Rahier won the Pharaoh in the fall, but then luck deserted him. The 1986 Paris-Dakar, in which organizer Thierry Sabine suffered a fatal accident, once more began with difficulties for the Belgian. After a fall and various punctures, he found himself only in 11th place. He then began catching up rapidly until, at high speed, he came upon a stream bed running perpendicular to his path of travel. Though he managed to clear the first channel, his heavy machine smashed into the second with its front wheel. Loizeaux, arriving at the scene shortly thereafter, managed to get his dazed teammate back on his feet and effect makeshift repairs on the bent motorcycle.

Demonstrating true grit, Rahier now fought his way back to eighth place. Only to end up, like Hau, stranded in the Assekrem Mountains, having run out of fuel. When transmission problems finally threw the two-time rally winner back into 14th place, Rahier could no longer find anything good to say about his employer. He announced his separation from BMW while still in Africa, accusing Hau of having left him in the lurch with a

Above: *Eddy Hau at the 1986 Paris-Dakar, at which he ended in eighth place.*

Far left: *Hubert Auriol in 1983 on his 67-horsepower 1000.*

Left: *Gaston Rahier (left) and Eddy Hau before the start of the 1985 Paris-Dakar.*

blown tire. He ended the ill-fated race in eighth place.

After the chaotic events of that Paris-Dakar rally, whose very rationale for continued existence was not only (momentarily) cast in doubt by the death of its originator, BMW decided to disband the factory team. Yet, this was not a complete retreat from off-road racing. Interested private parties could order a Paris-Dakar replica on an R 80 G/S base (starting at 29,000 DM) from HPN. BMW provided starting money and various bonuses. For Eddy Hau, BMW's exit from such events brought an extended involuntary exile as he could not find another competitive motorcycle on favorable terms. Rahier's hard feelings toward BMW soon abated. He took on the Bavarians' factory machines, founding his own team with support from Marlboro, Michelin, and Elf. With the HPN-modified machines, now displaying upside-down forks, the Rahier crew already gave a good accounting of itself at the Egyptian dress rehearsal. Despite a monumental crash and a foot injury, Rahier ended the 1986 Pharaohs Rally in third place. In 1987, the team boss managed to ride into Dakar in third place. Then things went quiet around the glorious rally BMWs.

1992: Jutta Kleinschmitt, fastest lady on two wheels

In 1988, French organizer Pierre-Marie Poli sent four very interesting machines to compete in the Paris-Dakar. He received the factory engines for the Rahier team from BMW in 1987. These were mounted on a light Kevlar carbon-fiber monocoque chassis. At a mere 172 kilograms dry weight, they were the Dakar's lightest twins. Yet this time the "Ecureuil" racers did not place very high.

In the following years, the desert extravaganza attracted a lot of negative headlines through deaths and serious injuries, with even hardcore rally freaks criticizing its excessive demands. In 1988, Herbert Schek, now 55, and daughter Patricia already had to drop out at the first stage in Algeria. Nor did rally novice Jutta Kleinschmitt's (a former member of the German national ski, bobsled, and sledding teams) initial hard luck portend her later Paris-Dakar victory in a Mitsubishi (2001). Eddy Hau and Richard Schalber, on the other hand, traveling on HPN machines purchased with the help of BMW, gave a brilliant accounting of themselves. With no support from expensive service personnel, Hau took 12th place in the overall ranking and 1st in the marathon class for production machines. In 1989,

Above: *BMW engineer Jutta Kleinschmidt with the largely production R 100 GS Paris-Dakar before the 1992 start in Munich.*

Below: *Richard Schalber and Kleinschmidt with the GS 1000, set up by HPN, before the start of the Pharaohs Rally in 1990.*

Right: *Eddy Hau at the 1986 Paris-Dakar, in the course of which organizer Thierry Sabine perished in a helicopter crash.*

All photos on this page show Jutta Kleinschmidt at the Paris-Cape Town Rally of 1992, with her largely production R 100 GS Paris-Dakar. Despite a broken foot, the then-29-year-old won the women's category and took 23rd place in the overall standings. In 2001, she became the overall victor driving a Mitsubishi Pajero.

the German BMW riders only appeared outside the Paris-Dakar Rally. Thus, Schalber ended the Transpania Raid in 10th position on an R 100 GS, even managing to break into the phalanx of factory machines at the Pharaohs Rally.

In 1990, at the behest of the Munich BMW office, HPN built a new chassis with reinforced production frame and cantilever swingarm for the 1,043cc engine. Yet Schalber lost a lot of ground at the Transpania Raid because of technical problems with the machine. Jutta Kleinschmidt won in the over 600cc on her near-production

GS. It was only in January 1992 that the engineer Kleinschmidt, employed by BMW and with factory support, finally made her big breakthrough on the motorcycle. Despite a broken foot, she completed the rally, which now lead to Cape Town over 12,700 kilometers, 23rd in the overall ranking. She placed 5th in the marathon class and was fastest woman of the race on a R 100 GS merely distinguished from the production model by its White Power shock and additional tanks. There's no doubt that the successes of the first Paris-Dakar years contributed

to the reputation of BMW enduros as motorcycles reliable even under the most extreme conditions. The Bavarians sustained themselves on this image for a number of years, abstaining from the ostentatious investments that factory racing involvement necessarily demands. Yet by the end of the 1990s, the blue-and-white's rally flame flared up once more.

Rallyesport racing from 1998: Comeback with the F 650 RR

The end of BMW factory involvement in rallyesport after four Paris–Dakar victories with twin-cylinder boxer machines (1981 and 1983 with Frenchman Hubert Auriol and 1984 and 1985 with Belgian Gaston Rahier) was regretted especially in France, Spain, and African countries. So much greater the satisfaction when the Bavarians announced their return on New Year's Day 1998 after a 13-year hiatus, kicking off the celebrations for "75 Years of BMW Motorcycles" in worthy style.

That time, however, on the start line at the Place d'Armes in Versailles there no longer stood the brawny boxers but graceful off-road machines based on a single-cylinder F 650. All four machines were intended to reach the finish in Dakar; BMW wanted to be represented in the top five of the overall standings with at least one F 650 RR. In all, 10,245 kilometers awaited the competitors, along which 6,388 kilometers of special stages. Organizing the gigantic, 20th edition of the desert extravaganza was ex-champion Hubert Auriol.

His motto: "Back to basics. The Dakar must once again become a racing adventure."

▌1998 start:
Bad luck and stupid breakdowns
The machines had been built up with technical support from BMW, by the Richard Schalber Company in Munich. Schalber, 1979 German off-road champion and successful 1980s rally rider on the BMW boxer, had gone into business for himself with his technology and tuning company, becoming the boss of BMW's new rally team in 1998. The F 650 RR now only shared a few parts with the production model. It weighed 168 kilograms and with the liquid-cooled single-cylinder four-valve engine tuned from 48 to 80 horsepower reached a top speed of 180 kilometers per hour. A couple of 17-liter tanks mounted on both sides at the front and a 20-liter tank rear provided a total volume of 54 liters of fuel and thus the range necessary for desert racing. As customary since the beginning of the 1990s, the BMW machines were also

Top: *Broken dreams at the reborn Paris-Dakar, 1998. Andrea Mayer never made it to Dakar, anymore than the other three BMW riders.*

Above: *The 1998 BMW team (left to right): Jean Brucy, Oscar Gallardo, Andrea Mayer, Edi Orioli, and team boss Richard Schalber.*

Right: *Oscar Gallardo at the 1998 Paris-Dakar on F 650 RR.*

Below right: *Richard Sainct on the improved F 650 RR rides to victory in 1999. The 700cc and 75-horsepower RR had little left in common with the production F 650 of the time.*

equipped with a GPS navigation system, which did much to prevent riders from getting lost.

The Schalber team's top rider in 1998 was the 35-year-old Italian businessman Edi Orioli, four-time Dakar winner in 1988, 1990, 1994, and 1996 on a Honda, Yamaha, and Cagiva. The other team members also had Paris-Dakar experience, including the 32-year-old Spaniard Oscar Gallardo, sociologist and second in the 1997 overall standings. The 35-year-old motorcycle mechanic Jean Brucy, from south of Paris, had come in fifth at the 1996 rally.

The fourth man was a woman: Andrea Mayer, from Hiemenhofen, freelance journalist, travel guide, instructor at the BMW Enduro Park in Hechlingen, and as such a BMW employee. On January 2, 1998, she celebrated her 30th birthday in the saddle on the road to Dakar. She had already undergone her Paris-Dakar baptism by fire in 1996, when, despite a fall and dislocated shoulder, she rode into the finish as winner of the Ladies' Cup and 45th in the overall standings. Of 140 competitors, only 50 had finally visited the beach at Dakar.

Hopes of again winning the 1998 women's rankings were dashed three days before the goal after Mayer burned out her clutch in deep sand. The factory comeback, which kicked off with so much optimism, also went pear shaped in other quarters, the other three factory BMW's having dropped out with technical defects. A rock shattered the motor housing on Orioli's BMW, Gallardo had to quit following a broken shock absorber and chain, and because of a ruptured frame rear end, Jean Brucy only crossed the finish line as 35th. The proud winner (for a total of six victories) was Frenchman Stéphane Peterhansel on his 850 twin-cylinder Yamaha.

▌ Granada Dakar 1999: Meticulous preparation

In 1999, the Bavarians really put themselves to the test. Intent on shuffling the deck, they went for their second try in the desert rally, which now began in Granada, Spain, ending as before, in Dakar, capital of Senegal. Once again, four F 650 RR (Rally Raid) were brought to the start, this time with strict factory supervision under the auspices of the newly founded BMW Motorcycle Team Enduro, with project leaders Willi Rampf and Richard Schalber at its head. This time, the people from Munich were pretty sure of their chances. "We want to be in the battle for the top places," Schalbert declared. A test run at the Dubai Rallye in November 1998 had proven that the

Above and right:
Frenchman Richard Sainct, the happy victor, with his F 650 RR (above) at the Dakar beach in January 1999. Apart from a defective tire, the BMW, with the number 12, ran more than 9,000 kilometers without a problem.

motorcycles were now sound: Oscar Gallardo had ridden the F 650 to a fifth place; Andrea Mayer won the women's ranking, placing 27th in the overall field of 102 participants.

While Gallardo, Brucy, and Mayer started again for BMW, Edi Orioli was no longer onboard; at the last minute, he had opted for KTM. In his place, the Bavarians had signed Richard Sainct. The 28-year-old Frenchman from St. Affrique and 1989 European enduro champion had already ridden the Paris-Dakar six times (fifth place in 1996) and won the Atlas Rally in 1998.

▌ Heat-resistant single-cylinder with 700cc and 75 horsepower

The F 650 Rallye had been redesigned in many respects. For example, the single-cylinder engine with displacement increased to 700cc now developed 75 horsepower at 8,500 rpm, yielding a top speed of 180 kilometers per hour with the correspondingly set-up five-speed transmission.

The jets of the two Mikuni carburetors had been modified in such a way that the engine could develop its peak power in high heat. With its 300 millimeters of travel front and rear, ground clearance of 295 millimeters, a wheelbase of 1,550 millimeters, and tire dimensions of 90/90x21 or 140/80x18, the F 650, at a dry weight of 168 kilograms, was optimally equipped for endless full-throttle stages over sand and scree, which had to be primarily ridden in a standing position. This rendered the considerable saddle height of 980 millimeters, a largely theoretical value.

This time, two tanks left and right, each with a 13.5-liter volume, along with a rear tank holding 17.5 liters (44.5 liters, i.e., considerably less than in 1998) would have to do. Two single-disc brakes (300 millimeters diameter front, 200 millimeters rear) stopped the machine. The telescopic fork was a mix of Showa and White Power parts; the rear shock strut came from White Power.

▌ A tough battle against KTM superiority

Despite excellent preparation, from the start the question arose whether the BMW team could stand up to KTM's superiority. The Austrians came to the race with nine factory riders (including stars such as Heinz Kinigadner, Kari Tiainen, Thierry Magnaldi, and Fabrizio Meoni), six support team riders, and

Above: *In 1999, Jean Brucy ran cover for his compatriot Richard Sainct, crossing the finish line himself in 20th place.*

Right: *A thirsty Sainct at the stage finish. The Frenchman hardly shows the strain.*

more than 60 private riders on the 640 LC4. For support, 12 trucks and 12 tons of materials stood at the ready, including 30 spare engines, 450 tires, and 12,000 liters of special fuel. BMW made do with a couple of service trucks, an extra F 650, and vital replacement parts consumables.

Following initial KTM stage victories, BMW began to close in. After Kinigadner landed in the hospital with a spinal injury sustained while overturning and the KTM of six-time enduro world champion Kari Tiainen

Left: The four-valve boxer underwent its baptism of fire as the R 1100 GS/RR at the Tunisia Rally of 1999.

Below left: The BMW team after arrival: Oscar Gallardo (34), winner Sainct, and Jean Brucy (6).

▌1999: Sainct wins with a four-minute lead

His pursuers weren't so lucky: Magnaldi overturned, Meoni broke his ankle, Cox injured his elbow. The remaining KTM riders certainly deserve credit for their relentless pursuit of Sainct despite the pain of their injuries. But at least as admirable was the fact that the Frenchman managed to hold his tiny lead of only four minutes and nine seconds to the end, thus winning the world's hardest rally for BMW.

"Oh, when the Sainct goes marching in . . ." intoned BMW's media department in the euphoria of victory. KTM rider Thierry Magnaldi rode in second, followed by teammate Alfie Cox. Still, F 650 rider Oscar Gallardo managed 9th place, Jean Brucy came in 20th, and Andrea Mayer rode in 21 hours, 13 minutes, and 43 seconds after the victor, taking the 32nd position, an amazing performance, under the circumstances.

At the prologue, the courageous journalist's BMW had sunk into a waterhole, leaving her in last place. An incredible race to catch up then brought the lady a long ways back toward the front of the race. When a serious fall about a third into the more than 9,000 kilometers course threw Mayer back once again. With heavy bruising of her eyes, a couple of sprained cervical vertebrae, and intense pain she finally crossed the finish line.

▌Tunisia 1999: Boxers officially return to major rally start line

Memories of the four legendary Dakar victories with BMW twin-cylinder boxers between 1981 and 1999 came alive at the Optic 2000 Rally, held in Tunisia from April 10 to 18. At this contest, BMW factory rider Oscar Gallardo first tested the prototype of a racing boxer on an R 1100 GS base. In spite of a botched start at the first stage in Sardinia, during which the electrical system quit following several knee-deep river crossings, the Spaniard worked himself up in the following days from 197th to 34th place. All the while, the

had gone up in flames, Oscar Gallardo took the lead on the F 650 RR. One of the reasons he managed to win the fourth stage was that teammate Jean Brucy had selflessly offered him the rear wheel of his F 650 after Gallardo suffered a blown tire. In second position, Richard Sainct now even made possible a BMW double lead, which lasted until the seventh stage. But then the man from Madrid ran out of luck. He waited

in the desert for hours with a defective battery, losing crucial time. Richard Sainct's hour had come: With grim focus he rode his BMW at the head of the race. Biting at the Frenchman's heels, however, were KTM riders Magnaldi, Meoni, and Alfie Cox, the South African. Despite the grueling psychological and physical stresses, Sainct managed to hold on to his wafer-thin lead of a few minutes without falling.

The BMW team for the 2000 Dakar-Cairo Rally with a single and boxer. Left to right: Sainct, Mayer, Gallardo, Brucy, Schalber, Hauser, Deacon, and Lewis.

rally boxer amazed as much through its performance as it did with its durability and riding characteristics.

The victory went to Richard Sainct on a BMW F 650 RR, three months after his Dakar triumph. With this, he once again relegated KTM stars Meoni, Kinigadner, and Magnaldi to follower positions, thereby proving that his Dakar victory had been more than just a lucky accident.

This remarkable boxer prototype had been set up by the high-end Bavarian HPN shop (named after the three company founders Alfred Halbfeld, Klaus Pepperl, and Michael Neher). In the end, the machine only had the engine design in common with the standard GS; the 1,085cc displacement motor and the matching six-speed transmission came from the R 1100 S. A light-alloy plate replaced the oil pan; the separate oil tank migrated behind the alternator.

The complex injection system was replaced by two sturdy Bing VV carburetors with 40-millimeter bore. With CDI ignition and special two-in-one exhaust system, the four-valve boxer eventually developed 85 horsepower at 7,000 rpm. This was power aplenty, as the R 1100 GS/RR had

a curb weight of only 200 kilograms, thus 100 pounds less than the basic model. The double-loop tubular frame was a wholly new design. The narrow 21-inch front wheel was not suspended with the home-baked Telelever but featured a White Power upside-down fork with 43-millimeter stanchions and cross-country capable 300-millimeter of spring travel.

One notable HPN special part was the handmade, light-alloy single-sided swingarm with directly hinged, multi-adjustable White Power shock, also with 300 millimeters of travel. As in the F 650 RR, an 18-inch rear wheel transmitted the power to the ground. Handmade also, the 28-liter front tank with integrated water container, along with the additional 8-liter rear tank. There's more! Öhlins steering damper, custom fiber fairing with double headlights and high windshield, rally cockpit featuring tripmaster, and GPS.

∎ Dakar-Cairo 2000: Successful appearance with two boxers and four single-cylinders

If Tunisia had merely been a warm-up for the rally boxer, BMW was in earnest at the next Dakar. It sent the twin cylinder to the start line for the first time in the 15 years since Gaston Rahier's last boxer victory, in duplicate and under the designation R 99 RR. For now, unlike in Tunisia, the motor only featured 900cc of displacement. Yet,

Above: *The 75-horsepower F 650 RR, with which Sainct won in 2000.*

Below: *The R 900 RR with 90 horsepower.*

carburetor technology imparted it higher output per liter and more zip. Ninety horsepower came to life at 8,200 rpm.

This time, five speeds sufficed for the power transmission. The gas tanks had been expanded to 30 and 10 liters, respectively; at 995 millimeters, saddle height shattered all records. Dry, the rocket tipped the scales at 190 kilograms. Otherwise the Dakar boxer, again from HPN, matched the Tunisian prototype. The boxers were ridden by 37-year-old engineer and motorcycle dealer John Deacon, from Cornwall, U.K., and 31-year-old motorcycle journalist and multiple Six Days winner Jimmy Lewis, hailing from Costa Mesa, California. Both new recruits to the BMW Motorcycle Team Gauloises had solid Dakar experience and could look back to numerous successes as independent riders. The whole enterprise was an act of bravado; that it would pay off soon became apparent.

Once again, the spearheads of the BMW legion were the four F 650 RR single-cylinder racers, which in principle matched the 99 models, reaching 75 horsepower, though they had been further developed in detail. They now featured a couple of 12-liter tanks to the sides and three 7-liter rear-end tanks side and middle, which

A full commitment and a little luck:

Above: *Sainct on the F 650 RR roaring to his 2000 victory.*

Right: *Jimmy Lewis on the R 900 RR. Despite loads of power, the heavy boxers could not keep pace with the agile single-cylinder machines.*

Above: In 2000, the irrepressible Andrea Mayer made it to her destination despite loads of problems.

Left: Oscar Gallardo battled his way to a respectable second place on the single-cylinder BMW.

raised the overall fuel volume to 45 liters while providing improved weight distribution. The 2000 RR had a dry weight of 168 kilograms. The powerful singles were entrusted to the team, which had been so successful in 1999: Richard Sainct, Oscar Gallardo, Jean Brucy, and Andrea Mayer. Responsible for technology and organization, as usual, was Richard Schalber, now supported by Berthold Hauser, BMW's new motorcycle racing boss.

▌ By ship to Africa

From the outset it was clear that this time around the members of the BMW team, as last year's victors, would be the quarry. Archrival KTM had rearmed as never before. And the route really had it all: It was designed for high speeds and held more than a few surprises in store. Rally boss Hubert Auriol had thought of something else: This time,

following technical acceptance in Paris on December 28, all 200 motorcycles (including side-cars and quads), 135 off-road cars and buggies, and 63 trucks traveled by ship to Africa, where the starter's gun went off on January 6 in

Dakar, the race's erstwhile destination. Then it plunged straight east, through Africa, ending 17 days and 10,000 kilometers later on January 23, 2000, in Cairo. But before this, grueling trials and unexpected adventures beckoned.

As in the previous year, the fight would essentially take place between BMW and KTM. The Austrians sent not one but two factory teams to the race: the A-team comprised Heinz Kinigadner, Joan Roma, Jordi Arcarons, Fabrizio Meoni, and Giovanni Sala who were equipped with brand-new single-cylinder factory bikes. The B-team, with Kari Tiainen, Alfie Cox, and Jurgen Mayer, rode 1999 machines. But once more, despite its best efforts, the rally was not run under a good star for KTM. "Shortly after the start, KTM was already beset by the carburetor, then the piston plague," reported Robert Kauder in *Motorrad*. "New Keihin carburetors caused the A-team major headaches, then a new supplier's pistons wreaked havoc with inconsistent contraction and expansion behavior." The first one to drop out was Spanish KTM rider Jordi Arcarons, with mechanical breakdown. Meoni and Sala were forced to abandon shortly thereafter because of falls. All riders struggled with gigantic clouds of dust thrown up by fast off-road vehicles. The experience often resembled flying blind at speeds in excess of 160 kilometers per hour. At his seventh attempt, Heinz Kinigadner had to abandon his dream of at least riding into the finish after suffering a femoral neck fracture in a nasty fall.

The only victim among the BMW riders was John Deacon. He crashed his Boxer R 900 RR already on the fifth stage near Ouagadougou, so severly that he had to be flown to a hospital in Cairo. The diagnosis: a fractured hip and a dislocated shoulder. Andrea Mayer, who immediately administered first aid to her teammate, then experienced her own less-than-gentle encounter with the African earth three days before the finish. Though she

wasn't injured, the engine of her F 650 RR never ran the same. This proved such a handicap that she was only 35th in Cairo, though arrive she did.

▌ Terrorist threat brings air bridge to Libya instead of Ténéré crossing

Things went appreciably better for the other four BMW bikes, even if victory seemed far from ensured at the start. Though Richard Sainct, the previous year's champion, won the first stage, KTM's Spanish rider, Joan Roma, already took the lead on the second day; by the sixth stage, he had extended it to 22 minutes over Sainct.

This development was initially taken in stride in the BMW camp. Then, on January 11 an ominous announcement came from French diplomatic circles warning of an ostensible terrorist

plot by the Groupe Islamique Armé (GIA). Hubert Auriol stopped the caravan in Niamey; together with race management, he then took a bold decision: stages seven through ten through the Ténéré were cancelled, to be replaced by an air-bridge to Libya. Over four days, three hastily chartered Antonov 124 aicraft ferried the whole rally, kit and caboodle, into the land of Muammar Khaddafi. The flying titans even had space for the helicopters and trucks. Not surprisingly, the cost ran into millions.

And no one could rejoice at the involuntary air stage. Not the participants, who felt cheated of the race's most spectacular and demanding segment, and not the the business people and local populations in suddenly left out Niger.

After landing, the BMW team had only seven days to make up KTM's lead. Responding to sport boss Berti Hauser's laconic instructions, "full throttle!" they now hurtled Egyptward through the desert in quadruple formation at more than 160 kilometers per hour, on the 879-kilometer 14th stage from Khofra to Dachla, Joan Roma, and his KTM hard on their heels.

While the BMW boxers and singles took the sizzling inferno in stride, the same could not be said of the KTM. Roma's engine eventually gave up the ghost, taking with it the dream of victory. Even the competition commiserated with the desperate ex-favorite. Berti Hauser of BMW: "A sad end for the magnificently riding Spaniard." For the teams of four off-road auto racers, the stage ended in the hospital. At full throttle, they had torn over a dune and landed 15 meters below.

▌ 2000: Quadruple BMW victory after KTM rout

After Roma's departure, the road was wide open for Sainct and company. At noon on January 23, Sainct, Gallardo, Lewis, and Brucy (their order in the final standings) rode by the pyramids, BMW flags flying high, and into the finish. They had worked a triumph unparalleled in the rally's then 22-year history. Freshly appointed BMW Motorcycle chief Marco von Maltzan exulted, "First, second, and fourth

Above: *Jubilation in Cairo after a quadruple BMW victory (left to right): Mayer, Lewis, Sainct, Gallardo, and Brucy.*

Right: *Sainct, the 2000 winner, and Auriol, winner in 1981 and 1983. In 2003, Sainct switched to KTM and won again. In 2004, he was killed in an accident.*

Right: *At the 2000 Paris-Dakar Rally, Jimmy Lewis wrote a new chapter in boxer history by coming in third in Cairo on his R 900 RR.*

Above: *R 900 RR boxers flying in formation before the start of the 2001 Paris–Dakar; Despres is at left and Lewis is at right.*

Right: *The 2001 Gauloises BMW motorcycle team with the R 900 RR. From left: Hauser, Lewis, Mayer, Deacon, Roma, Despres, and Schilcher.*

places for our F 650 single demonstrate that the F 650's victory of the previous year was no fluke. And the boxer also made an impressive comeback."

▮ 2001: Luck runs out on the final run

Four riders went to the start on the R 900 RR: new recruits Spanish ex-KTM pilot Joan "Nani" Roma, the Frenchman Cyril Despres, and old hands Jimmy Lewis (United States) and John Deacon (U.K.). Andrea Mayer (Germany) embarked on the 10,825-kilometer odyssey with a technically unchanged F 650 RR. BMW had hired KTM International's ex-chief, Norbert Schilcher, as the new team boss.

Organizer Hubert Auriol had reacted to criticism by making the rally more competitive again, limiting the number of service workers along with service infrastructure. Four marathon stages lead far from airfields and civilization; riding

skill would once more take precedence.

The rally boxers were again set up by HPN, with weight optimized in numerous details. A titanium spring on the shock and a magnesium rear-axle housing reduced the R 900 RR's dry weight exactly to the mandatory minimum weight of 190 kilograms. In the wind tunnel, BMW engineers had considerably whittled down the machine's wind resistance while improving rider protection. The twin-cylinder engine, reworked by Munich tuner Helmut Mader, now developed 90 horsepower and delivered muscular torque throughout the speed range. Four tanks held a total of 54 liters of fuel (main tank: 34 liters; central tank under the seat: 10 liters; left and right rear tanks: 4 and 6 liters). The special Michelin tires were again filled with puncture-proof BIB-foam. In the previous year, however, the synthetic foam had tended to dissolve at 180 kilometers per hour and high temperature.

What amounted to the Dakar's dress rehearsal, Dubai's Desert Challenge from November 7 to 11 drove up expectations: victory for Lewis, places third and fourth for Despres and Deacon, and a win in the women's class for Andrea Mayer. Only Roma's luck was bad: He had dropped out on the last day, while in the lead, because of a defective ignition.

The decisive event, however, the 23rd Paris-Dakar, meant to bring BMW its third consecutive victory, saw all its brightest hopes fade like a desert mirage. This time nothing could stop KTM: with the Italian Fabrizio Meoni, the Austrians gained a well deserved victory, also taking the next four places. The first BMW came only in sixth place, John Deacon's R 900 RR, followed by Jimmy Lewis's boxer. Cyril Despres was back in 13th place. Consolation came, once again, from Andrea Mayer, who dominated the women's ranking (30th place in a field of 142 participants). The overall 2001 rally victory went to Jutta Kleinschmidt and co-pilot Andreas Schulz on Mitsubishi, Kleinschmidt thus became the first woman to win the long-distance race.

Everything had looked so good for the blue-and-whites. Nani Roma took three stage victories on his R 900 RR and had reason to hope for an overall victory in the two-wheel category. But on the tenth stage, he made a braking error and flew over the handlebars. The boxer landed on Roma's right leg, and he landed in the hospital, ending his involvement in the contest. Already on the fifth day, Jimmy Lewis injured his wrist, and on the last, he broke his collarbone. John

Deacon's chances of victory vanished after problems at the start and a time penalty. Whoever had hoped that BMW would take the defeat in stride and step back to the plate in 2002 was sorely disappointed. The management cancelled the entire Dakar program, leaving the field uncontested to the competition.

Fatal accident after the BMW exit

By bowing out, BMW had probably taken the right decision. In the following years, the desert rally's image underwent a steep decline, primarily because of accidents that killed spectators and cost two ex-BMW riders their lives. On August 8, 2001, 10-time British enduro champion John Deacon

Top: Andrea Mayer won the 2001 women's ranking on the single-cylinder F 650 RR.

Above: After Jutta, Lewis could not bring the R 900 RR over the finish line.

died in a fatal crash at the Master Rally. Three-time Dakar winner Richard Sainct (KTM in 2003) broke his neck in a crash on September 29, 2004, in a special stage of the Pharaohs Rally in Egypt. Fabrizio Meoni, Dakar winner in 2001 and 2002 on KTM, died January 11, 2005, in a fall during the Paris-Dakar. According to unofficial statistics, a total of 24 motorcyclists, 21 race-car drivers, 28 co-drivers and team-members, 23 spectators, 4 journalists, and 1 policeman perished at the Paris-Dakar and other major rallys.

HP2 factory involvement

Renewed involvement in the Paris-Dakar was out of the question (at least at press-time). With their HP2, especially developed for hard off-road use, the Bavarians nevertheless did not hesitate to venture onto difficult terrain. The successful premiere took place in May 2005 at the infamous Erzberg Race.

BMW Motorcycle Enduro Team Feil competed in Austria with top-tier riders Simo Kirssi, Jimmy Lewis, and Christian Pfeiffer, the previous year's victor. With a phenomenal second run on Saturday, the Finn Kirssi secured the overall victory in the Iron Road Prologue in a field of more than 1,000 competitors. He ran the 13.3-kilometer course over rough rock and scree in a new record time of 00:09;02.67. The Dakar tested American Jimmy Lewis placed fifth; Pfeiffer took second place. In June 2007, the HP2 won the royal class and the prologue at the Erzberg race, once again with Simo Kirssi in the saddle. Under Berti Hauser, four more factory HP2s took good places.

It wasn't only in Austria that the HP2 met with fast success. In July 2006, with factory rider Kirssi joining Casey Yarrow, BMW entered the 84th edition of the U.S. hill-climb event to the 4,300-meter summit of Pikes Peak (Race to the Clouds). In Colorado, in the off-road factory team's first participation in the 21-kilometer course with 156 curves, the Californian won the Exhibition Class for motorcycles with diplacements above 750cc. Rookie Yarrow placed fifth in the unofficial overall ranking, while breaking the course record. Kirssi followed at seven seconds, also at an average speed of almost 100 kilometers per hour. With these successes, BMW had sufficiently proven the HP2's potential on the international scene. Its second iron in the fire was the 450 Sport Enduro (see pages 152-153).

Above left: *Chris Pfeiffer on the factory-HP2 enduro at the 2006 Erzberg Rodeo. The track at Pikes Peak in Colorado was equally dusty.*

Left: *HP2 racer Jimmy Lewis in 2005 at the Erzberg, where he came in fifth.*

Off-road and street GS specials

The fascination exerted by the BMW enduros can be enhanced with tuning procedures. All GS models are popular in sidecar rider circles. Because the trend to customized motorcycles has only increased in the past few years, the tuning industry has been inspired to the most varied modifications by the four-valve versions, as it once was by the two-valvers. From moderately optimized standard motorcycles to fun bikes with street tires, by way of rally machines, there's a lot on offer.

Describing the full breadth of the current offering would take us far beyond the confines of the current chapter. We will thus confine ourselves to a few select examples, while honoring the pioneers of the craft. It should be self-evident that, depending on the level of complexity, tuned examples can cost up to twice the price of a basic model. This is especially true of sidecar machines, for which anything is possible, from simple conversions with standard fork and wheels to off-road capable special trikes.

▌ Schek: Enduros for real off-road racer

For many years, Herbert Schek was one of the people who really counted in off-road racing. He took part in the Six Days a whopping 25 times; in 1967, at Garmisch, he won the gold medal. Besides this, the German had been European champion twice, and 11-time German champion (sometimes also on Maico machines). His close relationship with Maico yielded a super-light off-road bike that combined the boxer with chassis parts from the Swabian manufacturer. These efforts then also greatly contributed to the development of the G/S. As if this were not enough: For BMW France, Schek set up the motorcycle on which Frenchman Hubert Auriol won the 1983 Paris-Dakar Rally. For the factory team around Gaston Rahier, which took part in the Paris-Dakar in 1984, Schek built four machines, went to the start himself, and won the marathon ranking.

While the two-valve boxers remained in production, Scheck was among the most renowned tuners for

private clients. He developed a 1,010cc conversion with 67 horsepower on an 800-engine basis. The R 100 GS also got extra juice from Schek, though it retained the standard machine's 980cc displacement. With the Krauser four-valve heads, 70 horsepower at 7,300 rpm was possible for both variants. For the front suspension, the customer had a choice of the original fork with retrofitted air assistance, or various special forks with up to 280 millimeters of spring travel. In addition, a Monolever swingarm with 5-centimeter extension was available. In the interim,

Schek had largely retired from business. His daughter Cornelia now manages the company. It continues to service the tuning market with conversions and special parts.

▌ HPN: High-tech racers for the desert

Hubert Auriol bagged his first Paris-Dakar in 1981 on a GS that shared hardly anything with the standard machine. The machine had been set up under contract by the HPN tuning company, founded in 1979 and based in Seibersdorf, Bavaria. HPN stands

Above: A GS HPN set up for the 1984 Paris-Dakar Rally by HPN.

Left: A two-valve GS from the early 1990s, tuned and rendered rally-worthy by Richard Schalber.

for Alfred Halbfeld, Klaus Pepperl, and Michael Neher. The latter left the business some time ago.

HPN-prepared machines won at the 1982 and 1985 Paris-Dakar, took first place at the Pharaohs Rally in 1984, in the 1985 1,000-kilometer Baja California Race, and have won numerous marathon rankings. The likes of Hubert Auriol, Gaston Rahier, Eddy Hau, and Richard Schalber have won on BMW boxers tuned by HPN. In 1999, HPN was back in the news: BMW contracted the team with setting up the desert boxer on a four-valve basis (see pages 166-173). HPN currently supports BMW Team's racing involvement at the Baja race, the Erzberg Rodeo, Pikes Peak, and so on.

But who are HPN's private clients? "They are racers and long-distance riders who buy our skills in all possible variations," explains Klaus Pepperl. "Depending on the application, our clients can choose between different tuning kits and a range of off-road accessories. From basic conversions with reinforced frames, special Cardan shafts, and White Power upside-down forks to dual Paralever swingarms and different engine-tuning options, just about everything is possible." For example, Rahier and Hau's Baja racer was replicated as a 196-kilogram racer.

To this day, frame and suspension optimization lies at the core of HPN tuning, but HPN's rally experience also has performance-enhancing effects. The two-valve boxer of the time was inspired by the 1986 Paris-Dakar machine and developed about 65 horsepower for 1,043cc of displacement.

HPN did not leave it at a mere shortening of the cylinders and installation of forged pistons. Much effort was invested in securing engine and transmission lubrication under extreme conditions and in reinforcing the transmission.

As HPN is involved to this day in BMW's off-road activities, tuning for four-valve motors, including the HP2, is available to the latter's clientele. A wide range of frame reinforcements and items such as a 23-liter tank are already on offer for the light boxer. The aim is almost always the same: enhanced off-road and competitive capability.

Above: *For years, HPN built rally-winning motorcycles on a two-valve GS base.*

Above right: *WUDO's ultra-light and aesthetically pleasing scrambler prototype from 1995.*

Right: *A Schek BMW from the early 1990s, with 1,010cc, 67 horsepower, and a special chassis.*

WUDO: Fun-bikes on the GS

BMW dealer Helmut Wustenhofer's involvement with the blue-and-white brand goes back to 1975. To hold on to his customers in the competitive Rhein-Ruhr region, he early on developed tuning kits and special accessories, also for the Munich enduros. As a racer, Wustenhofer still tuned his motors himself in the early 1970s. It was only in the 1980s that for economic reasons he partly adopted the developments of his dealer colleague Fallert, later also drawing tuning parts from Siebenrock. Four special GS conversions demonstrate the versatility of WUDO in the 1980s and 1990s. The Ivory R 100, with its half-fairing and extended seat, was set up as a travel-enduro. Like the Ivory, the Hot Chocolate model was upgraded with a White Power suspension. With its narrow-profile tires and a six-speed transmission featuring a long transmission ratio, this 75-horsepower racer nevertheless felt most comfortable on asphalt. The stripped-down Speedster muscle bike is based on the 1000 Paralever GS. In 1995, a lightweight scrambler with an off-road capable special chassis displayed great similarity to the original GS. For the big four-valve GS bikes, besides various accessories, Wustenhofer developed a dual-ignition system, shortly before BMW began equipping its 1150 GS with this improvement, standard.

In contrast to the factory system, WUDO's kit lent itself to problem-free and economical retrofitting for the 1100 and 1150 models produced until 2002. As their cylinder heads do not offer any space in the timing chain housing area, the two spark plugs must be located on the upper side. Parallel adaptation of ignition and other electronic systems is required. Responsible for all this work was the ignition specialist Rudolf Kallenbach (QTech), also with a long-standing dedication to optimizing boxer engines. For the current 1200 as well as its forerunner, WUDO also offers fun bike conversions with 17-inch street tires and convenient accessories. A special item for the R 1150 GS is the nifty shorter sidepipe exhaust weighing a full 8 kilograms less than the original, manufactured for WUDO in the Netherlands by BSM.

Fallert: FM boxer with vertical shafts

As early as 1926, the father of well-known boxer specialist Werner Fallert founded a BMW dealership. Fallert Jr. took on its management early on. In 1970, the company moved to Achern, dedicating itself increasingly to development and marketing of accessories for BMW motorcycles, along with the tuning of boxer engines. Participation in numerous reliability runs and off-road competitions developed a close relationship to racing.

Fallert was very active as a designer. In the 1970s, when he suspected that BMW would stop dedicating further effort to boxer development, he embarked on construction of a new

Above: *A Witec four-valve RC 1100 Rally chassis, late 1990s.*

Above right: *An R 1100 GS in long-distance trim by WUDO.*

Right: *This R 1100 GS was converted to a moderate fun-bike with small front wheel.*

engine. His FM boxer with 1,000cc displacement had a cylinder angle of 170 degrees, which made it, strictly speaking, a wide-angle V-twin. Two valves in each cylinder head were actuated via vertical shafts and single cam control; the crankshaft featured a center bearing.

Fallert's masterpiece developed 105 horsepower in its carburetor version; trials with injection yielded a few extra horsepower. Yet Fallert had to recognize that mass production at market prices was illusory, and so he eventually shelved the project. Still, racer Konrad

Stuckler won a few events on the powerful FM. There was a PR effect, as a result of which many customers now wanted tuned boxers. Fallert responded with development of sophisticated kits to boost displacement and performance for the BMW R models.

He brought the 800 two-valve engine to 971cc, while holding output to 50 horsepower through installation of reducers in the intake nozzle; though torque band in the lower speed range improved markedly. Maximum torque increased by more than 10 percent to 67.5 Nm at 4,000

rpm. With shortened cylinders, special pistons, and some detail work, Fallert conjured 65 horsepower from the same displacement. A lighter crankshaft and 40-millimeter Bing carburetors boosted performance to 80 horsepower. With Mikuni carburetors and roller tappets, which Fallert developed from an idea by designer Ludwig Apfelbeck, 90 horsepower was within reach.

▌ Fine tuning for two- and four-valve boxers

With their double-joint swingarm, the GS models provided the basis for Fallert's thoroughbred street machines. A prime example being the curve-loving Dolomiti, featuring an 18-inch front wheel. Special fork triple clamps, cast PVM three-spoke wheels, a special half fairing, and a semi-raised two-in-two muffler were some of the Dolomiti's salient features.

For the R 1150 GS, Fallert developed a tuning package with modified cylinders and pistons, reworked heads, and altered-valve timing. For a compression ratio of 11.3:1, the boxer developed more torque and 98 horsepower. A tuning chip is also available for models built before 2000. In the later 1150s, engine management is already supported by an optimized chip, ex-works. For the 1200, there is an exhaust system with legal 103 horsepower. Meanwhile, Hans-Peter Huber and Dirk Hagenmeier have taken over management of the Baden agency.

▌ Wunderlich: Real variety

Erich Wunderlich originally made a name for himself with upgrades for the Yamaha XT/SR 500, but since the 1990s, BMW models have taken center stage. The company advertises the largest accessories program for the brand, and it goes without saying that GS models get their fair share. Especially in demand are high-quality aluminum case sets, light-alloy engine protection plates, and windshields.

What Wunderlich has up his sleeve for the four-valve machines becomes apparent, for example, in the R 80 GS Basic-inspired Basic Beast. Among the individually available conversion parts figure a touring windshield with Hella headlight, ergonomically correct seat, crash bars, large hand protectors, LED taillight, and a special side stand. With chip tuning, a different pre-silencer, and a Remus exhaust, Wunderlich boosts the 1100 boxer to 96 horsepower

Opposite top: *Werner Fallert's 1989 Dolomiti, with a 75-horsepower two-valve boxer.*
Opposite bottom: *A Fassbender fun-bike on an R 1150 GS base.*

Left: *The R 1200 GS with full Wunderlich long-distance travel set on a 2006 tour through Spain. Note the aerodynamically optimized cases and special tank with extra headlights.*

Below: *The R 1200 GS Jararaca by Wunderlich, 2007.*

Bottom: *2007 Wunderlich R 1200 GS with fine details and special two-tone paint job.*

and maximum torque of 113 Nm. On an R 1200 GS base, Wunderlich offers the SilverX tourer, as well as the Jararaca special models. Lacking the characteristic beak, with a dynamically styled cockpit, 19/17-inch lower-profile tires, and wave brake rotors, this conversion, named after a venomous South American snake, comes off very mean. A high-lift camshaft and other refinements ensure that the machine lives up to its name.

On the other hand, the 10-kilogram lighter R 1200 GS-WR appeals to hard enduro riders. Dirk Thelen won a respectable fourth place at the 2005 Agadir Rally on its racing version, against a slew of much lighter one-cylinder KTM's. The WR features approximately 40 millimeters more ground clearance, this in addition to an engine guard, high-strength BEHR aluminum rims, raised handlebars, wave brake rotors, and ultra-light ICP fairing parts.

▌ **Touratech: Roaring start with the GS**

Since 1999, Touratech has mainly dedicated itself to the F single-cylinders. Hard enduro and rally conversions are company founders' Herbert Schwarz and Jochen Schanz's area of predilection. Their rally experience largely flows into development of their tuning parts. Here Touratech can point

to impressive successes. For example, with their Touratech F 650's, team rider Gilles Algay and motorcycle journalist Michael Griep for the first time rode BMW machines with fuel injection into the finish.

At least as much as through its chassis optimizations, the Black Forest duo made the name Touratech a household word in GS circles with its "IMO" digital tripmaster and sturdy Zega aluminum travel cases. Two conversions on an R 1100/1150 basis diplay the Touratech repertoire. As the Desierto, the four-valve boxer with 41-liter tank and a redesigned front end with dual headlights becomes a long-distance enduro for the remotest tracks. In contrast, the ReVamp, presented in 2003, with its 22-liter plastic tank, front and rear end with altered appearance, and a 15-kilogram weight reduction is more fleet footed than the original. In 2002, with its TB 652, Touratech jumped the gun on the new Xchallenge by presenting a version of the F 650 GS slimmed down by a good 30 kilograms, along with a client version of the 2002 Rally single-cylinder.

▌AC Schnitzer: Luxury conversions from Aachen
The major auto and motorcycle dealer's tuning shop is increasingly focused on two- and three-wheeled vehicles. In this, AC Schnitzer has limited its GS model conversions to upgrades for sporty street riding. The off-road

segment is covered in its capacity as authorized dealer for Touratech. When it comes to enhanced street riding fun, 17 inches are almost mandatory. Matching the V-performance wheels, AC has custom rims at the ready. Add to this adapted side coverings, front mudguards, cockpit fairings, and Remus "Revolution" exhausts. The firm offers a similar kit for the R 1150 GS.

In concert with White Power, AC Schnitzer developed EDS Chassis Tuning. This system enables the rider to adjust the chassis from the cockpit via a push-button, even while in movement, to current payload and road conditions. ACS also attended to the F 650 CS. In order to upgrade the Scarver's looks, the tank bag received a redesigned cover, and the front end was modified.

▌Specialty shops from Michel to Rösner
Besides the above-mentioned specialists, Gunther Michel dedicated himself in earlier years to upgrading BMW enduros. Michel has set up numerous racing machines, including powerful BoT racers.

Top right: *A heavily laden Wunderlich-modified R 1200 GS on a long Asia tour, 2006. Everything on this machine was custom.*

Above and right: *In 2006 in Aachen, AC Schnitzer presented an HP2 as an aggressive supermoto with small front wheel and special street tires.*

The Wunderlich GS in Spain, 2006.

For the two-valve engine, the company offered tuning levels up to 1,042cc and 75 horsepower, along with specialties such as dual ignition. Michel optimized the chassis with a redesigned suspension (fork springs and shock from White Power) along with wire spoke wheels.

Among insiders, the tuning shop of Fritz Lottmann also rates as top notch. The Munich tuner has worked closely with HPN and took a hand in the setup in successful engines for the winning machines of Eddy Hau and Richard Schalber, among others. Lottmann originated such tricks as the oil fill bore in the left cylinder cover, an oil pan spacer ring, along with mounting of the older boxers' rocker arms via thrust bearings. Nowadays, Lottmann's tuning program also covers the four-valve engines, down to the best-selling R 1200 GS.

Weight reduction with a simultaneous increase in rigidity is a goal also shared by Hebert Gletter. For the two- and four-valve boxers, he developed tubular stainless steel rear ends that are as graceful as they are

sturdy. The tuner's (earlier employed by Schek) bag of tricks also features exhaust components and custom triple clamps. Schalber equally stresses lightweight construction in his two-valve GS trimmed for hard enduro, also available with upside-down fork. The star feature: the lightweight rear frame can be replaced in minutes with the original for riding with a passenger. The lightweight alloy triple clamps, a special front brake, and the raised exhaust also contribute to weight reduction.

Originally dedicated to Honda's African Twin, the African Queen later also took on the R 1100 GS. With its light, one piece fairing and 21-inch front wheel, the Bavarian Queen's appearance tends to rally; various components underscore this direction. The Bavarians also offer accessories for the newer GS models, along with the F 650 GS.

With the fun bike or rather supermoto wave, the four-valve GS increasingly got "short legs," or small wheels with narrow-profile tires. A number of variations on these curve-eaters were offered by BMW dealers such as Fassbender (Krefeld), WUDO

(Holzwickede), ABO (Wuppertal), Mertinke (Frankfurt), Rosner (Rodermark), Kuhn (Uhingen), or the Kassel agency under the direction of current services general manager, Bernd Scherer. Sharp fun bikes on an R 1150 GS basis are also cranked out by Team Métisse (Auenwald), minus the controversial "duck bill" mudguard, with the R 1150 GS Strada, and by the Regensburg specialist PIA, with the GS/SM. The latter machine turns heads with a disc wheel and 190/50 tire on the rear. M TEC upgraded the 1200 Boxer as a supermoto or to the Black Pearl, with the aid of various carbon parts. Yet the fun bike camp split into two opposing factions: some tuners retaining the GS steering geometry, while others think it absolutely necessary to adapt the caster to the 17-inch front wheel.

Before BMW itself saw the gap in the market and offered its supermoto version of the HP2, others, like AC Schnitzer or Fassbender, had mounted the lightweight boxer on 17-inch wheels. The latter went on to bestow a small wheel to the F 650 GS, while he was at it. On the other hand, in 2007, M TEC presented an HP8 as an evolved SM-HP2 .

Right: *The WR2 on an R 1200 GS base by Wunderlich was described as aggressive.*

Below: *R 1200 GS street conversion by AC Schnitzer.*

Middle left: *WUDO 1200 fun-bike.*

Middle right and bottom left: *Scarver and R 1150 GS by ASC.*

Above: *F 650 GS "fun" by Fassbender.*

GS sidecars

The popularity of sidecar machines on a GS goes back a long way. Whereas the two-valve models were the predominant beasts of burden until the mid-1990s, nowadays, it's almost exclusively the four-valvers that are used for this purpose. Today as yesterday, the offering ranges from three-wheel soft enduros to rally-ready special machines.

The boxer sidecar machines can look back to a proud tradition in enduro racing, having sometimes even been converted to chain drive. Until the beginning of the 1970s, the brawny twin cylinders from Munich set the tone at most off-road racing events (see introduction, pages 5-21). When the first R 80 G/S appeared in 1980, a new trend was born in travel and rally sidecar machines on an enduro basis.

The first specialist to take on the G/S was the traditionalist British Wasp brand, which, along with EML, had once dominated the off-road segment. Wasp boss Robin Rhind-Tutt built a new chassis around the boxer engine, and welded a sidecar to it, which, in motocross fashion, merely featured a platform and a handrail. A pivoted fork provided front suspension. In the rear, the single-sided swingarm yielded to a dual-arm version with a couple of special Bilstein shocks.

Wasp's German importer and co-designer, Otto Hermeling, undertook to gain street authorization for the lug tire BMW three-wheeler, offering the Wasp conversion in several equipment variations. Included in the scope of delivery was a 40-liter fuel tank located under the aluminum luggage box,

which could be used as a seat. This not only extended the range of the boxer, which proved rather fuel hungry in sidecar application, but brought extra weight to bear on the side wheel.

The HU company also used the Wasp chassis to convert G/S and GS models. However, Horst Ullrich lengthened and reinforced the rear-wheel swingarm in his designs. He also altered the chassis geometry. Accessories such as an exterior oil filter, an oil cooler with thermostat, enduro fairing, and extra headlight made the HU-BMW a super three-wheeler for touring in difficult terrain. As an alternative to the twice-damped dual swingarm for rear-wheel suspension, Ullrich came up with a sophisticated cantilever version with progressive linkage; this was installed in

Sidecar machines on a two-valve boxer base.

Above: *A Walter three-wheeler, mid-1990s.*

Below left: *A Stern machine with Dnjepr sidecar.*

Below right: *An off-road design by Ullrich with Wasp chassis, early 1990s.*

his desert capable "Sable" special model, which tipped the scales at 282 kilograms.

The GS sidecar machine offered by EML dealer Berglar was more conventional in design. Like the Wasp conversions, it was based on a special chassis. To this, Berglar bolted the the EML car, in which the passenger enjoyed cramped protection, as in the

Sidecar machines with four-valve boxers in 2000.

Left: *HU-R 1100 GS Voyage with full-swing chassis.*

Bottom left: *A Wasp-R 1100 GS Tornado.*

Bottom right: *A Stern R 1100 GS "light" model.*

■ **In demand: Sidecar machines with four-valve engines**
Since the four-valve GS's first appearance in 1994, an extremely varied offering of corresponding sidecar conversions has developed. With its "Light" three-wheeler, Stern probably offers the most economical variant for beginners and occasional riders without serious off-road ambitions. Telelever and standard tires remain in use. As a full sport touring machines equipped with the custom RXS instead of the classic Lucky sidecar, the GS models feature a pivoted fork in front along with durable auto tires. The company also offers a sharp enduro version for expedition-style travel.

Besides Stern, only the new Dutch manufacturer TripTeq and R.O.S./Schepsky trust the Telelever. The latter, however, thoroughly reinforce it and adapt the steering geometry using different aluminum handlebars. This technology is also available from TripTeq. Hermeling/Wasp are the only ones to employ double-pivot steering, also used in the Tornado street sidecar machines. Their advantages (separate wheel guidance, springing, and steering) are offset by the serious offroad handicap of a much too narrow

off-road sidecars of the 1960s. Falk Hartmann had earlier constructed a somewhat similar three-wheeler. He had been active in off-road racing himself, also acting as representative for EML, today W-Tec, in Germany. His version of a three-wheeled street enduro also featured a polyester gondola but had 16-inch composite wheels.

Hedingham importer Uwe Schmidt designed his ETH off-road cruiser ("Enduro Touring Hedingham") around the boxer; its most striking feature was an aerodynamic front fairing. Helmut Walter now also offered a sidecar, with a rounded front end and a trailer. In contrast, Peter Sauer, finding enduro qualities in the R 100 R, combined these

with a genuine off-road sidecar. Ralph Kalich first modified the GS for a low-budget conversion with telescopic fork, custom wheels, and the cheap Czech Velorex sidecar, and then as the basis for a swinging Velorex sidecar machine.

Use of the Paralever remains controversial in the sidecar riding community. Yet economics at least speak in favor of retaining the original rear-wheel suspension. Experience confirms that its engineering strength is adequate for simpler three-wheelers and moderate yearly mileage. Whoever needs to travel with lots of baggage or ride fast off-road, however, is better off going with thorough conversions à la W-Tec/EML or HU.

turning circle. Because of this, the Wasp four-valver, which is also visually reminiscent of the street Tornados, is best suited for trail riding.

By contrast, HU and Mobec conversions allow professional off-road use. Horst Ullrich plants the four-valve boxer within an entirely new, fully welded chassis with sturdy dual swingarms. The steel wheels mounted with various tire variants are interchangeable (just like the shocks), which can be a life saver in the event of problems far from civilization.

▮ Mobec: Powered sidecar with viscous clutch

In the case of Mobec, the sidecar wheel is powered via an automobile viscous clutch. In this system, the rotational speed difference between both drive wheels determines the degree of power transmission to the right: The more slippage at the rear wheel, the more the sidecar wheel kicks in. This renders a differential lock, such as that found on rigid TWD drives, unnecessary. Moreover, the system guarantees performances on asphalt matching those of conventional, single wheel-driven sidecar machines. This is because, with Mobec's Duo Drive system, the sidecar wheel remains unpowered as long as the rear wheel retains full grip.

As a mechanical alternative to the Visco system, which Mobec also offers for two-valvers, individual designer Holger Frank developed a manually engageable side wheel drive. Power transmission occurs via driveshaft and chain. The tractive assistance is intended for use only on slippery terrain.

As the 1100/1150 in their time, the R 1200 GS is popular among sidecar

machine riders. And this despite initially coming in for criticism because of its CAN-bus onboard network's partial vulnerability to malfunction, and although the weight and performance advantages versus the R 1150 GS are less obvious. EZS was the first to use the 1200, in 2004, to present its new family Munro sidecar machine. It goes without saying that there were no tours through the bush in the program for this heavy two-seater with auto tires. The following year, W-Tec/EML's current one-seater, the S1, celebrated its premiere alongside R 1200 GS. Despite street tires, this combination already

Above: *The R 1100 GS Duo Drive Zero by Mobec with viscous-clutch sidecar drive.*

Bottom left: *A W-Tec machine with EML S1 sidecar on an R 1200 GS.*

Bottom right: *The Stern RXS on an 1150 GS.*

allows some brisk trail riding. Front-wheel suspension was handled by the custom ExtensoDive-telescopic fork with spring struts separated from the columns. The R 1200 GS's presentation was overshadowed by a tragic event at W-Tec/EML: company founder Hennie Winkelhuis, a pioneer of the modern

Dirk Thelen successfully competed in international rallies on an HP2 prepared by Wunderlich. This photo was taken in 2007 in the desert state of Qatar.

street and enduro sidecar machine, died on May 25, 2007, after a short illness. He was 59.

While the R 1200 GS is now converted by a number of sidecar companies, the same is unlikely to ever happen to the HP2. Its base price alone should preclude such an undertaking.

▌Small but good: F 650 with sidecar

In contrast to the popular GS models, the F 650 hardly found any friends in sidecar machine riding circles, and this despite all its obvious qualities. Even though Walter, Stern, Mobec, and Hermann's Motorcycle Shop's produced some very attractive combinations with their

single-seater touring sidecar. From 2002, Mobec also offered its fantastic Duo-Drive system for the F 650 GS and CS.

Yet the only one to produce a bona fide enduro version was Norbert Degenhardt. The old off-road hand invested great efforts in the single-cylinder BMW for racing, and his combination is actually street legal. Degenhardt integrated the single-cylinder into a modified ELM chassis and promptly won the 1998 German enduro championship with co-rider Carsten Bachmann. A year later, Armin Böhler rode the F 650 in the German motocross championship, to little effect against the dominant two-stroke machines.

New and improved: The R 1200 GS for 2008

The R 1200 GS, introduced in 2004, rounded out its impressive career with a production record. On July 27, 2007, only three and a half years after its launch, the 100,000th unit (including the Adventure) of the big enduro rolled off the Berlin assembly line. A few months later, at the Milano show in November, along with the entirely new parallel twin GS models (F 650 GS and F 800 GS), BMW presented a new edition of the best-selling boxer, thoroughly redesigned in many important details. It was again available in two versions, the R 1200 GS and R 1200 GS Adventure. Although few of the improvements of the second series were apparent at first sight, they were numerous. Most important: 5 extra horsepower, a reinforced six-speed transmission with altered ratios, secondary drive with a shortened gear ratio for improved acceleration, optimized chassis, and revamped tank–seat combination (for details, see box). The R 1200 GS/2 base price (excluding ABS and ESA) was 12,500 euros. The revamped R 1200 GS Adventure cost 14,000 euros.

BMW did well to make the world's most popular large enduro fit for additional years at the top with a

Right: *Luminous Namibia Orange for the front fender and tank cover.*

thorough revamp. The pressure from the competition had grown significantly over the last few years. Heavy hitters of the enduro scene, such as the Honda Varadero 1000, the KTM 990 Adventure Traveller, and the Triumph Tiger, were poised to relieve BMW of market share. With a large-scale comparative test through the Alps, the editors of *Motorrad* magazine aimed to settle the question of whether the 2008 modified R 1200 GS could assert itself against

R 1200 GS/2 features

- More dynamic drive with improved spunk in the upper rpm range
- Engine performance boosted by 5 percent to 105 horsepower
- Maximum engine speed increased to 8,000 rpm and a broader usable speed range
- Altered primary and secondary transmission ratios for markedly improved traction and acceleration
- Redesigned six-speed transmission with enlarged bearing sizes, as well as optimized shifting kinematics for even more precise selection
- Electronic chassis adjustment via the optional Enduro ESA (never before available on an enduro); additional gains in agility, touring, and offroad ability through individualized spring and damper tuning
- Electro-hydraulic spring pre-load adjustment of front and rear suspension as part of the Enduro ESA
- Optimized ergonomics through new butted aluminum handlebars together with new finger-protectors and a reconfigured seat
- Fuel-level indicator with broader measurement range
- Optimized battery charging, improved generator performance
- More dynamic design with highlighted enduro features
- Color variants: Titanium Silver Metallic, Slate Black Metallic Matt, Namibia Orange, and Tanzanite Blue
- Special equipment and customizing accessories (selection): Enduro ESA, BMW Motorrad Integral ABS (semi-integral and disengageable), RDC, ASC, chromed exhaust system, heated grips, additional headlights, finger protectors, pannier holders, cross spoke wheels, onboard computer with oil-level warning, anti-theft system with remote control, Vario cases, Vario topcases, tank-bag, softbags, inner bags, carbon-fiber front mudguard and rear splash guard, LED blinkers, Akrapovic sport muffler, extra-wide enduro footrests, handlebar crossbrace, tinted windshield, low rider seat (820 millimeter), or adjustable high (880–900 millimeter)

Left: *Tanzanite Blue. Both colors clearly have African origins.*

its competitors. The trial began in December 2007 and was published in the magazine's February 1, 2008, issue. Spoiler alert: With 695 points, the new GS prevailed over its rivals, head and shoulders! Still, the three-cylinder Triumph, which had matured over the years, managed to take second place while in earlier days it couldn't hold a candle to the GS. At 635 points, the Honda rolled in third, and the much-praised KTM came in a disappointing last, with only 617 points.

There are many reasons why the BMW so clearly outclassed the rest:

"Even off road, the 1200 puts up a tough fight."

It was the best machine in categories for frame and suspension, along with everyday riding, safety, and cost. In the engine category, it only had to surrender a few points to the more flexible and agile Triumph. Reviewer Thomas Schmieder summed it all up: "GS seal of approval: the BMW impresses with the greatest versatility. On the highway, it's as fast as it is stable, absolutely (long-distance) travel-worthy, and unbeatable in everyday riding. Even off-road, the 1200 puts up a tough fight. Well thought-out details intersect with the quartet's only shaft drive. For example, the handlebars move forward by rotating the clamps (as in the KTM). The . . . cases can

be adjusted in width via a telescopic mechanism of brilliant simplicity. . . . Tops: suspension adjustment, riding characteristics with passenger. . . . The best braking is found on the BMW and the Honda: especially good grip and modulation with the GS. . . . Once paid for, the GS is inexpensive in everyday operation: economical, with a mobility guarantee and 10,000 kilometer service intervals."

▌ The new GS—top bike in comparative test

Prominent among the now 105-horsepower twin-cylinder boxer's strengths were the extremely low fuel consumption of 5.1 liters per 100

kilometers super unleaded on the road and 6.2 liters per 100 kilometers at 130 kilometers per hour on the freeway. In mixed riding, the KTM, with its twin-cylinder 1-liter engine, consumed about 1 liter more. Yet, the boxer engine left a somewhat contradictory impression during testing: "Throttle up, throttle down—in sharp turns this may cause some anxiety on the BMW. Its performance is just out of this world—as long as the knock control system doesn't start curbing the boxer above 5,000 rpm. And the dry clutch simply stinks under heavy stress."

Acceleration was tested at 0 to 100 kilometers in 3.6 seconds, 60 to 100 kilometers in 4.0 seconds, and a top speed of 213 kilometers an hour—not bad for a machine weighing 244 kilograms (with a full 20-liter tank). Only the Triumph was spunkier (0 to 100 kilometers an hour in 3.4 seconds) and faster (220 kilometers an hour), its 1,050-cc engine developing 115 horsepower, thus a higher output per liter.

■ Hi-revving boxer engine, now with 105 horsepower

Though corporate press officers frequently lean toward hyperbole and like to make their products seem better than they actually are, you have to credit the BMW media team for presenting new developments in a factual and technically informative manner. The R 1200 GS/2 is a case in point. As seen above, statements were largely supported by professional motorcycle testers. BMW was certainly not off the mark with the following: "The new GS offers sovereign performance, the highest level of comfort, and a wide spectrum of applications for the longest tours. Improved sprinting ability and agility guarantee maximum enjoyment on twisting highways and mountain roads. Optimized chassis and suspension characteristics provide for superb riding characteristics on the road—and off."

As in precursor models, a torsionally stiff chassis, the Telelever front and Paralever rear suspension also provide first-class and secure riding characteristics for the 2008 GS. The extremely efficient brakes vouch for the highest level of security, even in critical situations, especially when combined with the optional 1,080 euro semi-integral ABS system. Emissions control by closed-loop three-way catalytic

Titanium Silver Metallic clearly contrasts well with the "matte" black of the seat, tank covers and front fender.

converter was, of course, standard. It probably doesn't need to be repeated that the dependable and maintenance-free Cardan drive has figured among the BMW boxers' strengths from way back. In keeping with tradition, BMW also offered a practical and thought-out luggage system for the second-generation R 1200 GS, along with custom accessories.

In construction, fundamental structure, power transmission, and air/gas mixture processing, the new R 1200 GS's engine was based on the R 1200 R motor. For use in the R 1200 GS travel enduro, this powerplant, tuned for high performance, was specifically modified, primarily in the area of motor management. If the 1,170-cc boxer engine of the precursor model had already offered majestic power development under all conditions and in every situation, the powerplant of the redesigned GS—unaltered in displacement (bore and stroke 101x73)—succeeded in upping the ante with respect to power. It now developed 105 horsepower (versus a previous 98 horsepower at 7,000 rpm in Germany, 100 horsepower everywhere else) and revved distinctly higher, with a rated speed of 7,500 rpm and maximum rpm of 8,000.

At 115 Nm, peak torque remained unchanged, though it now only became available at 5,750 rpm (versus 5,500 rpm previously). As a result of

View from the command post, a most comfortable ride that oozes security.

wholly reworked transmission ratios for all six gears, the GS now ran more dynamically, with enhanced sprinting ability in the upper half of the engine rev range, and more effectively across the entire range, as generally confirmed by the testing data.

Like past models, the new—now at 12:1, very high-compression—engine (1 Series: 11:1) can still be operated with 95-octane fuel. Set up to run on

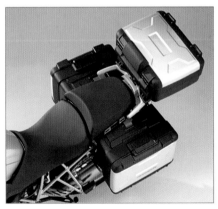

The skilled packaging of the new GS 1200 is nothing short of incredible. Everything is in the right place even if not all of it is easy to get at.

unleaded premium gasoline (RON 95), the motorcycle can also be operated on regular (RON 91) if necessary, without manual intervention, thanks to the knock control system (a useful feature while visiting faraway lands).

▌ New ratios and reinforced six-speed transmission

The redesigned six-speed transmission with enlarged bearing diameters and altered shaft clearances took account of the R 1200 GS's increased engine performance, expanded speed range, and potentially extreme operating conditions. With the forerunner model, damage to transmission bearings during hard, continuous operation had occasionally cropped up. Adaptation of transmission ratios to the more aggressive engine characteristics, along with shortening of the secondary transmission ratio from 1:2.82 to 1:2.91, resulted in distinctly better surge in the upper half of the engine speed

range, along with gains in efficiency, especially at low and medium rpm.

In the process of redesigning the transmission, the R 1200 GS also received an improved shifting mechanism. In plain English: The transmission shifts more smoothly and quietly.

Another GS premiere was ESA (electronic suspension adjustment), first available as an option on the K 1200 S from 2004. The enduro rider could now acquire this advanced safety technology at an extra 680 euros. Adapted to the special requirements of adventure travel, the system, rechristened "Enduro ESA," provided tuning of the suspension to meet the most varied operating conditions and payload situations at the push of a button. The ESA found on the K 1200 S allowed adjustment of the rear spring preload, besides electronic control of both front and rear shocks. But Enduro ESA had even more tricks up its sleeve, also featuring hydro-electric front shock preload adjustment, which provided distinctly improved bottoming-out protection off-road.

In detail, the GS's electronic suspension control distinguished between street and off-road operating modes and provided a range of specific adaptations according to rider preferences. By holding down the ESA button, the rider could "surf" between springing modes, and with a quick press, between the damping modes. The new handlebars of butted aluminum tubing were rider-friendly. As in the HP2 sport model, a couple of asymmetrically mounted clamps, rotating 180 degrees, allowed mounting in two ergonomically distinct positions. While the rear handlebar position guaranteed the best riding conditions for street and moderate off-road operation, the front handlebar setting proved particularly useful when the terrain required riding in standing position. The newly developed hand protectors, available as an option for the R 1200 GS and already installed ex-works on the R 1200 Adventure, were now directly mounted on the handlebars. For increased comfort, the seat upholstery was reinforced in the rider area.

With respect to the fuel level display, new sensor technology with an expanded measurement range and higher resolution was installed; this provided differentiated display already at maximum fuel level. Alternator performance was increased from 600 to 720 watts, and battery charging was optimized.

▌ New fairing design, fresh colors
With the slightly reworked design of fairing and its mounts, BMW wished to highlight the R 1200 GS/2's noticeably

improved dynamics. New stainless-steel covers were installed at the gas tank's forward section. The front mudguard's upper part was also new. The new look was rounded out by the now two-tone hand-protectors along with a redesigned guide vane for optimized ventilation. The reconfigured LED taillight and the white glazed blinkers had an up-to-date flair.

A range of new colors distinguished the current GS generation: fine Titanium Silver Metallic, noble Black Slate Metallic, powerful Tanzanite Blue, and luminous Namibia Orange. Cool, technologically suggestive surfaces, for instance on the silver front fender, the magnesium-colored, powder-coated fork sliders, or the magnesium-tinted head covers, reminiscent of the HP2, also contributed to the new look.

It goes without saying that BMW also provided a complete range

of special equipment and custom accessories for the new GS. These could either be ordered ex-works or subsequently installed by the dealer.

Visually, the 2007–2008 GS is distinguished from its precursor primarily by the new design of tank cover and mudguard.

Technical innovations in the second-generation R 1200 GS models are an engine with 5 extra horsepower and the optional electronically adjustable chassis. The sturdy luggage rack comes standard; the depth-adjustable aluminum cases are extra. The new GS rides on light-alloy wheels from the factory.

The revamped R 1200 GS enjoys great worldwide popularity. Once again, the latest version of the BMW travel bestseller sets the standards for its class with respect to handling, performance, safety, and comfort.

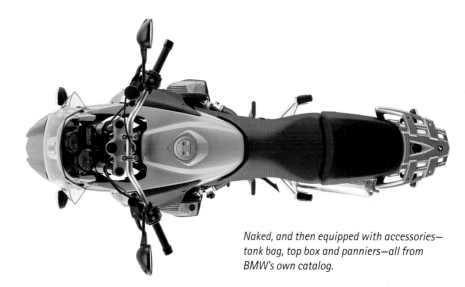

Naked, and then equipped with accessories—tank bag, top box and panniers—all from BMW's own catalog.

The 100,000th R 1200 GS

On July 27, 2007, the BMW R 1200 GS, together with its Adventure variant, set an impressive record: the 100,000th R 1200 GS rolled off the line in Berlin. Of these, 84,373 were standard GS machines and 15,627 were Adventures. No other BMW motorcycle had ever been built in such numbers in such a short time. This makes the BMW R 1200 GS the most successful BMW motorcycle of all times.

For years, the precursor model, R 1150 GS, had already held first place in registrations. From 1994 to July 2007, a total of 219,468 GS models of the four-valve boxer generation were produced.

BMW
Werk Berlin

100.000 BMW R 1200 GS.
Die erfolgreichste BMW aller Zeiten.
27. Juli 2007

July 27, 2007. An historic day, as the 100,000th R1200 GS leaves the production line in Berlin. From left: Hermann Bohrer, Vice-President of the Berlin plant, H-P Kemser, Head of Assembly, Volker Schmidt, Staff Association.

R 1200 GS Adventure Series 2

In November 2007, BMW presented what was already the third edition of the muscular long-distance travel enduro for globetrotters and adventurers: a modified R 1200 GS Adventure. Like the revamped basic model, the Adventure, weighing in at an unchanged 256 kilograms (on a full 33-liter tank), offered the typical GS mix of riding dynamics, touring, and off-road capability. Here, also, power and torque were boosted, and off-road qualities and long-distance comfort were further improved.

The 1,170-cc boxer powerplant was technically identical to that of the standard model. We won't get into the question here of whether or not increased engine speeds make sense in countries where only lower-quality fuels are available and poor road conditions dictate a moderate riding pace. In keeping with its purpose, and in contrast to the standard GS, an Adventure tends to be ridden more over rough track than on asphalt.

The reworked and reinforced six-speed transmission was, of course, also found on the Adventure. BMW just wouldn't be BMW if it hadn't managed to squeeze the most out of a well-stocked component parts bin. The customer could optionally order the Adventure with an especially short first gear if he or she placed a premium on above-average off-road climbing and

maneuvering abilities. The standard gearbox was ready set up with a shorter ratio in all six gears—just as in the basic model. The secondary transmission, at 1:2.91, was also shorter. Enlarged bearing diameters and modified shaft clearance provided extended service life in the conditions of extreme stress encountered on equipment-shredding long-haul travel.

At 210 millimeters front and 220 millimeters rear, the Telelever/Paralever suspension spring travel was again 20 millimeters longer than in the standard GS. This is a must for a motorcycle with such a radical field of application. As a first, BMW now offered the "Enduro ESA" suspension adjustment system as an option. This allowed pushbutton alteration of springing and damping to the most varied operating and payload conditions. As long as it's operating correctly, such a system surely is an advantage. Yet if it breaks down in the middle of nowhere in South America or Asia it can turn into a major headache. World travelers have long adhered to the principle of less is more. It will be interesting to see how many Adventure buyers end up shelling out the extra 680 euros for the ESA.

It remains, however, that ESA is a neat thing, per se. For the additional (in relation to the four-cylinder K 1200 sprinter) electro-hydraulic spring, preload adjustment of the front

The Adventure packs an increased frontal area than the regular GS but all to good effect.

Below: *The Adventure comes with increased weight but increased off-road capability and carrying capacity.*

GPS in the line of sight but cleverly not in the way. Note hand guards.

suspension provides clearly improved bottoming-out protection in off-road use. This is without the usually associated street-riding disadvantages, such as reduced negative shock travel or increased saddle height. As seen in the previous chapter, the "Enduro ESA" differentiates various street and off-road modes, within which the rider can program him or herself.

▌ Design modified with restraint

The Adventure's design, with its typical off-road components, remains unaltered in its basic orientation, though it was modernized in various respects. While

The Adventure, seen here with optional alloy cases, shared all the same changes for 2008–09 as the plain R 1200 GS.

the tank area was taken over from the previous model unaltered, there was an effort to impart in the Adventure an even more aggressive look, with a reconfigured upper front mudguard and a modified air-cooling vane. Though the white LED taillight and white blinkers represent concessions to motorcycle fashion, they're certainly nice to look at. New colors and surfaces gave the 2008 Adventure model a fresh look. Magnesium Metallic Matte highlighted the machine's technological bent, while red underlined its sporty side. One clear difference with the basic model was the two-tone seat matched the corresponding overall color scheme.

The second-series R 1200 GS Adventure rolled to the start with the standard equipment inherited from its forerunner model. That is, it was

considerably expanded in relation to the basic GS. Thus, its 33-liter tank allowed extremely long stages. At a constant speed of 90 kilometers per hour and a fuel consumption of 4.6 liters per 100 kilometers (calculated on the test bed), its theoretical range is about 750 kilometers. This meant that the new R 1200 GS Adventure could theoretically cover greater distances than any of its competitors. In real life, however, fuel consumption was more in the range of 6 to 7 liters per 100 kilometers, for the machine's fully loaded weight took its toll. Yet, at 7 liters per 100 kilometers, the range was still a proud 470 kilometers. With such distances over rough tracks, the rider is usually exhausted long before the gas. BMW increased the payload of its new model by 10 kilograms.

On fast freeway stages, the rider could be thankful for the high and wide windshield, which deflects the airflow largely without turbulence and provides effective protection at high speed, especially to the head and upper body. The machine reached speeds of well over 200 kilometers per hour, though this is not recommended with cases mounted. Specially configured flaps mounted behind the windshield also reduced the air current in the lower-back area. Thanks to its adjustable tilt angle, the windshield could be adapted to the sitting position for riders of all sizes. Wide enduro footrests, along with adjustable foot brake and shift levers, took account of widely varying conditions, above all in enduro operation. They also provided adaptation to individual riding styles as well as to various types of rider boots. Even more than with the standard GS, the new, adjustable aluminum handlebars did justice to the difficult conditions encountered in long-haul travel and extreme touring, far from any paved roads. The hand-protectors, now mounted directly to the handlebars, were also a practical accessory.

■ **Heavy-duty engine guard, variable seat**

As in earlier Adventure models, a sturdy stainless-steel tubular structure protected the tank and engine from the consequences of involuntary contact with the ground or boulders, especially off-road. In addition, high-grade aluminum guards protected valve covers from the marks of hard riding. Sturdy and practical luggage fixing options were featured onboard, along with the tough stainless-steel luggage rack, which could receive the optional aluminum topcase.

The Adventure is factory ready for pretty harsh off-road work. Plenty of accessories are available from both BMW's own catalog and from others to enable you to go the extra mile.

In spite of the knobby off-road tires, the Adventure could still be pedaled pretty fast on the street.

Essential features of the BMW R 1200 GS Adventure 2 Series versus the R 1200 GS basic version are listed below:

- 33-liter tank for extended range
- Larger, adjustable windshield
- Tank, engine, and valve cover guards
- Sturdy stainless-steel luggage rack
- Multi-adjustable seat
- Hand protectors, standard
- Extended spring travels for incrcascd off-road capability
- Cross-spoke wheels ex-works
- Extra-wide rider footrests, adjustable shift, and brake levers
- Maximum weight increased to 475 kilograms

Discretely modernized and stronger by 5 horsepower, but otherwise as sturdy as ever, the latest R 1200 GS Adventure is the ultimate dream bike for globetrotters and those who pine for the open road.

Despite its considerable weight and imposing dimensions, the 2008 R 1200 GS remains an amazingly maneuverable and forgiving motorcycle, off-road as well as on.

Now as before, the dual-section seat (adjustable in the driver's section) provided an optimal riding position. In the raised setting, at a 915-milimeter saddle height, it offered the comfort of a continuous seating surface without gradations, allowing the rider the necessary freedom of movement off-road. In the lowered position, the 895-milimeter saddle height guaranteed good ground control and secure footing at stops. A special seat configuration, markedly narrowed at the front, also contributed to this.

Street wheels for the HP2

For clients wanting maximum fun out of their HP2, not just off-road but also on the street, BMW began offering a 17-inch wheel set with street tires in March 2006. The delivered wheels included a black powder-coated front rim with dimensions of 3.5x17 inches (normal spoke with inner tube), mounted brake rotor, and a black powder-coated rear-wheel rim with dimensions of 4.0x17 inches (cross-spoke, tubeless). The wheels were mounted with Continental Road Attack tires (120/70 front and 150/70 rear), standard. Adapted fork protectors and installation instructions were also included. This second wheel set was now available on a new BMW HP2 (total price 16,900 euro). There was a 900-euro rebate if the set was declined. Retrofitting of previously delivered machines was also possible.

With the HP2's street wheel set, BMW enlarged the scope of safe enjoyment of the HP Megamoto.

Model updates for 2009

■ 2008-on R 1200 GS/Adventure: More power

Other changes included a new double-butted aluminium handlebar, new hand protectors, and a redesigned seat giving improved ergonomics, while a new sensor system for fuel display gave a more accurate reading from maximum, and alternator output increased from 600 to 720 watts. New stainless steel deflectors around the fuel tank, an LED rear light, and white indicators improved the looks. Colors: Titanium Silver Metallic, Dark Slate Metallic Matt, Tanzanite Blue, and Namibia Orange. The Adventure had the same updates but added an optional shorter first gear for tackling tricky, confined terrain.

Thus there are expected to be fewer major changes for the 2009 model year.

The biggest GS was still a tall motorcycle, though the lower seat option for 2009 put it within reach of more riders.

Some things didn't change. The 2008 R 1200 GS Adventure remained a superb big enduro.

It was on the road that the 2008 Boxer's power increase was most noticeable.

▌ G 450 X: Production enduro

In 2008 (as an '09 model) the G 450 X was launched as a production version of the 450 Sport Enduro. It retained the DOHC 449cc single, and the coaxial swingarm pivot and drive sprocket.

The engine was built for BMW by Kymco of Taiwan, and in production form was fully EU3 compatible. Thus the G 450 X, although a hard-edged off-road bike, was also road legal, coming fully equipped with lights and indicators, as well as meeting all emissions and noise legislation. Fully adjustable Marzocchi upside-down front forks were part of the standard package, along with an Ohlins rear monoshock.

BMW envisaged the G 450 X as a bike that could be raced on weekends, appeal to serious trail riders, and capable of being used on the road daily if need be. One interesting aspect of the G 450 X was the quick capability of a significant power upgrade. As standard, it offered 41 horsepower but could be easily boosted to 52 horsepower for racing simply by swapping a reversible plug in the wiring harness. There was also a 26-horsepower version for novice riders. Available only in Racing White, the G 450 X represented a harder edged alternative to the softer G series 650s.

Left: *BMW saw the new 450 as a serious weekend competition bike, also road legal.*

Below: *G 450 X power unit was a modern, compact four-stroke, made for BMW by Kymco.*

A key feature of the G 450 X was the concentric gearbox shaft/ swingarm pivot.

▌G-series: Little change

The 652cc G-series singles were hardly changed for 2008 and 2009, though all three models now had low-seat options, down to 910 millimeters (Xchallenge), 860 millimeters (Xmoto), and 800 millimeters (Xcountry). The Xcountry also came in Sunset Yellow and acquired span-adjustable control levers.

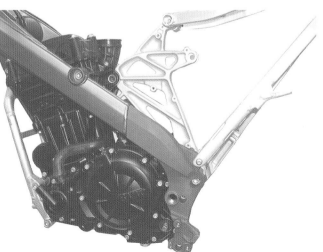

Above: *Xcountry remained the "friendliest" option among the G series singles. Sunset Yellow is the color for 2009.*

Left: *652cc single bolted snugly into the alloy frame shared by the X-series bikes.*

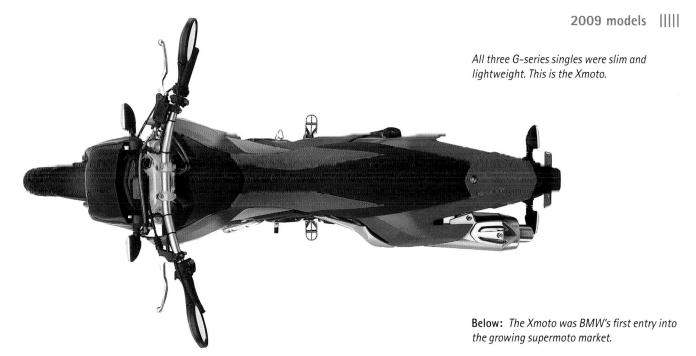

All three G-series singles were slim and lightweight. This is the Xmoto.

Below: *The Xmoto was BMW's first entry into the growing supermoto market.*

■ The middle man: F 650/800 GS 798cc "Rotax Twins"

Almost as soon as BMW launched its middleweight 800cc twins, the F-series 800 S and 800 ST, there was speculation that a GS version would follow. It arrived in March 2008, but the surprise was that there were two versions. Despite its name, the new F 650 GS used the same 798cc engine as the full 800, albeit in a softer state of tune and mounted in a more road-biased chassis.

Both bikes were based around the parallel-twin motor developed by BMW with Rotax and built by the Austrian engine maker. Unlike in the earlier F-series, it was mounted at 8.3 degrees to the vertical, to allow space for the F 800 GS's larger 21-inch front wheel and longer suspension travel. However, like the street bikes, it retained the "third con rod" counterbalancing system, which BMW said offset most of the vibration of the 360-degree crankshaft while consuming less power than a conventional gear-driven counterbalance shaft. Another innovation was a small heat exchanger mounted above the oil filter, which took up less room than a conventional oil cooler.

In fact, the whole engine was extremely compact, with offset chain drive for the twin overhead camshafts (four valves per cylinder) and fuel injection via a Bosch BMS-K system that included an oxygen sensor and three-way catalyst, plus secondary air injection on the F 800 GS. BMW claimed a low fuel consumption of 3.8 liters per 100 kilometers for the 800 GS (3.7 liters for the 650) and the same 85 brake horsepower as the F 800 S/ST, but at 500 rpm lower.

■ Chain but no belt

Two of the S/ST features was a toothed-belt final drive and single-sided swingarm, but the middleweight GS replaced both with a conventional chain and twin-sided cast-aluminium swingarm, which pivoted on needle-roller bearings directly in the engine crankcase. The six-speed gearbox was unchanged.

Chassis-wise, the GS used an all-new tubular steel space frame in which the engine was solidly mounted, with a steel subframe carrying the seat and 16-liter fuel tank. With this GS aimed at a lower price bracket than the flagship R 1200 GS, the suspension reverted to conventional

Above: *The new GS twins could come specified with factory luggage.* **Below:** *Both 650 and 800 shared the same instrument pack and optional GPS.*

Marzocchi forks (non-adjustable) with a Showa rear monoshock (preload and compression damping adjustable, the former via an easy-to-reach knob). Twin 300-millimeter Brembo front disc brakes were fitted to the 800 GS, gripped by twin-piston calipers, and backed up by a single 265-millimeter rear disc with single-piston caliper. BMW's two-channel Bosch ABS system was among the long list of options. The company evidently saw the 800 GS as a serious off-roader, as it wore a 21-inch spoked front wheel with a 90/90 dual-purpose Bridgestone tire and a 150/70 17 tire on the rear.

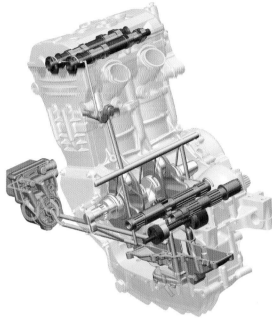

Above: *Rotax twins featured an innovative and compact oil cooler, clearly visible here above the filter.*

Below: *The 2008-on F-series GS neatly filled the gap between the G-series singles and GS-series Boxer twins.*

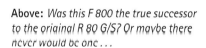

Above: *Was this F 800 the true successor to the original R 80 G/S? Or maybe there never would be one . . .*

Milder brother

The F 800 GS was treated as a true alternative to the big R 1200 GS (albeit smaller and more manageable off-road), but the new 650 was different. Around 1,500 euro cheaper than its big brother, it was intended as an entry-level bike, a replacement for the single-cylinder F 650 GS, easier to ride and more inclined toward road than off-road manners.

Most significantly, different camshafts with lower lift and softer timing reduced power to 71 horsepower, with torque peaking at 4,500 rpm, giving a nice broad spread of power from low revs. The softer tune of the engine also allowed it to do without the 800's secondary air system, as there was a lower volume of unburnt gases. The transmission and front suspension were unchanged, but the 650 wore a 19-inch cast-aluminium front wheel (with more road-biased tires at both ends) and a single 300-millimeter Brembo disc. At 820 millimeter, its seat was significantly lower than the 800's, with a further option down to 765 millimeters.

All in all, the new F-series GS twins filled a distinct gap in the range, offering an easy to live with motorcycle (the 650) and, in the 800, perhaps a true successor to the original R 80 G/S.

Above: *The F 650 GS was more road orientated than the 800. Some actually preferred its on-tarmac steering.*

Left: *BMW hoped the new F 650 GS—like its single-cylinder predecessor—would appeal to women riders.*

Technical data: Two-valve boxer 1980–1996 (1)

MODEL	Sales designation	R 80 G/S	R 80 G/S PD	R 65 GS	R 80 GS	R 100 GS	R 100 GS PD	R 80 GS/2	R 100 GS/2
	Built from/to	1980-87	1984-87	1987-90	1987-90	1987-90	1988-1/96	1990-94	1990-94
	Prod. units	21,334	2975	1334	3938	12,063	9007	6660	8736
MOTOR	Type	Twin cylinder four-stroke boxer engine, air-cooled							
	Displacement in cm³	798	798	650	798	980	980	798	980
	Bore x stroke mm	84.8x70.6	84.8x70.6	82x61.5	84.8x70.6	94x70.6	94x70.6	84.8x70.6	94x70.6
	Output hp/kW/rpm	50/37/6500	50/37/6500	27/20/5000	50/37/6500	60/44/6500	60/44/6500	50/37/6500	60/44/6500
	Max. torque Nm/rpm	56.7/5000	58/4000	43/3500	61/3750	76/3750	76/3750	61/3750	76/3750
	Compression ratio	8.2 : 1	8.2 : 1	8.4 : 1	8.2 : 1	8.5 : 1	8.5 : 1	8.2 : 1	8.5 : 1
	Valve actuation	ohv, 1 central chain-driven camshaft under the crankshaft							
	Valves per cylinder	2 controlled via tappets and rocker arms							
	Carburetor	2 Bing/32 mm	2 Bing/32 mm	2 Bing/26 mm	2 Bing/32 mm	2 Bing/40 mm	2 Bing/40 mm	2 Bing/32 mm	2 Bing/40 mm
	Ignition	Battery, contactless, electronic; secondary air system (emissions) from September 1990							
	Alternator	12V/280W	12V/280W	12V/280W	12V/280W	12V/280W	12V/280W	12V/280W	12V/280W
	Battery	12V/16Ah	12V/20Ah	12V/20Ah	12V/25Ah	12V/25Ah	12V/25Ah	12V/25Ah	12V/25Ah
	Starter	Electric 0.7 kW (plus kick-starter to 1987)							
	Lubrication	Eaton trochoid oil pump, Micronic filter cartridge							
	Oil volume l. (wo/w filter)	2.25/2.50	2.25/2.50	2.25/2.50	2.25/2.50	2.25/2.50	2.25/2.50	2.25/2.50	2.25/2.50
	Oil cooler	none	none	none	none	yes	yes	none	yes
POWER TRANSMISSION	Clutch	Single-plate dry clutch							
	Transmission/gearshift	5-speed/foot	5-speed/foot	5-speed/foot	5-speed/foot	5-speed/foot	5-speed/foot	5-speed/foot	5-speed/foot
	Rear-wheel drive	Cardan shaft, enclosed, with torsional damper, 1 universal joint			Cardan shaft, enclosed, with torsional damper, 2 universal joints				
	Secondary transmission ratio: 1	3.36	3.36	3.34	3.09	3.20	3.20	3.09	3.20
FRAME, SUSPENSION, BRAKES	Frame type	Double-loop tubular steel frame with removable bolt-on rear section							
	Front suspension	Telescopic spring fork							
	Springing/damping, front	Coil springs, hydraulic damping							
	Swingarm	Monolever single-sided swing arm			Paralever single-sided swing arm				
	Springing/damping, rear	1 side-mounted hydraulically dampened shock							
	Spring travel front/rear mm	200/170	200/170	200/170	225/180	225/180	225/180	225/180	225/180
	Rake angle, in degrees	62.5	62.5	62.5	62.5	62.5	62.5	62.5	62.5
	Caster, mm	115	115	114	101	101	101	101	101
	Wheel, front	1.85x21	1.85x21	1.85x21	1.85x21	1.85x21	1.85x21	1.85x21	1.85x21
	Wheel, rear	2.50x18	2.50x18	2.50x18	2.50x17	2.50x17	2.50x17	2.50x17	2.50x17
	Tire, front	3.00 R21	3.00 R21	3.00 R21	90/90 T21	90/90 T21	90/90 T21	90/90 T21	90/90 T21
	Tire, rear	4.00 R18	4.00 R18	4.00 R18	130/80 T17	130/80 T17	130/80 T17	130/80 T17	130/80 T17
	Brake, front	1 rotor, 264 mm	1 rotor, 260 mm	1 rotor, 260 mm	1 rotor, 285 mm	1 rotor, 285 mm	1 rotor, 285 mm	1 rotor, 285 mm	1 rotor, 285 mm
	Brake actuation, front	Hand lever, hydraulic, 1 fixed caliper							
	Brake, rear	Simplex drum-brake 200 mm diameter							
	Brake actuation, rear	Foot-lever, mechanical, rods			Foot-lever, mechanical, cable				
DIMENSIONS, WEIGHT	Length, mm	2230	2230	2230	2290	2290	2290	2290	2290
	Width with mirrors, mm	1000	1000	1000	1000	1000	1000	1000	1000
	Handlebar width, mm	820	820	820	830	830	830	830	830
	Height, mm	1150	1150	1150	1165	1345	1345	1345	1345
	Wheelbase, mm	1447	1447	1447	1513	1513	1513	1513	1513
	Saddle height, mm	860	845	860	850	850	850	850	850
	Ground clearance, mm	218	200	218	200	200	200	200	200
	Curb weight, kg	191	205	198	210	210	236	215	220
	Max. total weight, kg	398	398	398	420	420	420	420	420
TANK	Tank volume in liters	19.5	32	19.5	24	24	35	24	24
PERFORMANCE	Fuel consumption L/100 km at 90 km/h	4.7	4.7	5.0	4.7	4.9	4.9	4.7	4.9
	at 120 km/h	5.5	5.5	6.2	6.6	6.9	6.9	6.6	6.9
	Max. theor. range, km	350	580	310	360	350	500	360	350
	Accel. 0-100 km/h	8.8	8.8	9.4	6.0	4.8	4.8	6.0	4.8
	Top speed, km/h	168	168	146	168	180	180	168	180
PRICE	Price at series launch	8,290 DM	10,120 DM	9,200 DM	11,950 DM	12,990 DM	15,190 DM	12,800 DM	14,950 DM

SIGNIFICANT MODIFICATIONS: R 80 GS/2: also available with 27 hp (20 kW) or 34 hp (25 kW). R 100 GS "Paris-Dakar": from October 1994, only available as Classic Edition

Technical data: Two-valve boxer 1980–1996(2)

MODEL	Sales designation	R 100 R	R 80 R	R 80 ST	R 80 GS Basic
	Built from/to	1991-1/96	1992-94	1982-85	1996
	Prod. units	19,989 inc. Mystic*	3444	5963	3003
MOTOR	Type	Twin-cylinder four-stroke boxer engine, air-cooled			
	Displacement in cm³	980	798	798	798
	Bore x stroke mm	94x70.6	84.8x70.6	84.8x70.6	84.8x70.6
	Output hp/kW/rpm	60/44/6500	50/37/6500	50/37/6500	50/37/6500
	Max. torque Nm/rpm	74/3500	61/3750	56.7/5000	61/3750
	Compression ratio	8.5 : 1	8.2 : 1	8.0 : 1	8.2 : 1
	Valve actuation	ohv, 1 central chain-driven camshaft under the crankshaft			
	Valves per cylinder	2 controlled via tappets and rocker arms			
	Carburetor	2 Bing/32 mm	2 Bing/32 mm	2 Bing/32 mm	2 Bing/32 mm
	Ignition	Battery ignition, contactless electronic; secondary air system			
	Alternator	12V/240W	12V/240W	12V/280W	12V/280W
	Battery	12V/30Ah	12V/25Ah	12V/25Ah	12V/25Ah
	Starter	Electric 0.7 kW			
	Lubrication	Eaton trochoid oil pump, Micronic filter cartridge			
	Oil volume L (wo/w filter)	2.25/2.50	2.25/2.50	2.25/2.50	2.25/2.50
	Oil cooler	yes	none	none	none
POWER TRANSMISSION	Clutch	Single-plate dry clutch			
	Transmission/gearshift	5-speed/foot	5-speed/foot	5-speed/foot	5-speed/foot
	Real-wheel drive	Cardan shaft, torsional damper, 2 universal joints		1 universal joint	2 universal joints
	Secondary transmission ratio: 1	3.09	3.20	3.36	3.20
FRAME, SUSPENSION, BRAKES	Frame type	Double-loop tubular steel frame with removable bolt-on rear section			
	Front suspension	Telescopic spring fork			
	Springing/damping, front	Coil springs, hydraulic damping			
	Rear suspension	Paralever single-sided swing arm		Monolever	Paralever
	Springing/damping, rear	1 side-mounted hydraulically dampened shock			
	Spring travel front/rear mm	135/140	135/140	175/153	225/180
	Rake angle, in degrees	61.5	61.5	62.5	62.5
	Caster, mm	137.5	137.5	129	101
	Wheel, front	2.50x18	2.50x18	1.85x19	1.85x21
	Wheel, rear	2.50x17	2.50x17	2.50x18	2.50x17
	Tire, front	110/0 V18	110/80 V18	100/90 H19	90/90 T21
	Tire, rear	140/80 V17	140/80 V17	120/90 H18	130/80 T17
	Brake, front	Dual disk, 285 mm diameter	1 rotor, 260 mm	1 rotor, 285 mm	
	Brake actuation, front	Hand lever, hydraulic, fixed caliper			
	Brake, rear	Simplex drum-brake 200 mm diameter			
	Brake actuation, rear	Foot-lever, mechanical, cable		Foot lever, rods	Foot lever, cable
DIMENSIONS, WEIGHT	Length mm	2210	2210	2180	2290
	Width with mirrors, mm	1000	1000	1000	1000
	Handlebar width, mm	830	830	715	830
	Height, mm	1090	1080	1150	1345
	Wheelbase, mm	1513	1513	1465	1513
	Saddle height, mm	800	800	845	850
	Ground clerance, mm	140	140	190	200
	Curb weight, kg	218	217	198	218
	Max. total weight, kg	420	420	398	420
TANK	Tank volume in liters	24	24	19.5	19.5
PERFORMANCE	Fuel consumption L/100 km				
	at 90 km/h	4.9	4.7	4.6	4.6
	at 120 km/h	6.6	6.5	5.3	6.4
	Max. theor. range, km	360	370	360	355
	Accel. 0-100 km/h	4.8	6.0	6.0	6.1
	Top speed, km/h	180	168	174	171
PRICE	Price at series launch	13,450 DM	13,450 DM	9,490 DM	15,500 DM

SIGNIFICANT MODIFICATIONS: R 100 R: only 1 front brake rotor to 1992. All R 100 models: October 1994 to January 1996, only as Classic Edition.
R 80 R: also available with 27 hp (20 kW) or 34 hp (25 kW).   * R 100 R Mystic 1993-1/1996, 3,650 units, with R 100 R, except handelbar width 810 mm, saddle height 790 mm, curb weight 215 kg, 13,350 DM

Technical data: Four–valve boxer from 1994

MODEL	Sales designation	R 850 GS	R 1100 GS	R 1150 GS	R 1150 GS Adventure	R 1200 GS	R 1200 GS Adventure	HP2 Enduro	HP2 Megamoto
	Built from/to	1998-99	1994-99	1999-2003	2001-2004	since 2004	since 2005	since 2005	since 2006
	Prod. units	1954	43,628	57,834	16,233	71,035	10,058	2899	not available
MOTOR	Type	R 259 twin-cylinder four-stroke boxer, air- and oil-cooled; models 850, 1100, 1150, HP2 without balancer shaft, model 1200 with balancer shaft							
	Displacement in cm³	848	1085	1130	1130	1170	1170	1170	1170
	Bore x stroke mm	87.5x70.5	99x70.5	101x70.5	101x70.5	101x73	101x73	101x73	101x73
	Output hp/kW/rpm	70/52/7000	80/60/6750	85/62,5/6750	85/62,5/6750	98/72/7000	98/72/7000	105/77/7000	113/83/7500
	Max. torque Nm/rpm	77/5500	97/5250	98/5250	98/5250	115/5500	115/5500	115/5500	115/6000
	Compression ratio	10.3 : 1	10.3 : 1	10.3 : 1	10.3 : 1	11.0 : 1	11.0 : 1	11.0 : 1	11.0 : 1
	Valve actuation	1 overhead chain-driven camshaft per cylinder head		HC, 1 overhead chain-driven camshaft per cylinder head					
	Valves per cylinder	4 controlled via short tappets and rocker arms							
	Fuel-injection	Electronically controlled Motronic MA 2.2 injection system; 1150: MA 2.4			Motronic BMS-K	Motronic BMS-K	Motronic BMS-K	Motronic BMS-K	
	Ignition	Digital, coasting cut-off; Lambda-controlled three-way metal catalytic converter				Digital, coasting cut-off; Lambda-controlled three-way metal			Catalytic converter
	Alternator	12V/700W	12V/700W	12V/600W	12V/700W	12V/600W	12V/720W	12V/600W	12V/600W
	Battery	12V/19Ah	12V/19Ah	12V/14Ah	12V/19Ah	12V/14Ah	12V/14Ah	12V/12Ah	12V/12Ah
	Starter	Electric 1.1 kW							
	Lubrication	Double oil-pump, wet-sump lubrication							
	Oil volume L (wo/w filter)	3.50/3.75	3.50/3.75	3.50/3.75	3.50/3.75	3.70/3.95	3.70/3.95	3.70/3.95	3.70/3.95
	Oil cooler:	Inner oil-cooling							
POWER TRANSMISSION	Clutch	Single-plate dry clutch 180 mm diameter; 1150: 165 mm							
	Transmission/gearshift	5-speed/foot	5-speed/foot	6-speed/foot	6-speed/foot	6-speed/foot	6-speed/foot	6-speed/foot	6-speed/foot
	Real-wheel drive	Cardan shaft (encapsulated) with torsional damper, 2 universal joint							
	Secondary transmission ratio: 1	3.00	3.20	2.82	2.82	2.82	2.82	2.82	
FRAME, SUSPENSION, BRAKES	Frame type	Tubular treillis frame with cast light-alloy, load-bearing engine			Tubular steel frame, load bearing engine		Tubular steel frame, non-load bearing engine		
	Front-wheel suspension	Telelever fork with triangular steel longitudinal control arm				Improved Telelever, light-alloy handlebars		Marzocchi USD fork	
	Springing/damping, front	Hydraulically damped, adjustable central shock				Hydr. damp. adj. central shock		Springs, hydr. damping adjustable	
	Rear-wheel suspension	Paralever single-sided swing arm			Paralever stage II	Paralever stage II	Paralever stage II modif. + 30 mm longer	Air spring-damper system/shock	
	Springing/damping, rear	Hydraulically damped, adjustable central shock				Hydr. damp. adj. central shock			
	Spring travel front/rear mm	190/200	190/200	190/200	210/220	190/200	210/220	270/250	160/160
	Rake angle, in degrees	64.0	64.0	64.0	64.0	62.9	63.8	60.5	61.4
	Caster, mm	115	115	115	121	110	97.6	127	95
	Wheel, front	2.50x19	2.50x19	2.50x19	2.50x19	Cast light alloy 2.50x19	2.50x19 3.50x17	1.85x21	Cast light alloy
	Wheel, rear	4.00x17	4.00x17	4.00x17	4.00x17	Cast light alloy 4.00x17	4.00x17 5.50x17	2.50x17	Cast light alloy
	Tire, front	110/80 H19	110/80 H19	110/80 H19	110/80 B19	110/80 H19	110/80 R19	90/90 x 21 M+S	120/70 ZR 17
	Tire, rear	150/70 H17	150/70 H17	150/70 H17	150/70 H17	150/70 H17	150/70 R17	140/80x17 M+S	180/55 ZR 17
	Brake, front: Dual disk, perforated, 305 mm diameter, optional ABS			Evo brake, dual disk, 305 mm, (ABS)		1 rotor 305 mm	2 rotors 320 mm		
	Brake actuation, front	Hand lever, hydraulic, four-piston fixed caliper							
	Brake, rear	Single disk 276 mm diameter, optional ABS		1 disk 276 mm diam., optional ABS		1 disk 265 mm			
	Brake actuation, rear	Foot lever, hydraulic, dual-piston floating caliper							
DIMENSIONS, WEIGHT	Length mm	2196	2196	2196	2180	2210	2250	2350	2330
	Width with mirrors, mm	917	917	920	980	915	955	880	
	Handlebar width, mm	900	900	903	903	871	950	828	
	Width, mm	1400	1400	1400	1400	1380	1380		
	Wheelbase mm	1509	1509	1509	1501	1519	1511	1610	1610
	Saddle height, mm	840/860	840/860	840/860	900	840/860	895/915	920	890
	Ground clearance, mm	210	210	210	210	217	217		
	Curb weight, kg	243	243	249	253	225	256	197	202
	Max. total weight, kg	450	450	450	450	435	465	300	300
TANK	Tank volume in liters	25	25	22.1	22.1 or 30.0	20	33	13	13
PERFORMANCES	Fuel consumption L/100 km								
	at 90 km/h	4.6	4.6	4.5	4.5	4.3	4.6	4.1	4.6
	at 120 km/h	5.7	5.9	5.7	5.7	5.5	6.1	5.5	5.2
	Max. theor. range, km	485	475	433	433 or 590	408	620	270	265
	Accel. 0-100 km/h s	5.0	4.3	4.0	4.3	3.4	3.4	3.2	3.4
	Top speed, km/h	185	195	195	192	205	200	200	215
PRICE	Price at series launch	18,750 DM	17,450 DM	20,250 DM	11,500 euro	11,762 euro	13,500 euro	16,000 euro	17,330 euro

SIGNIFICANT MODIFICATIONS: R 1100 GS also with 78 hp (57 kW). Closed-loop catalytic converter optional from 1993, standard from 1995. R 850 GS also with 34 hp (25 kW). R 1200 GS outside Germany with 100 hp/74 kW. 2008-on R1200GS and R1200GS Adventure have more powerful 105hp/81kW/62.7Nm version of 1170cc engine, with 12.0:1 compression ratio and 8000 rpm limit. Also optional electro-hydraulic suspension adjustment as part of the enduro ESA system. Secondary transmission ratio shortened from 2.82:1 to 2.91:1. 2008-on HP2 Megamoto compression ratio 12.0:1, no change in power/torque outputs.

Technical data: Two-valve single 1925–1966

MODEL	Sales designation	R 39	R 2 *[1]	R 4 *[2]	R 3	R 35	R 20	R 23
	Built from/to	1925-27	1931-36	1932-37	1936	1937-40	1937-38	1938-1940
	Prod. units	855	15,207	15,295	740	15,386	5000	9021
MOTOR	Type	Single-cylinder four-stroke, air-cooled						
	Displ. cm³	247	198	398	305	342	192	247
	Bore x stroke, mm	68x68	63x64	78x84	68x84	72x84	60x68	68x68
	Output hp/min-1	6.5/4000	6/3500	12/3500	1/4200	14/4500	8/5400	10/5400
	Compr. ratio	6.0 : 1	6.7 : 1	5.7 : 1	6.0 : 1	6.0 : 1	6.0 : 1	6.0 : 1
	Valve control	ohv, 1 chain-driven camshaft, pushrods, rocker-arms						
	Valves per cyl./position	2						
	Carburetor/port mm	BMW/20	Sum/19	Sum/Register/25	Sum/Register/25	Sum/22	Amal/18.2	Amal/18.2
	Ignition	Solenoid	Battery	Magneto flywheel	Battery	Battery	Battery	Battery
	Starter	Kick-starter						
POWER TRANSMISSION	Clutch	Single-plate dry clutch						
	Transmission/gearshift	3-speed/hand	3-speed/hand	3-speed/hand	4-speed/hand	4-speed/hand	3-speed/foot	3-speed/foot
	Real-wheel drive	Cardan shaft, unenclosed						
FRAME, SUSPENSION, BRAKES	Frame type	Double-loop tube	Double loop pressed-steel frame				Tubular frame, bolted	
	Front suspension	Laminated spring, tubular swing arm	Laminated spring, pressed-steel swing arm			Telescopic fork, undamped		
	Rear suspension	Rigid						
	Wheels, front/back	Spoke						
	Tires, front/back	3.5 x 27	3.0 x 25	3.50 x 26	3.50 x 26	3.50 x 19	3.00 x 19	3.00 x 19
	Brake, front	Inner brake shoe 150 mm	Drum 180 mm	Half-hub drum			Drum 160 mm	Drum 160 mm
	Brake, rear	Outer brake shoe:	Drum 180 mm	Half-hub drum			Drum 180 mm	Drum 180 mm Cardan
DIMENSIONS, TANK, PRICE	Length mm	2050	1950	1980	1980	2000	2000	2000
	Width mm	800	850	850	850	800	800	800
	Height mm	950	950	950	950	950	920	920
	Curb weight kg	110	110	137	149	155	130	135
	Tank volume in liters	10	11	12	12.5	12	12	9.6
	Top speed, km/h	100	95	100	100	100	95	95
	Price	1,870 RM	975 RM	1,150 RM	995 RM	995 RM	725 RM	750 RM

MODIFICATIONS: *[1] R 2 model 1932: Amal carburator 18.2 mm, frictional damper front; model 1934: 8 hp/4500 rpm, covered generator. Model 1935: new tank and headlight with ignition lock. Model 1936: wider mudguards. *[2] R 4 model 1933: 4-speed transmission with hand-operated gearshift. Model 1934: 14 hp/4200 rpm, covered alternator. Model 1936: new "standardized gearbox", 4-speed

MODEL	Sales designation	R 24	R 25	R 25/2	R 25/3	R 26	R 27
	Built from/to	1948-50	1950-51	1951-53	1953-56	1956-60	1960-66
	Prod. units	12,020	23,400	38,651	47,700	30,236	15,364
MOTOR	Type	Single-cylinder four-stroke, air-cooled					
	Displacement in cm³	247	247	247	247	247	247
	Bore x Stroke mm	68x68	68x68	68x68	68x68	68x68	68x68
	Output hp/min-1	12/5600	12/5600	12/5600	13/5800	15/6400	18/7400
	Compression ratio	6.75 : 1	6.5 : 1	6.5 : 1	7.0 : 1	7.5 : 1	8.2 : 1
	Valve actuation	ohv, 1 underneath, chain-driven camshaft, pushrods, rocker-arms					
	Valves per cyl./position	2					
	Carburetor/port mm	Bing/22	Bing/24	Bing/22	Bing/24	Bing/26	Bing/26
	Ignition	Battery					
	Starter	Kick-starter					
POWER TRANSMISSION	Clutch	Single-plate dry clutch					
	Transmission/gearshift	4-speed/foot/hand	4-speed/foot/hand	4-speed/foot/hand	4-speed/foot	4-speed/foot	4-speed/foot
	Real-wheel drive	Cardan shaft, unenclosed				Cardan shaft, enclosed	
FRAME, SUSPENSION, BRAKES	Frame type	Tubular frame	Tubular frame, welded, central tube, two main beams				
	Front suspension	Telescopic spring fork, long swing arm, 2 shocks					
	Rear suspension	Rigid	Plunger			Long swing arm, 2 shocks	
	Wheels, front/back	Spoke					
	tires, front/back	3.00 x 19	3.25 x 19	3.25 x 19	3.25 x 18	3.25 x 18	3.25 x 18
	Brake, front	Half-hub drum-brake 160 mm				Full-hub brakes	
	Brake, rear	Half-hub drum-brake 160 mm				Full-hub brakes	
DIMENSIONS, TANK, PRICE	Length mm	2020	2073	2020	2065	2090	2090
	Width mm	750	750	760	760	760	840
	Height mm	920	920	920	910	910	910
	Curb weight kg	130	140	142	150	158	162
	Tank volume in liters	12	12	12	17	15	15
	Top speed, km/h	95	97	105	119	128	130
	Price	1,750 DM	1,750 DM	1,990 DM	2,060 DM	2,150 DM	2,430 DM
MODIFICATIONS		none for the series					

Technical data: Four–valve single from 1993

MODEL	Sales designation	F 650	F 650 ST	F 650 GS	F 650 GS Dakar	F 650 CS Scarver	G 650 Xcountry	G 650 Xchallenge	G 650 Xmoto
	Built from/to	1993-99	1996-99	since 2000	since 2000	2001-2005	since 2006	since 2006	since 2006
	Prod. units	43,535	10,083	75,579	20,544	20,845	558	1416	433
MOTOR	Type	Single-cylinder four-stroke, liquid-cooled, balancer shaft							
	Displacement in cm³	652	652	652	652	652	652	652	652
	Bore x stroke mm	100x83	100x83	100x83	100x83	100x83	100x83	100x83	100x83
	Output hp/kW/min-1	48/35/6500	48/35/6500	50/37/6500	50/37/6500	50/37/6500	53/39/7000	53/39/7000	53/39/7000
	Max. torque Nm/min-1	57/5200	57/5200	60/5000	60/5000	62/5500	60/5250	60/5250	60/5250
	Compression ratio	9.7 : 1	9.7 : 1	11.5 : 1	11.5 : 1	11.5 : 1	11.5 : 1	11.5 : 1	11.5 : 1
	Valve actuation	dohc, 2 overhead chain-driven camshafts, hydraul. chain-tensioner							
	Valves per cylinder	4 actuated via tappets							
	Carburetor/fuel-injection	2 Mikuni BST33-B316 33 mm		Electronic BMS fuel injection, from 2004 BMS-C II with multipoint injection, also G 650 X-models					
	Ignition	Contactless dual-ignition;		Open-loop electronic cat.; Lambda-controlled 3-way catalytic converter; single-, from 2004 dual-ignition.					
	Alternator	12V/280W	12V/280W	12V/400W	12V/400W	12V/400W	12V/280W	12V/280W	12V/280W
	Battery	12V/12Ah	12V/12Ah	12V/12Ah	12V/12Ah	12V/12Ah	12V/10Ah	12V/10Ah	12V/10Ah
	Starter	Permanent magnet with reduction, 0.9 kW							
	Lubrication	2 trochoid oil pumps, dry-sump							
	Oil volume, liters	2.1	2.1	2.3	2.3	2.3	2.3	2.3	2.3
	Oil cooler	none							
POWER TRANSMISSION	Clutch	Multi-disk clutch in oil bath activated via cable							
	Transmission/gearshift	5-speed/foot							
	Real drive	O-ring chain							
	Secondary transmission:1 ratio:	2.94	2.94	2.94	2.94	2.93	2.937	3.133	2.937
FRAME, SUSPENSION, BRAKES	Frame type	Single-loop tube/sheet-metal part/rear section		Tubular bridge frame/rear outrigger, integrated oil tank (F 650 GS); G 650 X: oil tank behind cylinder + cast light-alloy + bolt-on parts					
	Front suspension	Showa telescopic fork with 41 mm diameter		Upside-down fork, 45 mm diameter					
	Springing/damping, front	Coil springs, hydraulic							
	Rear suspension	Dual swing arm of steel section, hinged on needle bearing lever system				Light-alloy single-sided swing arm		Light-alloy dual arm cast swing arm	
	Springing/damping, rear	Central shock with hydraul. damper, spring preload + adjustable damping				Gas-pressure shock		Air damping system	Gas-pressure shock
	Spring travel front/rear mm	170/165	170/120	170/165	210/210	125/120	240/210	270/270	270/245
	Rake angle, in degrees	62	62	60,8	60,8	62,1	61,5	62,5	61,5
	Caster, mm	116	110	113	123	186	116	118	98
	Wheel, front	2.15x19	2.15x18	2.50x19	1.60x21	3.0x17 LM	2.50x19	1.60x21	Cast light alloy 3.50x17
	Wheel, rear	3.00x17	3.00x17	3.00x17	3.00x17	4.5 x 17 light alloy	3.00x17	2.50x18	Cast light alloy 4.50x17
	Tire, front	100/90x19 57S	100/90x18 56	100/90x19 57S	90/90x21 54S	110/70 ZR 17	100/90x19	90/90x21	120/70x17
	Tire, rear	130/80x17 65S	130/80x17 65S	130/80x17 65S	130/80x17 65S	160/60 ZR 17	130/80x17	140/80x18	160/60x17
	Brake, front	Single disk brake, 300 mm rotor, double piston floating caliper, optional ABS from F 650 GS					320 mm, 4 piston		
	Brake actuation, front	Hand lever, hydraulic							
	Brake, rear	Single disk brake, 240 mm rotor, single piston floating caliper							
	Brake actuation, rear	Foot lever, hydraulic							
DIMENSIONS, WEIGHT	Length mm	2180	2160	2175	2189	2142	2185	2205	2155
	Width with mirrors, mm	880	880	910	910	915	907	907	907
	Handlebar width, mm	800	760	785	901	824	860	825	825
	Height to windshield, mm	1220	1,200 (ca.)	1,250 (ca.)	1,310 (ca.)	1380	n.i.		
	Wheelbase, mm	1480	1465	1479	1489	1493	1498	1500	1500
	Saddle height, mm	800	785	780	870	780	840-870	930	920
	Ground clearance, mm	210	180 (ca.)	210	250 (ca.)	151	n.i.		
	Curb weight kg	191	191	193	192	189	160	156	159
	max. Total weight, kg	371	371	380	380	370	335	335	335
TANK	Tank capacity/ of which reserve	17.5/2.0	17.5/2.0	17.3/4.5	17.3/4.5	15.0/4.0	9.5	9.5	9.5
PERFORMANCE	Fuel consumption l/100 km at 90 km/h	3.8	3.8	3.4	3.4	3.0	3.4	3.6	3.5
	at 120 km/h	5.3	5.3	5.0	5.0	4.5	4.8	5.1	5.0
	Max. theor. range, km	385	385	410	410	375	230	220	225
	Accel. 0-100 km/h s	5.4	5.4	5.9	5.9	5.1	4.0	4.0	4.0
	Top speed, km/h	171	171	166	166	175	170	165	170
PRICE	Price at series launch	11,400 DM	11,950 DM	12,950 DM	13,950 DM	14,950 DM	7,900 euro	8,200 euro	8,700 euro

SIGNIFICANT MODIFICATIONS: All GS and CS models also available with 34 hp (25 kW). F 650 and F 650 ST then with 34 hp/5700 rpm, max. torque 48 Nm/4200, max. speed 149 km/h. F 650 GS and F 650 GS Dakar then with 34 hp/6000 rpm, max. torque 51 Nm/3,750/min, max speed 147 km/h

Technical data: G 450 X and F 650/800 GS twins 2008 on

MODEL		G 450 X	F 650 GS	F 800 GS
	Built	since 2009	since 2008	since 2008
MOTOR	Type	Water-cooled, four-stroke, single cylinder	Water-cooled four-stroke, parallel-twin cylinder	
	Displacement in cm	449.5	798	798
	Bore x stroke mm	98 x 59.6	82 x 75.6	82 x 75.6
	Low output hp/kW/rpm	26/19/6500	34/25/5000	83/61/7500
	Standard output hp/kW/rpm	41/30/7000	71/52/7000	85/63/7500
	High output hp/kW/rpm	52/38/9000	n/a	
	Low max torque Nm/rpm	30/5750	57/3000	81/5750
	Standard max torque Nm/rpm	43/6500	75/4500	83/5750
	High max torque Nm/rpm	44/7800	n/a	
	Compression ratio	12:1		
	Valve actuation	Two overhead chain driven camshafts		
	Valves per cylinder	4/top-supported, actuated via tappets		
	Fuel injection	Electronic fuel injection		
	Ignition	Keihin engine management, closed-loop 3-way catalytic converter	BMS-K engine management, closed-loop 3-way catalytic converter	
	Alternator	12V/280W	12V/400W	12V/400W
	Battery	12V/7Ah	12V/14Ah	12V/14Ah
	Starter	Permanent magnet with reduction		
	Lubrication	Dry sump		
	Oil volume	n/a		
POWER TRANSMISSION	Clutch	Multi-disk clutch in oil bath, activated by cable		
	Transmission/gearshift	5-speed/foot	6-speed/foot	
	Rear-wheel drive	Pinion, O-ring chain		
	Secondary transmission ratio,	3.2 :1		
FRAME, SUSPENSION, BRAKES	Frame type	Bridge-type frame, stainless steel tubing	Tubular steel space frame, load-bearing engine	
	Front-wheel suspension	Marzocchi upside-down fork	Telescopic fork, 41mm diameter	Upside down fork, 45mm diameter
	Springing/damping, front	Coil springs, hydraulic		
	Rear-wheel suspension	Dual swingarm, aluminum beams		
	Springing/damping, rear	Ohlins shock with spring preload and damping adjustable	Central shock spring pre-load and damping adjustable	
	Damping system	Gas pressure suspension strut	Gas pressure	
	Suspension travel front/rear mm	300/320mm	180/170	230/215
	Rake angle, in degrees	61.8	64	
	Caster, mm	118.8	92	117
	Wheel, front	1.60 x 21	2.50 x 19	2.15 x 21
	Wheel, rear	2.15 x 18	3.50 x 17	4.25 x 17
	Tire, front	90/90-21	110/90-19	90/90-21
	Tire, rear	140/80-18	140/80-17	150/70-17
	Brake, front	Single disc, 260mm rotor, double-piston floating caliper	Single disc, 300mm rotor, double-piston floating caliper	Twin discs, 300mm rotors, double-piston floating calipers
	Brake actuation, front	Hand lever, hydraulic		
	Brake, rear	Single disc, 220mm rotor, single-piston floating caliper	Single disc, 265mm rotor, single-piston floating caliper	
	Brake actuation, rear	Foot pedal, hydraulic		
DIMENSIONS, WEIGHT	Length mm	2200	2280	2320
	Width with mirrors, mm	806	890	945
	Handlebar width, mm	n/a		
	Height to windshield, mm	1475	1240	1350
	Wheelbase, mm	n/a	1575	1578
	Saddle height, mm	955	765-820	850-880
	Ground clearance, mm	n/a		
	Curb weight, kg	121	199	207
	Max total weight, kg	280	436	443
TANK	Tank capacity/of which reserve	8l/0.75l	16l/4l	
PERFORMANCE	Fuel consumption, l/100km			
	at 90km/h	4.5	3.7	3.8
	at 120km/h	6.6	5.2	
	Max theoretical range, km	178	430	420
	Accel 0-100km/h, secs	n/a		
	Top speed, km/h	Approx. 145km/h	185	Over 200
PRICE	Price at series launch	6,462 euro	6,961 euro	8,482 euro

Data Conversion Formulae

In ensure the maximum accuracy of the original BMW-sourced technical data, originally created in the German language, the measurements remain in the original European form after translation.

The following formulae should allow easy and quick conversion to familiar American measurements

To reach the American measurement, take the European measurement and multiply it by the multiplier below. [Example: 10 centimeters (cm) times 0.3837 equals 3.837 inches (in).]

Centimeters (cm) x 0.3837 to reach inches (in)

Kilograms (kg) x 2.205 to reach pounds (lb)

Kilowatts (kW) x 1.3410 to reach horsepower (hp)

Liters (l) x 0.2642 to reach U.S. gallons

Liters (l) x 0.2199 to reach Imperial gallons

Kilometers (km) x 0.6214 to reach miles

Newton-meters (Nm) of torque x 0.7380 to reach foot-pounds (ft lb)

Currency Conversion Rates

Currency conversion rates are ever changing and thus any conversion rate given here may be wildly inaccurate when you read this. However, the conversion formulae given below remain a useful approximation. As at press time in early 2009:

Euros (€) x 1.41 to reach U.S. dollars ($)

Euros (€) x 0.96 to reach Pounds Sterling (£)

Index

■ **Hans-Jurgen Schneider, who first wrote about the BMW 80 G/S in 1980.**

Hans-Jurgen Schneider (born 1946) got his motorcycle driver's license in 1975—10 years after his auto license. Two weeks later, he bought his first motorcycle, a 1952 BMW R 25/2. In the 1980s, it was an R 80 G/S or nothing, of course. In the 1990s, he also obtained a K 1100 RS, and shortly thereafter an original 1973 R 75/5, which graces his garage to this day. As editor of *Auto Zeitung*'s motorcycle section, later as an independent journalist and managing editor of *Motorradfahrer* and *Motorrad News*, Schneider has ridden and tested all BMW models (besides the motorcycles of every other brand) coming onto the market from 1976 to 1996. These ranged from the R 100/7 and R 100 RS, the two- and four-valve GS models, to the R 100 R and R 1100 RS.

Countless miles of freeway, road, and trail were rolled over in the process, largely under harsh conditions. In testing, useful results of course only ensue when bikes are put through their paces. In all those years, the author only occasionally went down off-road, and with no serious consequences—thanks to his guardian angel and a sixth sense. From 1985, the Rhineland native has built his own publishing house, Schneider Text, which, remaining independent to this day, has published numerous motorcycle and scooter books, and continues to do so. In 1995, he moved to France with his family. All told, Schneider has authored more than thirty books on auto and motorcycle related subjects.

■ **"Sidecar-pope," independent journalist and BMW rider for decades,
Dr. Axel Koenigsbeck**

Dr. Axel Koenigsbeck (born 1952) lives in Wuppertal, where he is not only a practicing dentist, but a freelance motorcycle journalist, as well as the author of numerous specialized books on the brand and technical history of motorcycles—with and without sidecars. He's been riding since 1974 and is considered an expert in the areas of sidecar and special motorcycles. Koenigsbeck conveys the excitement of the three-wheel scene on his internet site www.gespann-news.de.

He's always had a weakness for the blue-and-white brand. From 1985 to 2003, he moved about on a Fallert-BMW R 80 G/S with 1,000cc. Since 1989, his fleet has included an Armec-BMW R 100 with Tremola sidecar. A production K 1100 RS came along in 2003. Yet Koenigsbeck is also a lover of elegant Japanese technology. Thus, his garage also houses a 1998 Honda CL 400, a Suzuki GSX 400 F Katana, a modified Kawasaki W 650 Scrambler, and a classic Yamaha XS 750 from 1978—in short, the gamut of far-eastern brands.

Photo credits
Front cover photo: Roy Oliemuller/BMW of North America, LLC
Title page photo: Max Kirchbauer/BMW Presse
All other photos: AC Schnitzer (4), BMW Historical Archives and Media Department [to 1980] (55), BMW Historisches Archiv/Knittel (18), BMW Presse/Kroschel/Mosch/Sautter (163), BMW Presse/Kirchbauer/Stoffregen (119), Franke (7), Gutsche (4), Hahne (1), HPN (3), Konig (8), Koenigsbeck (20), Kuhner (1), *mo* (1), Photo Agency Luxemburg(3), Scheibe (5), Schneider (35), Schröder (1), Witec (1), WUDO (1) and Wunderlich (7). BMW Presse via Schneider Text [photography on pages 187 through 196], via Peter Henshaw [on pages 197 through 204].

The authors and Schneider Text extend their thanks to all who have contributed to this book: Rudiger Gutsche, Stefan Knittel, Guido Bergmann, Frank Roedel of *Motorrad News*, Markus Biebricher, Stefanie Lowenstein, Hans Sautter, and Jurgen Stoffregen of the BMW Media Department.

Parker House Publishing Inc.,
1826 Tower Drive,
Stillwater, Minnesota 55082, USA
www.parkerhousepublishing.com

Copyright © 2009 English language text Parker House Publishing Inc.

Originally published in the German language (5th edition)
copyright © 2007 Schneider Text Editions Specialisees, Normandy, France.
Schneider Text production Valentin Schneider, Gabriele Schneider

ISBN-13: 978-0-9796891-7-8

English translation: Nicholas Marder
Book design: Chris Fayers
Cover design: Amy Van Ert-Anderson
Editors: Kristal Leebrick and Brad Vogt
Additional text: Peter Henshaw
Manufactured in China through World Print Ltd.

10 9 8 7 6 5 4 3 2 1